Deception in Se

THE WILEY SERIES
in
STRATEGIC HRM

Series Editor

Neil Anderson

Goldsmiths College, University of London, UK

Competency-based Recruitment and Selection
Robert Wood and Tim Payne

Deception in Selection
Liz Walley and Mike Smith

*Trust and Transition – Managing Today's
Employment Relationship*
Peter Herriot, Wendy Hirsh and Peter Reilly

Further titles in preparation

Deception in Selection

Liz Walley and Mike Smith

JOHN WILEY & SONS
Chichester • New York • Weinheim • Brisbane • Singapore • Toronto

Copyright © 1998 by John Wiley & Sons Ltd,
Baffins Lane, Chichester,
West Sussex PO19 1UD, England

National   01243 779777
International +(44) 1243 779777
e-mail (for order and customer service enquiries): cs-books@wiley.co.uk
Visit our Home Page on http://www.wiley.co.uk
or http://www.wiley.com

Other Wiley Editorial Offices

John Wiley & Sons, Inc., 605 Third Avenue,
New York, NY 10158-0012, USA

WILEY-VCH Verlag GmbH, Pappelallee 3,
D-69469 Weinheim, Germany

Jacaranda Wiley Ltd, 33 Park Road, Milton,
Queensland 4064, Australia

John Wiley & Sons (Asia) Pte Ltd, 2 Clementi Loop #02–01,
Jin Xing Distripark, Singapore 129809

John Wiley & Sons (Canada) Ltd, 22 Worcester Road,
Rexdale, Ontario M9W 1L1, Canada

Library of Congress Cataloging-in-Publication Data
Walley, Liz
  Deception in selection/by Liz Walley and Mike Smith.
    p. cm. — (The Wiley series in strategic human resource management)
  Includes biographical references and index.
  ISBN 0-471-97498-6 (paper)
  1. Employee selection. 2. Employee screening 3. Deception
  I. Smith, Mike (J. Mike) II. Title. III Series
  HF5549.5.S38W35 1998   97–43237
  658.3' 112—dc21   CIP

British Library Cataloguing in Publication Data
A catalogue for this book is available from the British Library

ISBN 0-471-97498-6

Typeset in Linotype Palatino 10/12pt by Stephen Wright-Bouvier of the
Rainwater Consultancy, Longworth, Oxfordshire
Printed and bound in Great Britain by Biddles Ltd, Guildford and King's Lynn
This book is printed on acid-free paper responsibly manufactured from sustainable
forestation, for which at least two trees are planted for each one used.

Editorial Advisory Board

Louise Allen
Personnel & Training Director
Tesco
Tesco House
P O Box 18
Delamare Road
Cheshunt
Waltham Cross
Herts   EN8 9SL

Professor David Wilson
Director of Research and Doctoral Programmes
Aston University
Aston Business School
Birmingham   B4 7ET

Professor David Guest
Department of Organizational Psychology
Birkbeck College
Malet Street
London WC1E 7HX

Professor Brian Towers
Department of Human Resource Management
University of Strathclyde
The Graham Hills Building
50 Richmond Street
Glasgow   G1 1XT

Steve Rick
Director
Human Resources Development
The Royal Bank of Scotland plc
P O Box 31
42 St Andrew Square
Edinburgh   EH2 2YE

Contents

Figures

Figures

Tables

Series Editor's preface

Strategic human resource management (HRM) has come of age. Fundamental and core changes in the nature of work and work organization have resulted in far-reaching and universally felt changes in the practice of HRM in industry. Many departments, formerly known under the generic title of 'Personnel Department', have reflected these inescapable changes by renaming the function the 'Human Resource Management Department'. But such changes in name alone do not reflect the more subtle, covert and pervasive themes of change that have afflicted the professional practice of HRM over the last decade or so. HRM has been transformed from being a welfare and administration-oriented service department to a strategically oriented and business policy-setting function which is responsible for much more than the hiring and firing of personnel.

Although the very term HRM has provoked numerous charges of being one of mere empty rhetoric, few would doubt that the demands upon specialist human resource management departments have changed beyond all recognition over more recent years. Flexible forms of working, ad hoc project teams, decentralization, outsourcing of functions and the development of budgets are all factors which have contributed to the coming of age of the HR department. Yet we are far from witnessing the final, logical outcomes to such driving forces for change. Indeed, HR is a function and profession in transition. For this reason, it is important and timely for HR professionals, consultants and practitioners to take stock of the current state of their profession and its concomitant methods, theories and procedures. For while the context within which HR is practised is changing rapidly, some would argue that the profession has struggled to keep pace with these drivers for change, and that simultaneously, while we have seen numerous attempts at innovative practice within HRM, there remains a stable backbone of traditional practice and practices in many industrial sectors.

The tensions within the HR profession have therefore become of paramount concern. Pressures towards cost-effectiveness and ultimatums to demonstrate the real world contribution of HR to any business enterprise do not sit easily alongside more academic treatises on what HR practitioners *should* be doing to stand at the forefront of innovative practice. In fact, some would argue that the practice of HR has become very much more market driven over the last decade, and that the professional status of the HR body has taken second place behind the acute and day-to-day pressures faced by all practising HR managers in their own organizational setting. This second tension, between theory and practice, is one that has arguably led to an increasing divide between researchers and practitioners in HRM. If this has indeed been the case, it is an unfortunate outcome, as each side of the profession can surely learn much from the other. Yet another tension concerns the professional responsibilities and reporting relationships of HR practitioners. Are HR managers primarily members of their own organization's management team, or qualified professionals bringing their own expertise to bear on this particular employing organization? Many practising HR managers will have felt this tension at some point in their careers, and the compelling pressures towards competitive advantage now in both the private and the public sectors of industry have resulted in HR professionals having to demonstrate the 'added value' of their work much more clearly than ever was the case in the past.

Given this changing context for the profession of HRM, the driving forces for business change, and the ambitions and career goals of practising HR managers, it is no surprise that those attempting to practise in the field in the late 1990s face a veritable barrage of conflicting pressures and role requirements. The HR manager has become everything to all employees: a member of the senior management team, a confidant and counsellor for employees, an expert professional belonging to a recognized professional body, facilitator of organizational change, and manager of her or his own HRM department staff, to name but a few of the predominant roles. This lack of role clarity has led undoubtedly to feelings of stress and being a 'Jack of all trades' among many personnel professionals. So where might the way forward lie? Although these conflicting pressures may well have led to role conflict, they have also opened up many doors of opportunity for practising at a strategic level within organizations. Organization development interventions, team building, stress management audits, senior managerial succession planning, employee reward systems, staff appraisal procedures, and contributing to the organization's vision and objectives are all areas which historically were absolute no-go zones for the 'people people' in traditional personnel departments. Yet nowadays, HR professionals are *expected* to make a definite and tangible contribution to many of these areas. It is therefore timely to examine the practice of HR under the title of 'Strategic HRM'.

The objective of the Strategic HRM Series is to bring together cutting-edge texts which examine and interpret some of the most pressing concerns for HRM practice in industry. All books in the Series have been written by eminent and acknowledged experts in their own field of practice, whether they happen to be based in academia, consultancy, or industry. Indeed, the authors contributing to the Series do originate from these three different backgrounds. The books attempt to bridge the academic–practitioner divide, but not in a bland matter-of-fact manner, rather, quite the opposite. Authors have been encouraged to be opinionated and to offer a personal commentary on what they as experts in their respective areas believe to be the predominant issues of concern for practising HR managers. Readers should therefore find all texts in the Series thought provoking, carefully considered, but reasoned position statements on the current state of the art of each area addressed by every book in the Series. Books have been written to be easily accessible to the reader, but, nevertheless, to challenge assumptions and traditional practices in HRM. It is my hope, as Series Editor, that every reader will gain something from each book within the Series; that readers will find as much to agree with as to disagree with in each text; but crucially, that all books provide a thought provoking account of changes within the HR profession. Although these house style guidelines have been worked to by all authors contributing to this Series, each volume will nevertheless show an individual style and format which is best suited to the material covered. A stringent editorial policy was therefore intentionally avoided, and indeed, the autonomy to present personal viewpoints, opinions and suggestions for improvement in strategic HRM was encouraged at all stages in the authoring and production process. Books cover a wide range of topics within strategic HRM, and therefore are not intended as 'best practice' how-to texts. Given this diversity of subject matter and approach, it is my hope that the authors have produced texts which will be of interest and concern to practising HR managers. In my view the authors have without exception done a diligent and splendid job in this respect and by so doing have contributed to the debate which promises to shape the future of strategic human resource management in this country.

Neil Anderson
Professor of Work Psychology

Deception, selection and fairness

1

What do Hugh Neil, Alison Durbar, Burger King and Levi's have in common? Like several other individuals and organizations, they all made the headlines for their behaviour in the selection procedure. Media coverage highlighted public interest in deception in the selection process and in its consequences.

The reports indicate that the deception practised varied in nature and intent. Alison Durbar claimed false qualifications to gain employment and a higher salary. Hugh Neil's curriculum vitae (CV) incorporated impressive flights of fantasy and he was selected as a prospective Tory MP. Students applying for work in Burger King's burger bars felt misled over their pay and conditions and Levi's admitted errors in handling internal staff during an assessment centre. These cases will be described more thoroughly during the book, but for now Alison Durbar's story is given in fuller detail.

The above examples and case study are thought provoking because they raise the following issues:

Case Study 1
ALISON DURBAR

In 1992 Durbar was appointed deputy head of Haslingden High School, alleging she had eight O levels, two A levels and a BA from the Open University. Shortly afterwards, she successfully applied for the head teacher's position with a salary of £39,153. She claimed an honours degree and said she was studying for a doctorate at two universities.

As a head teacher, she had an exemplary record and both morale and examination results in the school improved. She was described as having brought 'a breath of fresh air' to the school. Haslingden

Cont'd

is Lancashire's biggest school with 1,300 pupils and a £2.5 million annual budget.

However, she had lied on her application form and faked her qualifications. Governors of the school were alerted to discrepancies in her academic record and in December 1994 she was arrested by detectives at her home, later appearing in Manchester Crown Court. There she admitted obtaining her position by falsely claiming she had an honours degree and other qualifications. She also admitted a second charge of obtaining £4,017 by deception by lying about a teaching grade and alleging that she was on a different pay scale than the previous head teacher.

The prosecution maintained that she did not have an honours degree or diplomas, was not studying for a doctorate and had only six O levels and one A level.

In court she was described as 'a hard-working woman with gifts for teaching and organization. She was conscientious and diligent as head teacher. Everyone was impressed by her personality and industry'.

Judge John Burke QC told her: 'You invented your qualifications to get this post and as a result you dealt a death blow to your career.' He said that neither the school nor community had suffered by her false claims and 'It would be wrong to deprive you of your liberty. You are the ultimate casualty. You have thrown away your excellent record.' She was put on probation for one year and ordered to pay £2,000 costs. A spokeswoman said that the teacher was no longer employed by the organization.

- both individuals and organizations may engage in deception

- individuals who deceive are not necessarily villains but may possess many admirable qualities and be well regarded by others

- incidents of deception may be reported in the full glare of publicity

- deception has legal implications

- the consequences can be severe and far reaching at both personal and company level.

Facets of deception such as reasons, methods, extent and results need to be put in context. The nature of deception and the selection process are best outlined separately, before looking at their interrelationship.

DECEPTION AND SELECTION IN CONTEXT

What is deception? The Concise Oxford Dictionary defines the topic in the following way:

deceive	*(verb)*	Persuade of what is false, mislead (deceive oneself, juggle with one's own convictions, also be mistaken).
deception	*(noun)*	Deceiving, being deceived; thing that deceives, trick, sham.
deceptive	*(adjective)*	Apt to deceive, easily mistaken.

This implies that deception relates not just to the deceiver but also to the deceived – in other words, it is both active and passive. In the case of self deception the two may coincide.

Deception is not always blatant, intentional and obvious. Whilst it may be practised deliberately, it may also occur through ambiguity and omission. When challenged or discovered, the deceiver may frequently dismiss deception as jokes or genuine mistakes, attributed to the deceiver's errors or to the receiver's misunderstanding of information.

Individuals are likely to vary in their predispositions for dishonesty. Some will display almost total truthfulness; others will demonstrate persistent and sustained lying, with most people occupying the many intervening gradations. Whilst some people are more likely to deceive than others, situational influences can be significant. Within the selection framework there are many situational influences which may work against honesty.

The selection procedure

Superficially, selection seems straightforward and confined to two parties – the applicant and selector. An employer wishes to fill a job vacancy and through a process of recruitment identifies a number of likely candidates, selects the most suitable and consequently fills the position. Such simplification ignores other inputs and outputs of the process which are identified in the model of selection shown in Figure 1.1. It also overlooks the many people involved both directly and indirectly in the process. The number stems from two main factors – the increasing complexity of the selection methods being utilized and the outsourcing of some Personnel functions to external consultants and agencies.

Inputs

Inputs represent the individual and organizational efforts, cost and facilities required before the processes can occur. Candidates entering the process are not only external applicants seeking entry to the organization, but include current employees being selected for internal promotion, redeployment and redundancy. Mergers and acquisitions may necessitate employees applying and competing for their own jobs, whilst the growth of multinational companies involves selection for relocation of employees in a global arena.

Selection methods

Most selection involves three methods – the submission of an application form or CV, an interview and the use of references – sometimes referred to as the classic trio. These established techniques have been subject to change as attempts are made to improve the quality of the interview. At the same time, other more sophisticated methods have been developed, as seen by the growing use of psychometric tests, work samples and assessment centres. More unusual methods such as graphology enjoy a limited popularity.

Outcomes

The results of the process extend beyond the two main parties. Outcomes affect rejected as well as selected candidates, and the organization's treatment of all involved in selection can influence perceptions of the company's public image.

The exchange of information

Underpinning the whole of the selection procedure, the exchange of

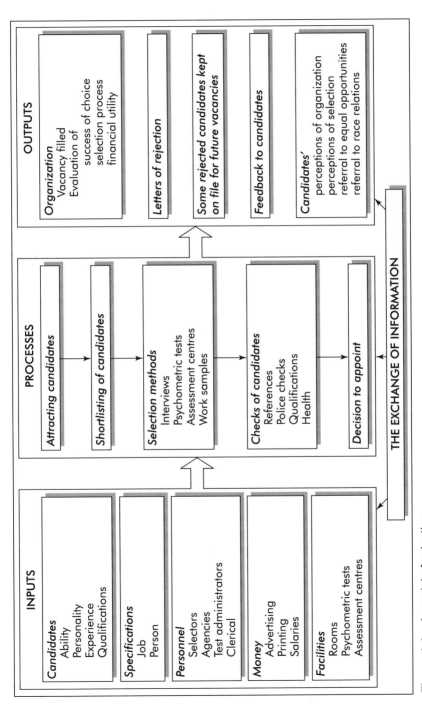

Figure 1.1   A model of selection

information is crucial to the decisions of both candidates and organizations. Applicants judge whether to enter the selection process, remain in it or retreat whilst selectors use information to determine short lists and the job offer.

Perspectives on the selection process

The convergence of a number of perspectives on selection underpins the models of deception guiding the philosophy of this book. These varying viewpoints are briefly described before examining deception in selection.

The conventional perspective

Many candidates and selectors are likely to share the conventional assumption that the selection process is controlled by the employer. His inherent power dictates the pace, style and ultimate decision making whilst the powerless candidate plays a reactive role.

Selection as a social process

Herriot (1989a) disagrees with the conventional perspective. He views selection as an interactive process consisting of a sequence of episodes, in which each party has the opportunity to make decisions about whether to continue or withdraw. For example, the organization despatches an application form. On receipt the candidate decides whether to discontinue or to complete the form. When it receives the completed form, the organization then decides whether to proceed with the application or withdraw from that candidate and another episode commences.

Both candidate and organization have expectations about the selection procedure, job and each other, and there is a reciprocal exchange of messages either implicitly or explicitly, impersonally or personally (Herriot, 1989a). The messages may not be received accurately or interpreted correctly. Perceptions of self and organization may change, determining whether the applicant continues the association with the organization and establishing the quality of that relationship. Herriot (1989a) believes that with time the accuracy and congruence of applicant and organization expectations will increase.

An economic and social perspective

The selection process does not exist in a vacuum and is not static. It reacts to change in society and the economy which partly control the power relationship within the process.

A fluctuating demographic position with fewer school leavers coupled with growing skill shortages in some sectors means that employment may switch from a buyer's to a seller's market. The shift to core and periphery workers, accompanied by a tendency to employ an increasing number of temporary staff, suggests that the current employment situation is in flux.

Similarly, changing legislation within Britain and the European Community contains strict provisions on discrimination and affects individual rights and privacy. Previous selection practices have been modified in the light of industrial tribunal decisions and compensation awards resulting from discrimination, especially of minority groups. This is augmented by the influence of pressure groups and a growth in politically correct behaviour with its emphasis on fairness and ethics.

The concepts of distributive and procedural justice

Organizational justice theory (Greenberg, 1990) distinguishes between procedural and distributive justice, which in the selection context corresponds to fairness of the selection process and the fairness of the hiring decisions (Gilliland, 1995). Leventhal (1980) suggested that evaluations of procedural justice comprise perceptions of the satisfaction or violation of a set of procedural rules which include consistency, the suppression of personal bias, information accuracy, ethical values and correctability.

Gilliland (1993) extended these concepts to the selection situation and proposed 10 procedural rules, summarized in Figure 1.2. These rules would appear to encapsulate the candidate's expectations about the selection process and her presumptions that the choice of candidate will be based on job related factors rather than on irrelevant whims such as colour of candidate's hair or shoe size. Equally, the applicant's expectations include being treated with reasonable dignity and not being subjected to unnecessarily stressful or humiliating practices. This does not preclude acknowledging differences in ability and experience between herself and competitors for the position, but consideration of these variables is expected to align with the fairness perspective.

Formal characteristics of the selection procedures

Job relatedness – the extent to which a test appears to measure content relevant to the job or appears to be valid.

Opportunity to perform – having an adequate opportunity to demonstrate knowledge, skills and abilities in the selection situation.

Reconsideration opportunity – having the opportunity to review score sheets, to challenge results or to retest.

Administrative consistency – consistency or standardization of administration of selection procedures over people and over time.

Explanation of procedures and decision making

Feedback – provision of timely and informative feedback on test results and the selection decision (or the provision of an accurate estimate of when feedback could be expected).

Selection information – information on and justification for the selection procedures and decision process.

Honesty – salient instances of candidness or deception during communication with the candidate.

Interpersonal treatment

Interpersonal effectiveness – the degree to which candidates are treated with warmth and respect.

Two-way communication – the opportunity for candidates to ask questions and offer input during interpersonal interaction.

Propriety of questions – the degree to which questions asked during the selection process are appropriate.

Figure 1.2 Gilliland's ten procedural rules of justice
Source: Gilliland (1983)

Fairness in selection

Arvey and Renz (1992) adopted a slightly different perspective of fairness. Like Gilliland, they identified two factors as being the processes and procedures used in selecting employees, and the nature and kind of the information used in forming decisions, each of which could cause fairness issues and problems. However, their third factor was the resulting outcomes of selection. The components of these categories involved different principles. The processes and procedures encompassed objectivity, consistency, selection not subject to manipulation, professionalism of personnel, confidentiality of data and review of applicant information. The nature and kind of the information used in forming decisions included the types of instruments and tools used in gathering such information. Outcome issues in selection incorporated fairness to individuals and groups who may be disadvantaged by the selection process and decision making.

A number of variables with different degrees of fairness was suggested by Arvey and Renz (1992). In Britain there are fairly widely shared perceptions of the fairness of using various types of information, such as knowledge and skill, accepted as legitimate means of distinguishing between applicants. Others, such as colour of skin are not only considered to be unfair but are also illegal. A possible categorization of the British situation is given in Figure 1.3. As would be expected, most variables fall between the two extremes and their acceptability depends on individual and organizational interpretation.

DECEPTION IN SELECTION

The complexity of the selection process plus the direct or indirect involvement of many people combine to increase the opportunities for deception and its handmaidens bias and unethical conduct. The potential sources of deception are illustrated in Figure 1.4.

Whilst candidates and employers are the most likely people to deceive one another, each may be deceived by various intermediaries who are, ostensibly, facilitating the process. Outside agencies and referees may mislead one or both of the main parties. Each participant has individual aims and objectives, hidden and overt agendas, is subject to pressures from others or organizational policy, and has to adapt to changing conditions. In this context it is not surprising that deception occurs.

Perceived to be fair	Could be fair or unfair	Perceived to be unfair	Focus of pressure group activity	Illegal
Knowledge	Personality	Political connections or affiliations	Age	Race
Skill	Physical attractiveness	Nepotism	Sexual orientation	Gender
Experience	Values	Religion		Disability
Ability	Interests	Marriage connections		
□ intellectual		Social class		
□ physical		Membership of groups		
		□ trade union		
		□ 'old school tie'		
		□ freemasons		

Figure 1.3 Suggested categorization of fairness in the British selection process

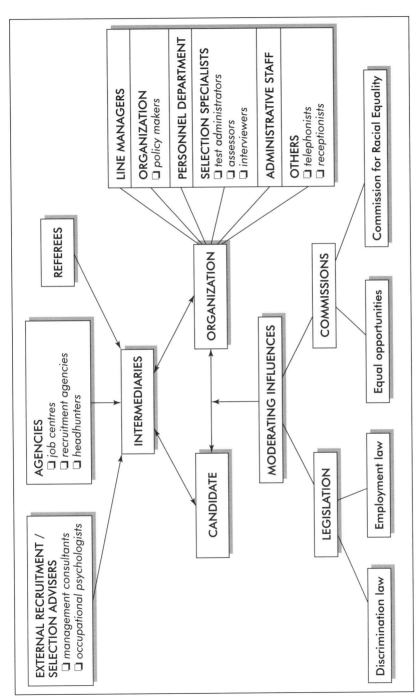

Figure 1.4 Potential sources of deception in the selection process

The organization itself may deceive, and be deceived, by the practices undertaken by its own employees or outside agencies on its behalf. The Personnel Department and management may have different attitudes to selection, with line managers and other staff involved in selection diverting from agreed procedures or those propounded in training sessions. Consequently Personnel staff themselves may be deceived, unless they discover that their espoused best practice is not given the total commitment they had sought, and believed they had obtained, from others associated in the procedures. Within their own department Personnel specialists may hold differing views on the validity and usefulness of selection methods, whilst the Personnel approach may contrast with the more scientific methods advocated by organizational psychologists.

A watching brief on the proceedings is kept by outside bodies such as the Equal Opportunities Commission and Commission for Racial Equality. These may intervene, usually on the job seeker's behalf, whilst the law gives recourse to either side should they feel aggrieved.

The nature of deception in selection

The exchange of complete, accurate information is fundamental to selection. The types of misinformation between candidate and selector are illustrated in Figure 1.5. Misinformation can permeate the whole of the selection procedure, beginning with the company's advertisement.

Deception occurs in individual methods and the selection process as a whole. It may happen unintentionally or deliberately. The types of deception, illustrated in Figure 1.6, differ between candidate and selector, though the exchange of inaccurate information and possible dishonesty is common ground. Selectors' deception operates by preventing candidates demonstrating their skills, broken contracts and poor interpersonal treatment. Similarly the choice of methods, the manner in which they are administered, the interpretation of results and the decision making can also mislead. Deceptive methods by the candidate centre on impression management, faking and the manipulation of selection methods. Candidates' deception may also include collusion with others involved in selection.

Impression management

Impression management describes the tactics used by individuals to con-

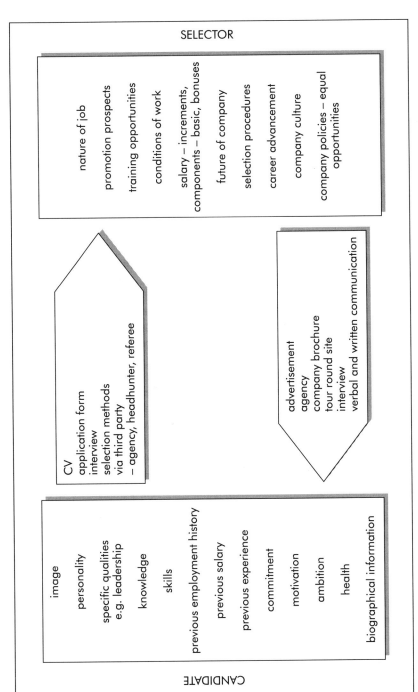

Figure 1.5 Types of misinformation in the selection process

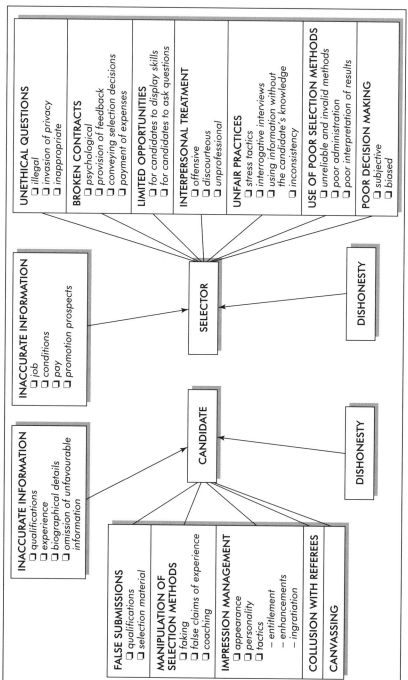

Figure 1.6 Types of deception in selection

trol the impressions they make, so influencing the subsequent image. Individuals hope that a favourable image will work to their advantage.

Self presentation strategies range from 'legitimate packaging' which highlights positive attributes to deliberate falsification. In the words of Rosenfeld, Giacalone and Riordan (1995) 'Sometimes impression management is truthful and accurate, other times it involves "false advertising" through the use of exaggeration, fabrication, deception and outright lying' (p. 7). Inflating one's extroversion may be more acceptable than magnifying the numbers and grades of qualifications.

In selection, a certain amount of impression management may be expected from both candidates and selectors. Selectors may 'sell' the job and organization whilst applicants will promote themselves in CVs or application forms. Social norms dictate that candidates make some sort of effort at the interview and comply with expected dress and behaviour codes. Failure to do so may be interpreted as a sign of disinterest, a lack of intelligence or ignorance of requisite social skills. However, deliberate distortion may be considered unacceptable.

Originally a *restricted perspective* of impression management viewed it as manipulative behaviour, in which intentional tactics are knowingly used by people for political gain. Recent *expansive perspectives* maintain that whilst impression management may be conscious and deliberate, it can also be a natural, if not automatic, facet of most people's behaviour and everyday life. In an organizational context, Rosenfeld et al. (1995) state 'Whether impression management is good or bad, ethical or unethical, really depends on why it is used and what it does; a decision that requires a judgement of the motives or consequences of impression management as used in a particular situation.' In selection, where an applicant is trying to obtain employment, self interest is the paramount concern and may involve the manipulation of the selector for the applicant's own purposes.

Impression management may be automatic or planned. The high stakes in selection ensure many candidates will pay attention to tactics and the selectors' possible reactions, including possible challenges to the image projected. Candidates may perceive courses in self presentation or interview training as a sensible and acceptable means of improving their impression management strategies. Selectors may think otherwise, arguing that once candidates stop, consider and actively plan their impression management strategies they are moving toward a more deceitful approach. In Fletcher's (1992) survey 5% of interviewers felt that training in effective interview presentation was dishonest.

Selectors following the expansive perspective may tolerate impression management, accepting it as an expected part of the selection procedure. Those subscribing to the manipulative approach may believe that a person who manipulates the truth for personal advantage during the selection procedure may continue with similar behaviour once appointed. Their view of the motives and consequences of impression management has moved it into the realm of deception.

Just as deception forms a continuum, so does impression management. Natural impression management, such as making the most of one's physical appearance and positive qualities, may not be done to deceive others and so corresponds with unintentional deception. Indeed, some could actually be self deceptive enhancement. Progressing along the continuum there is a fine line between the impression management tactics of embellishment, information filtering and falsification and this mirrors the exaggerations, deliberate omissions and lies which clearly form part of deception.

In Figure 1.7 impression management overlaps the continuum of deception. Its position is somewhat fluid, as the element of deception in impression management is largely controlled by the underlying motivation of the individual.

The aftermath of deception

People who practise deception to gain employment may see their dishonesty as a response to the selection procedure. They may feel that it is dictated by circumstances and justify it to themselves accordingly. Having achieved their purpose of gaining employment, their natural inclination for honesty may reassert itself. Alternatively their original dishonesty may be a typical and more stable characteristic which persists when they assume work tasks and responsibilities. Theft, fraud or general subterfuge may result and dismissal may be the ultimate sanction, necessitating re-recruitment with its associated costs, time and effort.

Employers may be unsure of which person fits which category. Doubts may be raised as to whether a person dishonest in one situation can be totally trusted in other circumstances, especially if their behaviour appears to have been governed by self interest. As the integrity of employees is often crucial, employers are concerned about the practice of deception. Candidates have similar concerns about the behaviour of a prospective employer. An employer who deceives during selection is unlikely to engender faith in organizational integrity, and concern may be felt about the future relationship between the organization and employee.

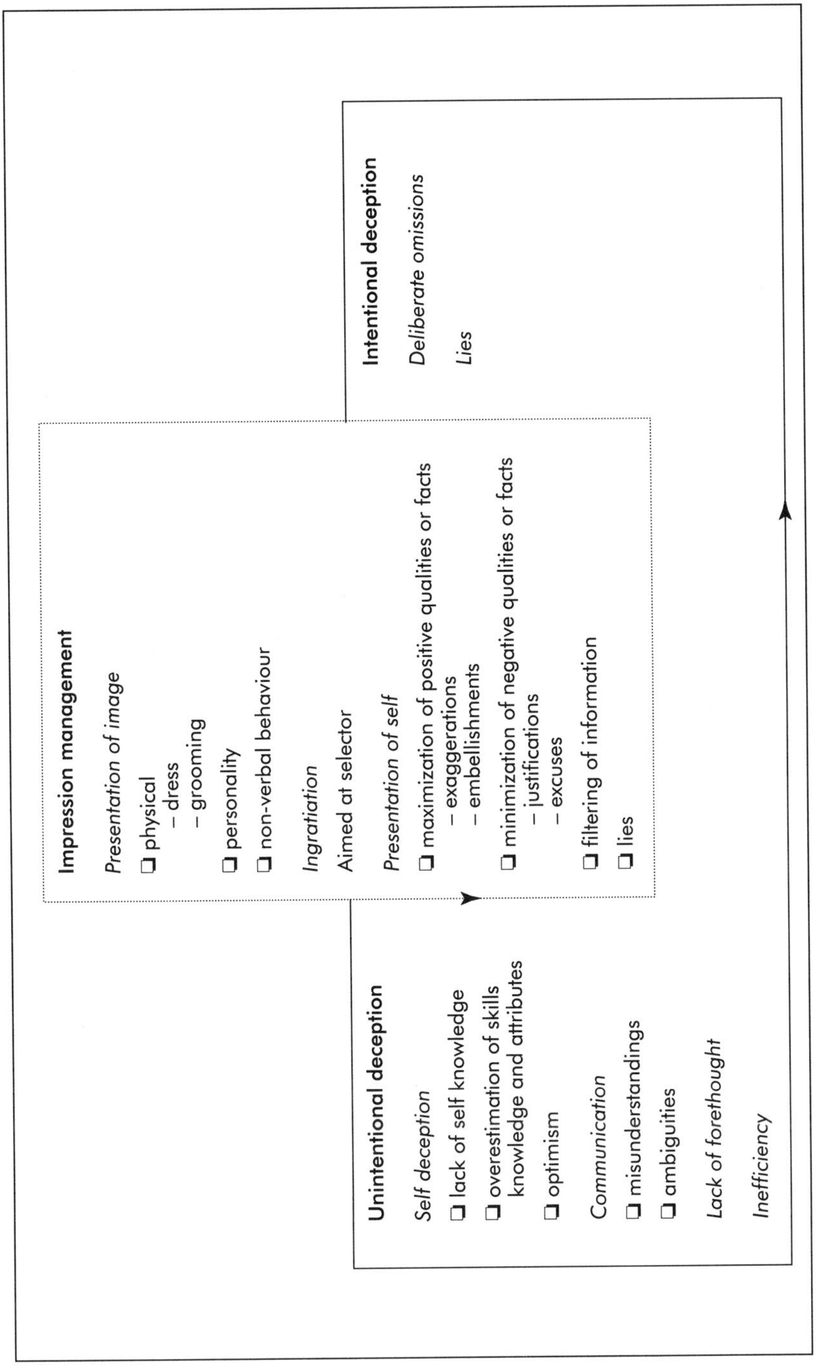

Unintentional deception

Self deception

❑ lack of self knowledge
❑ overestimation of skills knowledge and attributes
❑ optimism

Communication

❑ misunderstandings
❑ ambiguities

Lack of forethought

Inefficiency

Impression management

Presentation of image

❑ physical
  – dress
  – grooming
❑ personality
❑ non-verbal behaviour

Ingratiation

Aimed at selector

Presentation of self

❑ maximization of positive qualities or facts
  – exaggerations
  – embellishments
❑ minimization of negative qualities or facts
  – justifications
  – excuses
❑ filtering of information
❑ lies

Intentional deception

Deliberate omissions

Lies

Figure 1.7 The continuum of deception

Candidates may have misled selectors about their experience and abilities, so that productivity levels and quality suffer through the appointment of incompetent or unsuitable employees. Rudeness to customers and indifferent service typify unfavourable consequences of poor selection. The potential harm caused by a deceitful employer can have far-reaching financial consequences. A company engaging in dishonest practices is likely to damage its public image with devastating results, especially if the deception is broadcast to a wide audience through media attention.

The superficial results of deception are readily appreciated by Personnel and can be quite dramatic. However, the ramifications of deception are not always immediately apparent, so a chapter focusing solely on consequences is featured after a detailed examination of where and how deception occurs.

The extent of deception in selection

It is difficult to assess the extent of deception in employment. Many companies will not admit blatant bias such as discrimination against minority groups, even if it is recognized, because of its illegality (Gilliland, 1995). Personnel are understandably reluctant to acknowledge their own errors, instances of inefficiency and personal prejudices of which they may not even be aware themselves. Surveys investigating candidate honesty have been conducted (Fletcher, 1992; Keenan, 1983) but there is an inherent difficulty in believing their accuracy. How much faith can be placed in the honesty of the replies of candidates admitting a degree of dishonesty?

However investigations have been made into discrepancies of expectations between candidates and selectors and the accuracy of exchanged information (Herriot and Rothwell, 1981; Keenan and Wedderburn, 1980). More significantly, there is a considerable body of research on the validity and reliability of selection methods and concrete evidence of discriminatory practice is provided by the Equal Opportunities Commission (EOC) and Commission for Racial Equality (CRE). Personal interviews with job seekers and recruitment personnel have provided many examples of deception and the media frequently report newsworthy instances which may influence popular perceptions. Reference has been made to these in our case studies.

SUMMARY

Deception occurs against a background of perspectives of selection and justice. Procedural and distributive justice may be taken as representing the candidate's expectations of job related selection procedures, effective interpersonal treatment with two-way communication, honesty, the exchange of information and consistency.

Deception is both active and passive, affecting both the deceiver and the deceived. It may be practised by candidates and selectors but third parties may be influential. Recruitment agencies and referees may contribute to deception whilst legislative bodies may act as counterbalances. The organization may be deceived by the practices of its own staff, whilst training and good practice established by Personnel may be unheeded by others in selection. There is wide variety of types of deception, with inaccurate information and dishonesty being common to both selector and candidate. The candidate may make false submissions, manipulate methods and practise impression management whilst the selector may similarly use unfair practices in both the process and methods of selection.

Why do people deceive? 2

The reasons for deceit play a crucial role in the practice of deception and its consequences. They provide a valuable insight into the choice of misleading activities and procedures adopted by applicants and employers. Similarly, the choice of strategies to combat deception is helped by an appreciation of the underlying rationale.

There is a host of reasons for practising or conniving at deception and Figure 2.1 reveals that selectors and applicants often share the same motives. Each participant has personal open or hidden agendas, aims and objectives which may be furthered by deceit. Individuals do not operate in a vacuum but in a wider context in which they are subject to varying pressures and controls. Selectors are closely bound to the Personnel department, the established selection system and other organizational procedures and constraints. Current legislation, competitors and associated companies such as advertising and recruitment agencies are involved. The applicant's referees, colleagues, friends and family, the public plus the organization's customers and clients may also be interested and influential parties.

This chapter explores the continuum of deception. It starts by examining the circumstances in which non-deliberate deception, such as self deception and unwitting deception, occurs and then focuses on deliberate deception. Arguably most deception occurs when candidates and selectors wish to fill positions which would remain vacant if there was strict adherence to the truth. Political motives, pressure from others and commercial interests are also causes of deception and the difficulty in isolating reasons is apparent from the number of overlaps and common influences. The chapter concludes by considering justifications given for deception and the perceived likelihood of discovery.

NON-DELIBERATE TYPES OF DECEPTION

Self deception

In some cases people deceive themselves about their own character, attributes, behaviour and abilities. Consequently, candidates may seek and obtain jobs for which they are unsuitable, while selectors may have misplaced faith in their own abilities and the professionalism of the selection process. In deceiving themselves, individuals may embroil others who are convinced by the self deceiver's display of confidence.

Self deception occurs for several reasons. Key features are a lack of self awareness and the inability to see oneself through the eyes of others. The individual who considers himself to be thrifty may be regarded widely as a miser. Similarly, self deceivers are unlikely to appreciate their projected image and their effect on others. A person who is attentive to detail and methodical may extinguish spontaneity in colleagues and stifle creativity because his nit-picking propensities over-emphasize practicalities. Some individuals have a weak grip on reality. They may identify themselves with their desired image and verge towards a Walter Mitty type of fantasy life.

A contributory factor to self deception is the inability to learn from experience, especially as any feedback received can be ignored, discounted or reinterpreted. This is usually accompanied by supreme confidence in one's own abilities. The selector who is totally convinced of his expertise in interviewing attributes poor appointments to subsequent supervisory inefficiency, lack of training or changed circumstances rather than to the stereotyped judgements and biases which contributed to his poor judgement and decision making. A candidate may convince himself that he was a very close contender for a vacancy when in fact his skills fell far short of those required.

An unwillingness to acknowledge uncomfortable situations also subscribes to self deception, especially if unfavourable aspersions would result. A Personnel manager may prefer to maintain that the current selection process is professional and efficient when the reverse is true. To concede otherwise would necessitate recognition of personal ineffectiveness, mismanagement and shoddy standards.

People who are subject to self deception frequently make spontaneous, unconsidered decisions without reference to past experiences and the lessons that could be learnt. Intuitive reactions may be responsible for the gap between expectations and reality, whilst optimism may contribute to the 'triumph of hope over experience'. Consequently an applicant may genuinely believe that he can undertake proposed tasks, maintains such protestations despite the caution and doubts expressed by others and may convince a selector of his capabilities through his immense self confidence. Eventually the distance between perceptions and the ensuing reality becomes apparent, and both candidate and organization realize a mistake has been made. The following instance illustrates such self deception.

Reason	Candidate	Selector
UNINTENTIONAL DECEPTION		
Self deception	Misplaced faith in ability to do job	Misplaced confidence in interviewing skills
Poor preparation	No real motivation to gain job	Out of date or no job analysis, job description or person specification
Lack of forethought	About practitioners of travel, hours, etc in target job	Can the vacancy be filled in other ways, e.g. redeployment
Poor communication	Misunderstandings	Misunderstandings
INTENTIONAL DECEPTION		
Pressure from others	Pressure to get the job	From line managers to recruit rapidly, re expansion or seasonal fluctuations
To fill the vacancy	Deceipt to fit requirements	Enhance insecure and/or unattractive work and/or pay conditions
Concealing unfavourable information	Criminal record, poor health, being sacked from previous job	Possible reorganization, takeovers, dictatorial culture
Political agendas	To satisfy the conditions needed to receive the Jobseekers Allowance	'Lip service' to policy of external advertising when an internal candidate is 'earmarked'
	Use the process as 'practice' for 'genuine' applications	Internal power struggles among selectors
Financial reasons	To enhance future payment by exaggerating past earnings	To gain employees at the cheapest rate by 'fudging' salary details
Commercial reasons	Industrial espionage	Gain free consultancy from candidates' presentations
		To gain data from candidates about rivals

Figure 2.1 Reasons for deception

Martin, seeking his first employment, was advised that the job involved working three twelve hour shifts across Friday, Saturday and Sunday evenings. He could see several advantages in this arrangement, as he would have four free days to pursue other interests and see friends. The disadvantage of missing the social life of the weekend was discounted. Within a few weeks the difference between Martin's expectations and reality became increasingly obvious. The weekend social activities were missed more than anticipated while the tiredness from long hours of work detracted from his ability to enjoy his free time fully. Contact with friends during the early part of the week was also much less than he had expected. Martin left the job within six weeks.

Unwitting deception

Deception may occur through inadvertence. One person is deceived though this was not the intention of the other party and it may arise through misinterpretations of the truth. In other circumstances it occurs because of incompetence, differing points of view which generate contrasting expectations or a breakdown in communication. Alternatively the influence of other people may thwart procedures.

Incompetence may cause unwitting deception if selectors embark on selection without adequate forethought or preparation. Acting in good faith, a selector may advertise a vacancy, attract applicants and then realize that there are other ways of filling the position without appointing new staff. The aspiring candidates are therefore superfluous and have been misled by the process. Sometimes selection may be finalized before such recognition dawns. In these cases the successful candidate is installed in a job which may not be required or which undergoes swift modification in order to accommodate changing circumstances. A candidate may be equally rash. He may apply for shiftwork in a local firm without considering that the lack of public transport renders access to work virtually impossible.

Professional inadequacy may cause deception within the actual selection process. The absence of careful job analysis or the production of an incomplete job description can mean that key requirements are overlooked or unnecessary specifications are highlighted. As a result deception is built into the process. It is compounded through misleading advertisements which directly or indirectly specify such competencies. Applicants are misled by the job descriptions, believe that they would not qualify in their own right and massage the facts accordingly. Alternatively, selection can proceed to an advanced stage before such omissions are discovered, as exemplified below.

A firm wished to recruit a computer supervisor who would be based at head office but would also be responsible for operations in the surrounding satellite centres. A standardized job description and Personnel specification were available for the supervisor's position, selection followed its due course and the appointed candidate commenced work. Only at this stage was it appreciated that the appointed person could not drive. Mobility had not been required in the usual supervisory position and had been overlooked. The computer department felt deceived by the practices of Personnel staff and the candidate, pressurized into undertaking a concentrated course in driving, felt extremely unhappy about starting work with a disadvantage.

Ignorance of good practice may also cause deception in the choice of selection methods. Poor methods such as graphology or astrology, which are widely considered to be of low validity and reliability, may be utilized because of economy or current popularity. Lack of technical expertise may be combined with a failure to understand relevant principles. Consequently inability to appreciate the importance and necessity of standardized administration of psychometric tests can penalize some candidates. Alternatively robust selection methods are employed, but used unprofessionally, frequently involving questionable administration by untrained staff. Decisions may be made instinctively and without reference to acquired evidence.

Selectors and applicants may approach selection from different perspectives which generate contrasting expectations. The selector may favour utilitarianism. He believes that any tactics are justified in order to appoint the most appropriate candidate, and may therefore have no compunction in pressurizing candidates or using an interrogative style of interviewing. This stance may not be shared by the applicant, who expects selection to involve reasonable, humane treatment. As the two views are incompatible, unstated and therefore not subject to negotiation, it is likely that one party will feel aggrieved and deceived by practices which are perfectly acceptable to the other. The deception will be compounded if each party believes that his own viewpoint is universal. The following case serves as an illustration.

> Abigail was shortlisted for a routine administrative position and invited for interview. She expected this to follow a traditional pattern. Instead the interview transpired to be an in-depth session with a management consultant who wished to explore many personal matters with her, including her feelings on the death of her mother. Abigail emerged in a distressed condition and felt that she had been seriously misled. Had she had prior knowledge she would not have consented to such an experience. The consultant considered such tactics to be routine and unexceptionable.

Unwitting deception frequently occurs when there is a breakdown in communication. Ambiguous questions, whether written or verbal may prompt misleading responses which can be interpreted in several ways. The result may be that each person leaves an encounter such as an interview with different perceptions as to what occurred (Taylor and Sniezek, 1984), was said, discussed and the details and nature of any agreement reached. Eric's experience indicates such ambiguity.

> Eric was eighteen years old and applying for his first job. He was pleased with the progress of the interview and felt that he had made a good impression. He was delighted with the final question 'When could you start?' which was followed by a little more conversation and a concluding comment of 'We'll contact you tomorrow.' Eric couldn't wait to tell everyone of the new job he had just landed. As he left the room, the interviewer ticked the checklist columns on 'availability' and 'send immediate regret letter'.

Unwitting deception also occurs when selection decisions are subsequently subject to unforseen factors. Selector and candidate may act with sincerity and reach mutually satisfactory conclusions, only to find that their transactions were founded on quicksand. The actions and agendas of others may foil agreements, causing retractions and embarrassment. A selector may appoint in good faith, only to discover that political machinations render recruitment superfluous. A candidate, having been assured of family backing, agrees to the organization's proposals only to find that the expected support fails to materialize. The difference between theoretical discussion and reality can be great.

> When Dave told Janet of the proposed relocation from Brighton, Janet's reply consisted of a terse comment, 'I said I would move to the end of the world with you, but I didn't mean to Eckerslyke.'

DELIBERATE DECEPTION

Deliberate deception concerns the active manipulation of truth, personality and opinions in order to give a false impression. Strategies can involve the exaggeration of facts, their omission, the faking of other information and outright lying.

The cornerstone of deception in selection is that both employers and applicants wish to have a vacancy filled. Each may believe that if they were completely honest they would encounter difficulties in reaching their objectives or would not achieve ultimate success.

Applicant's deception of the selector

In order to obtain employment an applicant may deceive an employer for various reasons, and the degree of deception may be influenced by desperation to obtain the job, personal ambition and current economic position.

To increase the chances of gaining employment

The basic reason for much deception is the applicant's wish to gain a job which is believed to be unobtainable through strict adherence to the truth. Applicants may feel obliged to deceive selectors about their experience, qualifications, motivation and personality in order to make themselves appear attractive and closer to the ideal candidate sought by the organization. People seeking employment or promotion face an apparently insurmountable hurdle when they perceive a mismatch between the requirements of the desired job and their true capabilities and personal attributes. Such stipulations may cover clearly specified formal job requirements and more nebulous informal ones needed by either the job or the organization.

In addressing formal job requirements, the jobseeker may choose to exaggerate existing skills and experience until they reach the desired level. If this is not feasible, more drastic action may involve the complete fabrication of a whole range of features such as qualifications and past work experience.

Informal requirements may pose more difficulties. An applicant may perceive that firms seek certain personality features or a definite 'type' which the applicant does not naturally fit. Eager to satisfy the selector's demands and project the desired social image, the applicant may assume personal qualities which do not represent his typical personality.

To conceal unfavourable information

Frequently applicants believe they have some attributes which would deter employers from appointing them. These may include instances of past activities, previous behaviour such as violence and dishonesty plus apparently undesirable aspects of personality and background. For example, a man who has experienced difficulty in accepting the authority and orders of a female supervisor is unlikely to parade his chauvinism if he is interviewed by a female line manager. Equally the absence of requisite achievements, such as a clean driving licence, may be regarded as significant and such details may therefore be disguised, altered or omitted. In some cases omissions are justifiable. Applicants with criminal records are entitled not to disclose them if their convictions have been spent under the Rehabilitation of Offenders Act, 1974.

To conceal an unfair advantage

Candidates may also mislead fellow contenders and selectors by engaging in unfair practice, such as canvassing directors, undertaken to give them an advantage. Family connections, membership of particular societies or the 'old boy' network may all influence selection decisions unofficially. Such preferential treatment is informal, unacknowledged and could disqualify applicants, so candidates will endeavour to deny its presence and their potential collusion with influential members of the organization.

The wish to reach a particular stage of selection

Some deception occurs because the applicants wish to reach a particular stage of the selection procedure, usually the shortlist, and may direct their deception to accomplish this short term goal. Consequently, they may display an interesting and unusual personality in order to stand out from competitors. They may assume that selectors become bored when faced with many applications of equal merit and are readily swayed by details which make one application intriguing. A professed hobby of 'belly-dancing' has been known to produce the desired result.

For the excitement of the challenge

Some applicants may thrive on the challenge of selection. Deceptive tactics are acceptable weapons and adrenalin may flow in the attempt to emerge victorious with deception undiscovered. Candidates may relish the opportunity of outwitting selectors and enjoy their perceived astuteness.

Employers' deception of the applicant

Selectors may not share the candidates' views. As established members of the organization, their reputation may suffer if they take inordinate time to fill positions or make disastrous decisions which incur the wrath of other staff. They may therefore resort to deception for the reasons described below.

To fill the vacancy

Some selectors may deceive applicants in order to fill a vacancy. A dishonest, unrealistically favourable portrayal of unappealing situations may be considered essential to attract any applicants whatsoever. A poorly paid, dirty or tedious job without security and prospects is difficult to fill. Work which is normally attractive but occurs in unconducive surroundings or under the supervision of a bullying dictator may pose similar selection problems. Selectors may feel that if applicants knew the whole truth about the job and/or the organization the vacancy would remain unfilled. Such an outcome would be undesirable because of the costs incurred in re-advertising, repeating the recruitment exercise and a further investment of managerial time. Personnel may fear charges of incompetence if they fail to make an appointment.

At the other end of the spectrum, auspicious candidates may be lured by promised responsibilities, training, opportunities for advancement and other inducements which subsequently fail to materialize. This deceit may be practised so that appointed candidates bring added prestige to the company whilst simultaneously depriving competitors of the chance to employ their talents.

Employers may mislead candidates about the nature and duration of the selection process, reasoning that if candidates knew the full details they would not apply. This may occur when the methods used are of dubious quality, the procedure is prolonged or when the complexity of the process appears disproportionate to the position. An applicant seeking work as a receptionist may consider that two-panel interviews, a mini assessment centre and a thorough medical examination are unnecessarily demanding of his time and efforts, and would be reluctant to embark on such a process knowingly. A candidate expecting to be called for one interview and then being recalled for another two is similarly deceived.

The selector's personality

Selectors may deceive applicants because they view candidates with contempt or dislike, regarding them as mere adjuncts to organizational processes. This instrumental perspective negates personality, obligations and explanations and results in a disinclination to honour stated commitments. For example, promised feedback may not be delivered because it is not considered a high priority. It may be avoided because of inefficiency, disorganization or the fear that selectors may themselves be questioned about decisions which appear to lack objective justification.

Lack of professionalism or the necessary skills may contribute to the selector's reluctance and a laissez faire attitude may accentuate the attractiveness of inactivity.

In some cases candidates are misrepresented to other people, especially if ulterior or political motives operate within the organization. Such reasons for deception are described in the following section.

Political reasons for deception

Both individuals and organizations may have their own political agendas which effectively dictate certain courses of action. People are subject to the pressures, schemes and ambitions of others, which may necessitate their adoption of political strategies in the interests of self preservation. Political pressures influence applicants and organizational Machiavellianism may affect current employees, managers and Personnel staff.

Pressure on applicants

Pressure from others may lead applicants to practise deceit, especially over motivation to gain employment. Individuals may feel coerced into applying for jobs that they do not wish to obtain, that are of no interest and which would be rejected if job offers materialized.

In periods of unemployment, family pressure may be exerted on the jobless to get any type of work, regardless of personal inclination or disposition. This is especially true if the situation is aggravated by financial worries. Compulsion from one partner on the other, or from parents on young unemployed people, may cause the jobless person to deceive prospective employers about their ambition and interest in work generally and in that vacancy in particular. In this way their jobseeking activities gain a reprieve from domestic nagging and also satisfy the Department for Education and Employment (DfEE).

Under the stricter benefits regime, unemployed individuals are only entitled to a Jobseeker's Allowance if they can prove that they are actively seeking work. Without such evidence benefits are withdrawn. Accordingly, jobseeking activities, such as completion of application forms and attendance at interviews, may be undertaken with little or no intention to obtain work. Some jobseekers judge the differential between salary and benefits to be marginal, prefer to remain on benefit and therefore fulfil the conditions needed to achieve this.

In these cases candidates deceive employers and others. They go through the motions of pursuing jobs, to which they are indifferent, in order to appease external pressures. Occasionally similar situations occur within an organization.

The organization's use of the official selection policy for political reasons

Complex deception occurs when internal candidates wish to apply for other positions within the organization, especially if company policy dictates that all vacancies are advertised externally. Should the internal candidate be a highly favoured applicant, external candidates are deceived about the realistic availability of that particular job. Their presence is a formality, ensuring that prescribed procedures are followed and preventing allegations of 'favouritism'.

Alternatively management may consider the internal candidate to be totally unsuitable and the position is subsequently offered externally. Unless the internal candidate has been actively discouraged from pursuing his application, the procedure may raise false hopes in the internal candidate, deceive him as to the likely outcome and use company policy as a means of rejection. A similar situation may occur when a line manager is subject to pressure from an employee.

Pressure on staff within an organization

Employees may feel pressurized into applying for relocation or jobs involving promotion, as a manager or mentor may feel that such actions would be a good career move for the employee. The employee does not feel able or willing to disabuse a superior that such a plan is contrary to his own wishes and inclination.

In some cases there may be no opportunity for discussion. Applicants are entered for promotional selection procedures without consultation, as senior management may believe they are acting in their protegees' best interests. Alternatively the process may be automatic for people at certain grades or as part of corporate plans which are based on assumptions of the staff's total commitment and loyalty to the company.

In such circumstances candidates attempt to deceive selectors and others about their true motivation, commitment, ambition and career aspirations. Their actions may be prompted by self preservation and aimed at safeguarding their standing with senior managers.

The reverse type of deception may occur when internal employees pressurize a line manager to approve a proposed application for promotion. Doubts about the applicant's suitability or readiness for such a move place the line manager in a dilemma. If he agrees to the request, the candidate is misled about the chances of selection success and the selectors are misled by the line manager's endorsement of the application. Additionally, senior managers may question the line manager's judgement in supporting a poor candidate.

On the other hand, failure to support the application may prompt a discussion between line manager and employee on the employee's shortcomings. The line manager's rejection and feedback can cause the candidate to feel disappointed and aggrieved, which in turn damages their future working relationship. The line manager may conclude that it is more politic for someone else to determine the outcome, especially if he has any doubts about his own judgement.

Personnel staff themselves may be subject to the pressures of others. Line managers may have strong preferences for particular candidates which are unrelated to their performance in the selection procedure. Likewise senior managers can make their sponsorship of particular candidates known. Implicitly or explicitly, this may pressurize selectors to connive at unethical selection practices, especially if selection is used as an arena for political ambition.

Power games among selectors

Selection frequently involves staff of varying status and different departments. Selection methods such as assessment centres or panel interviews may give managers an opportunity to engage in a political power struggle. Selection decisions may therefore be subordinate to ulterior motives which may be contrary to the company's best interests. This may be particularly pertinent if selectors have vested interests in certain candidates which are not declared to fellow selectors.

Political strategies adopted for expediency

Selectors may be aware that legislation imposes certain constraints on the use and implementation of methods available in selection. This is especially apposite in the case of considering candidates from minority groups. Individuals may proffer lip service to such regulations without any intention of abiding by their spirit. Superficial compliance with the letter of legislation may be undertaken to avoid allegations of unfair practice and repercussions such as attendance at industrial tribunals, legal costs and subsequent compensation awards. The deception may be compounded if the guise of fairness is used to mask the selector's or organization's prejudices.

Expediency may also influence the organization's retention or release of existing staff. Employees may experience uncertainty about their current position in the organization. Redeployment, relocation, redundancies and promotion situations may all lead employers to deceive employees about their positions, security and long term future in the company. In the same manner employers may deceive employees and fellow employers on the matter of supplying references which would assist staff to gain employment elsewhere. Political interests may be paramount in retaining good employees whilst releasing poorer ones, as exemplified below.

> Teddy Toy Company had been a well established family business for the last thirty years, with a comparatively low staff turnover. Recently it had suffered from growing competition from the Far East and falling profits led to rumours of redundancies. Several staff were known to have applied for a job in the newly opened nearby branch of Trendy Toys. The production manager received reference requests for two of his staff – super efficient Clark and less reliable Len. He knew that if Clark left, productivity would fall and his own job would become much more difficult. Consequently, Len was given a good reference whilst Clark's reference was mediocre. Len got the new job.

Organizational pressure on recruitment agencies and headhunters

Occasionally organizational policy or individual staff may pressurize agencies to thwart the ethics of selection. Instructions may be given to agencies to supply only certain categories of candidates, usually in direct contravention of discrimination legislation and the agency's own code of practice. Such practices also mislead the agency's other jobseekers, who expect to be treated fairly and given every opportunity to gain employment.

Commercial interests can influence the agency's concurrence with such 'requests' and this additional reason for deception is described in the next section. The following scenario illustrates the interrelationship between political and commercial interests.

Smart recruitment agency had been operating for five years and had built up a reputation for fairness and efficiency. Consequently it could usually offer employers a good selection of applicants. One day, it was approached by a local senior manager seeking a sales manager. The CVs of several applicants were submitted. The immediate response consisted of an ultimatum 'I only want you to send me CVs from white men – if not I'll take the business elsewhere.' The agency declined to assist the employer and adhered to its equal opportunities policy. The vacancy was filled through another agency which prioritized profit ahead of ethics.

COMMERCIAL INTERESTS

Agencies and organizations all operate to make money and in some instances the desire or necessity to maintain profits may encourage deception in selection. Organizations may be unwilling to spend the time and money needed to implement fair and efficient selection procedures. Inappropriate, inexpensive selection methods may be used or adequate procedures may be adopted but devalued by lack of investment in essential training of administrators or parsimony in updating originally valid methods to accord with current circumstances.

External commercial bodies are increasingly involved in an organization's selection process and the consequent increase in competition heightens commercial awareness. A reluctance to engage in unethical practices, as described above, may have to be balanced against short term financial viability. Some agencies may feel unable to challenge unethical requests for fear of losing a client who can easily transfer business to a more accommodating firm.

The desire to make money encourages some agencies to engage in other practices of dubious honesty. Candidates may be deceived by advertisements for non-existent jobs which have been inserted by agencies anxious to maintain their supply of CVs. Similarly some agencies may forward CVs to employers without the candidates' consent, in order to gain the fee awarded by employers for supplying the 'first past the post' CVs.

The organization's wish to gain commercial advantage

The employing organization may deceive in order to achieve commercial advantage. During the selection process applicants may be asked, directly or indirectly, to disclose the practices of rival companies. Sometimes the exercise is entirely fictitious, and is orchestrated specifically to obtain valuable information about competitors.

Deception of candidates also arises when they are used as a source of free consultancy as shown in the following illustration.

> Barbara was very keen to obtain a junior position in a marketing company. Eventually she was shortlisted. She was requested to prepare a presentation on a case study which necessitated the development of a strong marketing strategy. After spending two days on research and preparation, Barbara duly gave the presentation but was not appointed. Shortly afterwards she recognized some of her key ideas in a press campaign. She felt that such a coincidence was beyond belief.

The candidate's ulterior motives

Occasionally applicants may wish to gain employment for ulterior, commercial motives. If successful, the newly appointed employee can infiltrate the firm and gain access to confidential material concerning process, production, marketing and other commercial strategies. Such information can then be used for nefarious reasons such as industrial espionage. The organization has therefore been deceived by the applicant's apparent motivation and may suffer financial loss. Alternatively, candidates may apply to competitor organizations in order to 'spy' on processes and gauge future strategies. They can then report their rival's position to their current employer in order to gain acclaim and personal advancement.

The above outline of reasons for deception has indicated that they are complex, interrelated and involve many people. Although organizational and commercial influences can have considerable impact, they are interpreted, internalized and propounded by specific individuals. Nevertheless, not all individuals in similar circumstances deceive others, as other factors may be influential. The key determinants appear to be attitude to the truth, the perceived justification for misleading others and the likelihood of discovery.

FACTORS AFFECTING ALL THOSE PRACTISING DECEPTION

Many people who deceive others in the selection process are not congenital liars but individuals who may believe that social norms prescribe the use of self advertisement and the use of impression management techniques. False modesty may be considered misplaced in interviews, especially if their unstructured format encourages self promotion and associated exaggerations. Deceivers' justification in giving false information frequently results from their past experience of selection and a calculation of the subsequent benefits and disadvantages of such deceit.

Attitudes to the truth and likelihood of discovery

Attitudes to the truth are related to personal attributes such as expediency, the development of conscience, upbringing, a disregard of rules plus the strength and nature of moral values. All help to shed light on why some people lie and others tell the truth, but the detailed examination of such characteristics is beyond the scope of this book. However, mention must be made of one characteristic which contributes to deception and this is an individual's reluctance to speak frankly.

Some people are unwilling to be honest in circumstances where the truth could be seen as unproductive, unpleasant or hurtful. This aversion may arise because of cowardice, innate politeness or a concern not to damage others' feelings. The desire to be diplomatic may result in the use of ambiguous language, so there is uncertainty about the real message being conveyed. Alternatively a key issue is avoided by concentrating on positive points and omitting negative factors. Such behaviour may be exhibited by both selectors and applicants, creating a climate of uncertainty which clouds selection.

Participants in selection may have no compunction in telling lies but may hesitate to do so because they fear discovery. This may be especially relevant if they suspect their behaviour will betray deceit or if they doubt their ability to deceive successfully. The absence of a good memory may cause the deceiver to forget previous falsehoods whilst lack of imagination may hinder further fabrication of material needed to sustain the original deception.

The likelihood of discovery of deception and perceived consequences may effect deception and influence the scale and methods adopted. Some people embark on deception without considering the consequences or

may think that the deception will not be discovered. Others may calculate whether discovery is likely, at what stage and the possible results.
The less risk they foresee, the more likely they are to deceive.

The perceived time span before discovery may be relevant, since it
could influence the strategies of deception and the organization's subsequent actions. Candidates may consider that they could 'bluff their way
out' if deception was detected at an early stage in selection. They may
reason that the chances of unmasking the deception once they are
appointed are minimal, and if this occurred they would already be in a
position of strength which would render dismissal unlikely. They may
choose to ignore the possibility of more serious consequences.

It would be unwise to conclude that deception is only practised by
people who have a scant regard for the truth. There is a continuum of
attitudes to honesty, ranging from people who consider lying to be totally unethical in any circumstances to congenital liars. In the context of
deception, the first group is of limited interest and the second group is
extremely difficult to handle because there can be little defence against
the determined 'con artist', though defence strategies can be strength-
ened as much as possible.

It seems that the middle of the continuum is the area in which most
deception occurs and is also the area in which detection is difficult because
of a mixture of honesty and dishonesty. Individuals who are usually honest may classify the occasional lie as being 'economical with the truth' and
the following section describes the ways in which they justify deceit.

Justification

Deceivers may feel that 'the end justifies the means' and their justification comes from a variety of sources.

Past experience – 'everyone does it'

Candidates who initially act with integrity in their search for employment, soon learn that other jobseekers do not employ the same values.
Deceit may enhance a rival's status and help competitors to gain employment in preference to honest individuals. The belief that 'everyone else
does it' prompts the adoption of misleading behaviour, albeit with varying degrees of reluctance. Deceit may be viewed as an option forced on
candidates by the actions of others so that they can compete on equally

dishonest terms. The belief that deception is widespread may render it less morally reprehensible, if not actually acceptable. Selectors may share this view. Previous encounters with dishonest candidates may encourage a blanket approach of distrust which penalizes honest applicants.

The selector's past experience of other applicants can be matched by the candidate's experience of employers. Employers may treat their staff, other candidates or the applicant himself in ways which create unfavourable opinions. The belief that some employers are governed by self interest and exhibit contempt for employees is compounded if an applicant perceives employers as acting unethically. Applicants may conclude that employers do not necessarily deserve to be treated with complete honesty.

Relevance of information sought by the employer

Again justification for deceit arises if a candidate genuinely believes that he is capable of doing the job but is apparently prevented from gaining employment because of arbitrary and unnecessary preconditions. Judging such stipulations to be irrelevant, he may believe that the specified job requirements are unfair, and therefore manipulates his own details in order to present himself in a favourable light.

Justification for dishonesty also occurs if an applicant feels that information sought by the employer, at any stage of the selection procedure, is not relevant to the job. Details of domestic arrangements may be a case in point. Such enquiries may be seen as personal, intrusive and in breach of legislation. As the candidate may not be in a position to challenge the need for such information, he may feel obliged to supply it, but not necessarily fully or accurately.

Fear of the employer misinterpreting information

Employers sometimes seek information which jobseekers regard as being sensitive and personal, as on health matters. Candidates may feel concerned that employers will reach stereotyped conclusions on issues of which they have little knowledge. Consequently they may disguise, minimize or totally conceal information that they feel could eliminate them from further selection stages. They feel justified in combating perceived unjustified employer prejudice.

Perceptions about the selection system

Candidates may feel that despite the apparent fairness of the formal selection process, appointments are in reality made on the basis of other criteria, such as the 'old boy' network. This may encourage someone without these connections to deceive employers. They feel that unfair practices deserve to be treated by equally irregular attitudes and adopt a 'fight fire with fire' approach.

Opportunist deceit occurs when enterprising applicants spot and exploit weaknesses in the selection system. They feel able to disclaim ownership of the ensuing duplicity on the grounds that it was the organization's fault for using an inefficient system. In this way a candidate with poor command of written English may feel justified in asking someone to complete the application form on his behalf as there are no instructions to the contrary.

Short term duration of the deception

The belief that the deception is only a short term measure, perhaps to get a candidate an interview, may also encourage people in deception. A plan of revealing the deception at interview or the knowledge that the deception will be immediately obvious may be seen as validation. Should events not turn out as planned, the applicant may then be forced to continue the deception in order to maintain apparent credibility, as illustrated by Sheila's case.

> Sheila was a lively, enthusiastic, experienced secretary with a young at heart attitude. She felt about thirty-five years old but was actually forty-eight. Having just finished a six month spell of temporary work, she noticed an advertisement for a local company which sought 'an experienced secretary aged 21–40'. Assessing herself to have the necessary experience, Sheila appreciated that she was unlikely to get an interview if she stated her true age, so rejuvenated herself by ten years on the grounds that should she get an interview everybody would notice the discrepancy. She was invited to the interview which was conducted by someone in her twenties. To her amazement, her age was accepted at face value. Her deception had been more successful than anticipated.

SUMMARY

In conclusion, self interest can be identified as the key reason why applicants and employers practise deception. Candidates want to gain jobs; employers want to fill vacancies. In some circumstances each party judges that its aims will not be achieved easily or readily if the total truth is known. Pressure from others, commercial interests and politics within an organization are all facets of this self interest. Accordingly some people practise deception as a means of solving their own problems and apply a number of arguments to justify their actions.

The employer's deception of the candidate

3

The selection process incorporates the provision of information, communication, treatment of candidates and relevant ethical issues such as professionalism, confidentiality and consistency. These factors apply to all applicants, whether shortlisted or not, and therefore the process operates independently of selection methods to some extent, so warranting separate consideration. Unlike other aspects of selection, the selection process is determined solely by the employer.

The initial stages of the selection process frequently embrace many potential and eventual applicants. As most jobseekers will not be shortlisted and involved in later selection methods, they form their impressions of organizations from the information and treatment they receive during this period. From a public relations point of view, this stage is crucial.

The organization's provision of information determines the number and quality of potential applicants. If selectors misinform applicants, they may be overwhelmed by applications from unsuitable jobseekers or good candidates may be lost. Lack of detail encourages inappropriate applicants and prevents self selection whilst deceptive information and treatment may deter auspicious contenders.

The chapter's starting point is an outline of the selectors' and candidates' different expectations. A more detailed analysis is made of employers' misrepresentations over the job, shown in Figure 3.1 and the selection procedures, summarized in Figure 3.2. This is followed by considering the treatment of candidates, with specific mention of dignity, consistency and confidentiality. Finally the chapter looks at the crucial role of communication.

THE CANDIDATE'S AND THE SELECTOR'S VIEWS OF THE SELECTION PROCESS

Candidates expect to be treated fairly and reasonably during selection (Arvey and Renz, 1992; Gilliland, 1993). They foresee receiving inform-

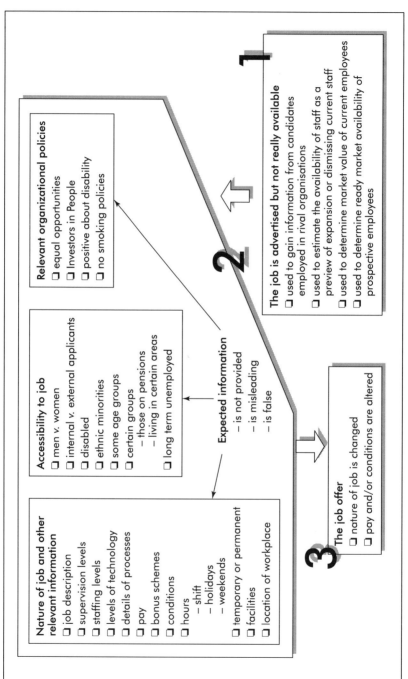

Figure 3.1   Deception of the candidate over the job

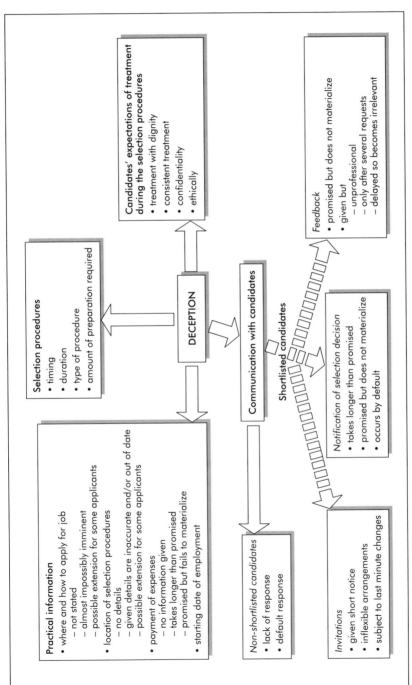

Figure 3.2 Deception of the candidate over the selection procedures

ation about the job as a priority, but value knowledge of the selection process and their own performance. They also hope for two-way communication and being treated with warmth, respect, honesty and ethical behaviour from selectors.

Candidates are probably realistic enough to know that such ideals are unlikely to operate universally. Nevertheless, they may still expect to be acknowledged as individuals who have invested time, effort and emotion in their applications, rather than being regarded as powerless, inanimate pawns to be moved at the organization's whim. Applicants' attitudes to selection affect their decisions, and if their expectations are unmet they are likely to feel misused and deceived, perceiving that justice has not been done.

Employers do not necessarily share the candidate's perspective, and may think they are doing applicants a favour by letting them apply. The candidates may not be seen in terms of personality and individuality, but more instrumentally as organizational 'fodder'. Consequently, there appears less need to treat candidates sympathetically, especially in a utilitarian culture where fairness may be considered irrelevant.

Selectors may be influenced by their wish to fill a job vacancy as speedily as possible, perhaps with minimum time, cost and effort. They may therefore deceive applicants in their representations of the job, selection procedure and exchange of information.

These perspectives influence the exchange of information. Candidates and organizations are unequal contributors, as candidates are asked to disclose much information whilst organizations are less communicative. Applicants need two types of information – primarily about the job but also concerning the actual selection procedure. Organizations may exhibit reluctance or lack of openness in providing realistic information in both areas. This inhibits jobseekers' decision making, as they can not determine their suitability for the job and likelihood of obtaining it, so are unable to self select.

As shown in Figure 3.3, the main sources of information to applicants – advertisements, agencies, brochures and site tours – are open to deception. They vary in the detail, amount, completeness and accuracy they provide. The job advertisement is often the first, and frequently the only source of information for many candidates, but it can be the starting point of deception, as seen from Figure 3.1.

Source of information	Misrepresentation and omissions
Advertisement	
Nature of job	Given in generalized terms or exaggerated. Few details of tasks and responsibilities.
Salary	Omitted, ambiguous, misrepresented, expressed subjectively, e.g. 'excellent' or on incomprehesible scales, e.g. JT3 POINTS 3–4. No indication of whether bonuses or commissions are involved.
Organization	May not indicate name, type of firm or location. Brief details may make identification virtually impossible. Anonymity may be preserved through box numbers or agencies.
Job requirements	Vague, subjective or unrealistic, e.g. a graduate aged 25–30 with at least ten years' experience. Qualifications may be inflated to reduce numbers of potential applicants.
Other details	Frequently omitted.
Organizational brochure	May be marketing propaganda rather than factually accurate.
A site tour	Selective presentation of favourable facilities, exclusion of inadequate facilities. Requests to see certain facilities may be ignored. Questions ignored or answered misleadingly.
Agencies	May exaggerate the job to appliants and/or not give organizational details. May not give the same information to all clients.
Details sent to applicants	Incomplete, inaccurate, out of date. Lack of information on relevant organizational policies.
Job description	Non-existent, unavailable, incomplete, inaccurate or out of date.
Person specification	Non-existent, unavailable, incomplete, inaccurate or out of date.

Figure 3.3 Sources of information about the job

THE ORGANIZATION'S DECEPTION OVER THE JOB
The existence of the job

Assumptions that the advert implies a real job opportunity may be incorrect, for the reasons summarized in Figure 3.1. Sometimes adverts refer to jobs which are available originally but later withdrawn, or occasionally the job never existed at all. Similarly the nature of the job, its requirements and salary may be changed during the course of the selection process.

The reasons for such deception are complex. In some instances both selector and candidate are misled by directors or senior management for political, financial and security reasons. Proposed mergers and reorganization may be concealed to maintain the normality of day to day organizational life. Routine recruitment, which is undertaken by selectors in good faith, may be overtaken by subsequent events, rendering such appointments unnecessary. Consequently the selector and appointed candidate become the casualties of forces beyond their control.

Hidden agendas may motivate an organization to advertise a non-existent vacancy for ulterior motives. These may include gauging the availability of potential staff or obtaining free consultancy through presentations prepared by candidates. Interviewing applicants currently employed by competitors enables organizations to gain valuable knowledge, such as product research, which can boost their organizational success whilst damaging rivals' prospects. Alternatively agencies may insert adverts as a means of getting CVs on file in order to satisfy client needs.

Information about the job

Candidates relying solely on the advertisement may have very limited information about the vacancy. They may wish to amplify details of the nature of the job, its scope, rewards and other information, as shown in Figure 3.1. The location and physical work conditions are relevant whilst future considerations such as promotion opportunities, job security and the organization's economic stability are also important.

The organization may supply misleading descriptions of the job and other relevant information through the advert and the other sources of information already mentioned. Lack of clarity, deliberate or unintentional, may occur if the advert gives mixed messages. An advert showing a photo of a woman telephonist and stating that jobs are open to both sexes may raise doubts and cynicism.

Salary is a frequent source of confusion and misinformation, intentionally or otherwise. Absence of salary details creates uncertainty. Candidates asked to include their salary details and/or expectations with their CV may feel that the organization's ploy is to appoint at the cheapest rate possible. Attempts to clarify ambiguities may not receive frank responses and organizational reluctance to divulge salary details may persist, despite further enquiries, as in Samantha's case.

> As an administrative assistant Samantha's annual salary was half the national average. Wishing to improve her position, she applied for several jobs, one of which appeared suitable but omitted salary details. Phoning to determine renumeration, she was told that the company's policy was to discuss salary only at the interview stage. She had encountered a similar situation previously, when the salary disclosed was lower than her current pay, so she persisted with her enquiries but met resistance. Eventually she was told that whilst exact salary details could not be declared, if Samantha revealed her current salary, further information could be provided. This occurred and as the salary was attractive Samantha pursued the application. At the interview selectors told Samantha that they had noted her preoccupation with salary, and she interpreted this comment as an unfavourable evaluation. Samantha felt the reluctance to disclose salary was unfair, unrealistic and potentially a waste of everyone's time.

Expected information about the job requirements, organization and relevant organizational policies may be unforthcoming. Candidates may feel disadvantaged by such ignorance and be unsure of whether they wish to proceed. There are more practical implications. A candidate could unknowingly apply for a position within his current organization or for his own position in a firm he has just left.

Accessibility of the job

Assumptions that an advertised job is open to all may be unfounded, as shown in Figure 3.1. Adverts may not indicate opportunities but compliance with organizational policy, and favoured status may be conferred on particular groups.

This is pertinent in considering external and internal candidates. Jobs may not be advertised internally and in the case of *Ramsden* v. *Advance Tapes (UK) Ltd* an industrial tribunal found this led to unlawful discrimination. Frequently preference may be given to an internal candidate or temporary employee who has already been identified as suitable. Company policy necessitates an advertisement, even though external candidates will not be considered and are effectively being manipulated to conform with procedures, as exemplified below.

> Jim applied for a job as a trainee housing officer with a large metropolitan borough. After six weeks he had heard nothing about the position and phoned to make enquiries. He was told bluntly that there had been sixty applications which had not even been opened as the temporary worker already covering the vacancy was going to be made permanent. The advert had been a routine procedure which satisfied the letter of company policy, not the spirit.

Open competition may be non-existent or very restricted. Succession planning may operate through executives secretly meeting to hand pick successors (Mabey and Iles, 1993). Potential applicants may be effectively ruled out without even knowing they were under consideration. Some jobs are never advertised but sourced informally through word of mouth, nepotism, membership of certain societies or the 'old boy' network.

The location of adverts may preclude some sectors of the community from learning of opportunities, as may informal recruitment methods which maintain the status quo of the existing workforce. Vacancies which attract applicants from all sectors of the community may actually operate certain restrictions. The organization may operate unofficial age restrictions or have a priority list, so that first consideration is given to internal applicants who are at risk of being made redundant or are seeking redeployment. Disabled applicants may be given precedence, followed by those who live within particular areas. Occasionally candidates may be disqualified from further consideration because they are on a job related pension. If such policies are not stated openly, the candidate is deceived about the chances of success.

In other circumstances inconsistency of availability is due to bias. Active deception may occur if some applicants are told untruthfully that jobs are 'filled' when the reverse is true. This may stem from differences in ethnic group, appearance or apparently foreign names on application forms. Noon (1993) studied racial discrimination in speculative applications to the UK's top 100 firms, and concluded there was a big gap between company policy and practice on equal opportunities. Similarly stereotyped views on 'men's work' and 'women's work' may cause some agencies to disqualify 'inappropriate' applicants by withholding details of male candidates for packing or secretarial jobs, traditionally seen as 'women's work'. They may adopt this view unilaterally or believe, rightly or wrongly, that it is shared by the client.

The job offer

Discussion of the nature and existence of the job may not occur until the job offer stage. Sometimes the job offered involves a change in type of work from the one advertised. Frequently this is not as challenging or interesting as the original position, and overall opportunities are fewer and less promising. On other occasions the essential job remains unchanged but other features, especially terms and conditions are altered at the last minute. Such adjustments are frequently less favourable than those portrayed initially.

Job offers may be made and accepted before deception is discovered. Candidates may be told that the offer is subject to board confirmation which never materializes. After persistent enquiries, the candidate realizes that either there never was a job or that this is the company's way of informing candidates that they have been unsuccessful. Similarly candidates may turn up for work, only to find that the job, and sometimes the organization, were the figment of someone's imagination.

THE ORGANIZATION'S DECEPTION OVER SELECTION PROCEDURES

Candidates value practical information and knowledge of the selection procedures, as these may influence decision making. Details of the timing, duration and location of selection, payment of expenses and selection methods are all relevant.

Practical information

Timing and duration of selection

Information does not always indicate a closing date for applications, so creating considerable uncertainty for candidates. On the other hand, submission by a stated date may be problematic if the timescale is short.

Shortlisted candidates may be given little notice of inflexible selection dates. This may be an insurmountable hurdle if timing coincides with pre-booked holidays or hospital appointments. Had candidates been advised earlier of provisional selection dates, clashes could have been identified and the candidate could have decided whether to invest the time and effort needed to apply. The position becomes more galling if companies expect last minute flexibility from candidates in order to accommodate their own needs.

Duration of subsequent selection may not be indicated. Through ignorance, the employed candidate may underestimate timing and the amount of absence required from work. Subsequent inability to conform with the expected selection programme may be construed as a lack of enthusiasm but extended absence from work could jeopardise current employment. Similarly candidates may be unaware of whether one or three interviews are involved.

Location

Location is important because of accessibility, distance and time implications. Often selection procedures are held in the workplace but offsite selection may occur in head offices, job centres or hotels. This makes it impossible to form opinions of the organization and particular work place conditions. Few candidates would choose to work in a place they have not seen and interviews may be conducted offsite simply to prevent candidates viewing an unattractive workplace.

Employers may not provide location details such as maps and availability of public transport routes and parking availability. They may consider that locating the site is a test of candidate initiative.

Payment of expenses

Expenses are a fraught issue for candidates, especially as they are frequently cloaked in uncertainty. Organizational policies vary tremendously and are rarely conveyed to applicants. Some companies reimburse all candidates, some pay the expenses of successful candidates, others pay only the expenses of unsuccessful candidates and still others do not pay any expenses. Organizations may lack a policy, may adopt an ad hoc stance or vary their observation of policies according to circumstance. Selectors may try to eke out departmental budgets by individual interpretations of policy, paying expenses only in response to candidate requests or to individuals judged to be travelling beyond the local area.

Candidates expecting expenses feel deceived if they are not forthcoming. This may occur if candidates fail to satisfy undisclosed conditions such as gaining travel receipts or because organizations do not honour their commitments. As a result candidates are financially disadvantaged.

Expenses may assume greater significance when combined with other selection variables. The candidate attending a fair, professional interview may accept the non-payment of expenses philosophically. The applicant involved in a five minute interview conducted for ulterior motives may be totally disgruntled, and consider that such treatment is only redeemable by financial recompense.

Knowledge of selection methods

Applicants rarely know details of selection. Whilst most adverts indicate how candidates are to respond, some exhibit imprecision. Shortlisted candidates may receive more information in the proffered invitation, though imminent selection procedures may remain unknown until arrival at the organization. This ignorance may prompt candidates to make incorrect assumptions and limits their preparation, which could affect their subsequent presentation of skills and abilities.

Whilst interviews are expected and accepted, psychometric tests and other selection methods are used less commonly and may cause anxiety. Some candidates may feel that they would not have proceeded with their application if they had known tests were involved, whilst others may have reacted enthusiastically. Violation of the principle of informed consent can be perceived as unfair and candidates may feel deceived.

Candidates are concerned with the face validity of selection methods. This involves their perceived job relevance, transparency and general acceptability in terms of fairness, objectivity, lack of bias and provision of opportunity to display their ability, skills and knowledge. Candidates may have reservations about the methods chosen. Methods such as interviews enjoy greater popularity than those with more scientific validity such as psychometric tests. Methods are often believed to be unfair and methods considered fair may be invalid.

An organization's choice of selection methods may be determined by tradition, cost, perceived effectiveness and possibly personal preference.

It may be influenced by knowledge of more modern methods such as bio-data or recent developments in traditional procedures such as the situational interview. Sometimes established methods continue without reviews of their validity and effectiveness.

Candidates may feel deceived if they are subjected to apparently ineffective methods such as graphology. Alternatively, they may feel pleased with the chosen method but dissatisfied with its operation. For example, candidates may be happy to be interviewed but not if stress tactics are used or the interview lasts five minutes.

TREATMENT OF CANDIDATES DURING SELECTION

Applicants expect to be treated with openness, especially in the provision of information, dignity, confidentiality and in a systematic, consistent way without bias to certain groups.

Treating candidates with dignity

Candidates expect to be treated with dignity and courtesy whilst waiting for interviews or participating in selection. Applicants arriving at an organization for selection procedures may be disconcerted to discover that they are unexpected. Their presence may be challenged and their arrival can cause consternation. Candidates' discomfort may increase if subsequent phone enquiries about them are conducted within their hearing. Candidates may be asked to wait in inappropriate places without a modicum of comfort or privacy and may then be totally ignored. During this period they may be surreptitiously observed by others such as receptionists who may contribute comments and opinions to selectors.

Disabled candidates may experience a range of indignities, often beginning with access to the building. A wheelchair-bound candidate may feel extremely demoralized and uncomfortable if access is limited and the only available means of reaching the interview room is by means of a service lift at the rear of the building. This does not bode well for good performance in selection. In some cases the insensitivity in dealing with disabled candidates is compounded by the organization's belief in the acceptability of the behaviour exhibited. The following example illustrates this.

Margaret had spina bifida and frequently used a wheelchair, though could manage without for short spells. She was highly intelligent and when she was notified of an interview appointment, she phoned the company to make sure they appreciated her position. She was assured that there was no problem and that suitable arrangements had already been made. On arrival she was somewhat disconcerted to discover that the interview was to be held on the third floor, but assumed that a lift was available. She was mistaken. The arrangements made to get her to the third floor consisted of her being physically carried there by Ron and George, two burly storemen from Maintenance.

Consistency of treatment

Candidates expect to be treated consistently over time, place, person and situation, since this is a fundamental tenet of fairness. Such treatment should ideally apply to all selection stages, including equality in decision making. Despite legislation designed to eliminate discriminatory practices, the continuance of bias breaches concepts of fairness.

Bias is often associated with stereotyped beliefs which are generally negative and results in unfair, unfavourable and inconsistent treatment of applicants. Consistency dictates that members of minority groups should be assessed fairly and receive the same treatment as majority applicants. However, they may have unequal access to jobs, and may encounter suggestive or racially offensive remarks, harassment or abuse when attending selection procedures. Consequently, candidates may feel deceived when they are unsuccessful because of attributes unconnected with their ability to do the job.

Confidentiality

Candidates may provide considerable personal and professional detail to the company but be deceived about its confidentiality. Application forms clearly headed 'confidential' may not be treated as such, nor may the personal information contained in the body of the form and the equal opportunities section. Incorrectly addressed forms may be opened by inappropriate staff and even when correctly returned, confidential information may be left in unattended offices which are accessed by non Personnel staff. Forms may be removed from the office, so that Personnel staff can read CVs on the train or at home. Equal opportunities information may be used for selection purposes, regardless of statements to the contrary, especially if incorporated in the main form or if a separate section is not detached.

Applicants' information may be augmented by test scores, interview notes and other information. This is handled during the selection process and may be retained afterwards, raising concerns over storage security. This is a significant and sensitive issue for internal candidates, especially if details are kept on computer with open access. The UK Data Protection Act 1984 covers the use of computers for applicant screening, and regulates the storage of personnel information held on computerized information systems. Certain rights are conferred on the applicant, such as the right to hold a copy of the details held on file and knowledge of the assessment criteria used. Whilst some companies inform candidates of this, such knowledge may not be openly available to the majority.

Confidentiality may be breached in other ways. Checks on candidates may be made without their express permission, even if this has been guaranteed on the application form. This may be particularly pertinent if informal checks are made, about which the candidate has no knowledge. Similarly organizations or agencies may be breaking established policy or assurances by contacting applicants at work.

COMMUNICATION WITH THE CANDIDATE

Communication is the vital link between organization and candidates and is central to exchanging information. The quality and tone of face to face encounters, phone calls and written correspondence furthers the candidate's insight into the company as it is indicative of the organization's attitude to people. Procrastination and excuses may all be deceitful, whilst contacting candidates at their current place of employment can be potentially disastrous if handled indiscreetly. Phone messages left with other family members can be problematic. One partner may not know of the other's job intentions and many teenagers are notoriously unreliable in correctly relaying messages.

The lack of communication

It is in the lack of communication that candidates appear to feel the greatest sense of ill use, and the greater their progress in the selection procedure, the greater their sense of injury. Candidates expecting communication about their applications may be disappointed by the complete absence of contact. Anxious applicants are concerned about the safe arrival of their applications but may be hesitant to pursue enquiries. If enquiries are made, promised responses frequently fail to materialize.

Jobseekers may not expect speculative letters to automatically generate replies, and lack of acknowledgement appears the norm. Replies that are received may be viewed cynically, especially if intimating that the writer's CV and particulars will be kept on file. Whilst for some companies this may be true, a number of organizations admit that this statement is included to soften the reply. The optimistic candidate is unable to distinguish between fact and fiction.

Notification of selection decisions

Conveying selection decisions appears to be extremely problematic. Some job advertisements state categorically that unsuccessful candidates will not be notified. However unless a time limit is also specified, uncertainty lingers. A candidate who has not heard within six weeks may safely assume misfortune, but for shorter periods hope may continue.

Candidates may leave the interview or final selection stage without knowing when appointment decisions will be reached nor when and how they will be conveyed. Frequently shortlisted candidates are told that they will be informed of the outcome within an allotted time, but the failure of organizations to keep to their word is very common, consistently summed up by candidates in the phrase 'They say they'll let you know, but they never do.' Recognition of not succeeding in selection tends to be achieved by default rather than positive action. The candidate feels deceived and of no consequence.

Feedback on the selection process

Feedback on performance during selection may also generate aggrievement, especially if employers deceive candidates about its provision. Promised feedback may not materialize, despite repeated requests from disappointed applicants eager to know details of their performance and suggestions on improvements. Eventually the candidate abandons hope. Alternatively feedback may be delayed so much that it becomes inopportune and irrelevant. Feedback may be bland, unhelpful or destructive if provided unprofessionally by an untrained member of staff who lacks tact and sensitivity.

SUMMARY

Applicants and selectors may have differing perspectives on selection and if employers adopt an instrumental attitude to candidates the exchange of information may be unequal. Candidates may feel disadvantaged by their lack of knowledge about the prospective job and organization. Sometimes candidates are deceived in details about the job, selection processes and practical considerations. Poor communication may contribute to misunderstandings. Candidates' decisions to proceed may be based on false premises and the selection process itself may be conducted for nefarious purposes.

Selectors may behave inconsistently towards applicants, who may be subject to bias and stereotyping. Candidates may be treated without respect and expected confidentiality may fail to materialize. There may be a failure to convey selection decisions to unsuccessful candidates and expectations of feedback may be disappointed. Further deception may occur in the choice of selection methods, their practice and subsequent decision making.

Application forms, CVs and agencies 4

The initial stage of selection, from the candidate's viewpoint, is the submission of particulars to the employer. Usually this is in the form of an application form, CV or letter, although details may be presented by phone. This stage is critical. Subsequent screening and shortlisting winnows the many applicants down to a manageable number for further selection procedures, though methods of shortlisting may be questionable. Candidates, appreciating the significance of the situation and anxious to make a good impression, may be tempted to varnish the truth in order to gain an interview and the opportunity to convince selectors of their suitability.

Not all candidates submit their CVs directly to organizations. Recruitment agencies and headhunters may play a crucial role as intermediaries between applicants and employers, so being in a position to deceive and be deceived by both parties during the process.

This chapter initially outlines the background of application forms and CVs before treating them as separate entities. An examination is then made of the ways in which candidates may deceive employers through their completion and submission of application forms and CVs, whilst mention is made of help available to candidates to optimize their chances of success. The selector's use of possibly discriminatory questions on application forms is described and deception in the handling of applications and shortlisting follows. The chapter's final section analyses the role of third parties, particularly recruitment agencies and headhunters.

THE BACKGROUND OF APPLICATION FORMS AND CVS

Application forms, references and interviews form the classic trio of methods most commonly used in selection in Britain and the use of both application forms and CVs is widespread. Keenan's (1995) investigation of the graduate selection methods used by 536 UK organizations revealed extensive use and the 1994 British Industrial Society survey of 428 member organizations found that 88% of respondents used application forms.

The main difference between application forms and CVs lies in the degree of control allocated to the candidate. Organizations design application forms to suit their individual needs and determine the format and content of information presented by applicants, so it is gathered systematically. This facilitates sorting, comparisons between candidates and shortlisting. The organization also dictates when and how application forms are distributed to candidates, usually as part of specific selection exercises. In contrast, candidates direct the style, format and content of CVs and this individuality can reflect the candidate's personality. As CVs are readily available to the candidate, they can be submitted at any time, irrespective of advertised vacancies, and they are frequently despatched on a speculative basis.

Candidates use these measures to persuade employers that their details match the requirements of the job. Few applicants expect to obtain employment simply on the basis of a CV or application form, so most regard these measures as a means of reaching the interview stage where they can promote themselves in a good light. Candidates are aware that if the application form or CV creates a bad impression or fails to include relevant information, the interview and therefore job are unlikely to materialize. Consequently they use these tools to sell themselves and open the door to personal contact with a prospective employer.

For employers, application forms and CVs are often the first source of information about job applicants, and can be used to measure characteristics against the criteria of personnel specification. The information can be used by selectors to identify and shortlist the most promising candidates. The Industrial Society showed that application forms are the main method of shortlisting candidates for interview and Keenan (1995) reported that 94% of respondents used application forms for initial pre-selection purposes.

APPLICATION FORMS

Most application forms follow a prescribed format of questions. Certain factual information may be considered essential, such as biographical data, educational background, qualifications and employment history. Beyond these basic details the employer may seek additional information which frequently involves open questions or essay type answers and sometimes a short personality test. Employers may also request medical information and ethnic details, which may or may not be part of an equal opportunities monitoring section.

Deception of employers

To the employer, the submission of a completed application form implies that candidates wish to be considered as serious contenders for a vacancy. This in itself can be misleading, as not every application is a demonstration of genuine intent. Some completed application forms are tendered for ulterior motives such as pacifying family demands, appeasing outplacement consultants and satisfying the DfEE conditions in order to claim Jobseekers' Allowance. Other candidates may have minimal motivation and limited expectations of success. Such people may be applying for several jobs, wish to keep all options open or engage in practice applications before undertaking more significant and realistic job search. They may have little intention of taking the job, especially if it does not really meet their personal requirements in terms of location, salary and other criteria.

Candidates may not regard themselves as committed competitors if they perceive an enormous chasm between their circumstances (particularly qualifications and experience) and the job requirements. However, if they nearly match most of the requirements they may find themselves in the predicament exemplified below.

A vacancy for a machine operator is advertised with a stated requirement of four GSCEs. Bill, an experienced worker with two GCSEs, thinks that he is perfectly capable of doing this work, considers that the qualifications are unnecessary for the job and believes that they have been included as a means of reducing the number of potential applicants. Bill therefore has to choose between not applying for the job, applying honestly and risking rejection or applying with a false claim of four GCSEs, in the belief that his experience is more relevant than formal qualifications and he can persuade an interviewer accordingly. Should he decide on the latter course he has embarked on a deception which he may have to maintain throughout the selection process.

In these circumstances the candidate does not know whether the company is adopting a compensatory or non-compensatory method of shortlisting. If the organization will compensate insufficient qualifications by experience, the candidate has a chance of success. If the company will not compensate for fewer qualifications and uses this criterion as an absolute measure, the candidate will be discounted however good his experience and other attributes. The candidate's uncertainty may therefore encourage deception.

Applicants wish to portray themselves as ideal candidates, which may engender varying degrees of deception. It is believed that a candidate may create a favourable impression in three main areas:

• the completion of the application form

• the accuracy of replies

• impression management strategies adopted in answers to open questions.

Completion of the application form

In this context, applicants may mislead selectors in two ways. They may seek advice on the content, nature and general input of information or they may ask others to physically complete the form on their behalf. Some candidates will do both.

Candidates may photocopy forms, complete the duplicate copy and then ask advisers, teachers, relatives or significant others to check content and suggest improvements. Fletcher's (1992a) research into the ethics of job search revealed that such activity was acceptable to undergraduate candidates but 20% of interviewers felt it was unfair for candidates to get help in completing the application form. Presumably they would argue that the impression given by the form is not an accurate reflection of the candidate's power of expression, and would feel duped by such procedures.

Applicants may ask others to complete the form on their behalf for various reasons. Inability to read the questions may occur through learning difficulties or limited comprehension of English if not the first language. Physical problems with handwriting may stem from disability whilst others may believe that their illegibility or poor spelling will have adverse effects. Sometimes candidates may find it formidable to answer more complex questions because of problems in self expression.

Accuracy of replies

Information on the application form may be erroneous. Inexactitude may occur through candidates' mistakes. Alternatively, deliberate deception may occur if applicants believe that truthful answers would produce negative effects. Consequently more proactive information management strategies may be adopted.

Unwitting deception

Applicants may unintentionally give misleading answers because they find some questions confusing, ambiguous or containing unfamiliar jargon. If unsure of the answers, they may lack the time or inclination to work out the correct response – mature applicants may not readily recall A level grades achieved thirty years earlier – and provide 'guestimates'. Other questions necessitate subjective self assessments e.g. 'Would you describe your fluency in a foreign language as excellent, good, average or poor?' and may prompt the candidate to wonder what criteria are being adopted, and whether a week's holiday in Torremolinos bestows above average fluency.

Some requested data may appear irrelevant to the job or invasive of privacy, so applicants may withhold the requested information for ethical reasons, as in the case of details about the age and gender of an applicant's children. Similarly a prospective computer programmer faced with a broad question about health e.g. 'Do you have any health problems?' may judge that the employer is not really interested in her flat feet and so omits these details. Applicants may feel justified in prevaricating if they believe questions to be illegal, as in questions about one's spouse.

Sometimes selectors may be deceived because a literally true response to a poorly designed question may not convey the situation accurately. The question 'Do you possess a full driving licence?' may elicit a positive reply and the candidate may not consider himself to be misleading in failing to disclose eleven penalty points. Occasionally relevant questions may be omitted, so that inappropriate staff are appointed to positions of trust without disclosing previous convictions, since the application form did not request such disclosures.

Information management strategies

In order to create a favourable impact, the candidate may choose to manipulate information by two strategies. The first is to enhance positive information such as experience, skills and personal qualities. The second approach is to engineer negative details, usually through minimization or omission. Candidates may discount their absence of experience, attempt to disguise their lack of certain qualifications specified as essential job requirements or substitute others which they feel are equally acceptable. Alternatively, selective filtering of information involves concealing negative attributes, such as possession of a criminal record or driving disqualification, which they feel would damage their chances of success. An interesting strategy, sometimes adopted by older and/or more qualified people who perceive their over-qualification as a problem, is to minimize positive information.

Biographical section

Although a few candidates may use false names and completely false identities, most applicants find the biographical section is straightforward to complete. However, some candidates may feel uneasy about age, and the addition or subtraction of a few years may ensure that candidates meet the requirements specified in advertisements. Candidates may substitute relatives' addresses if their own is in an area considered undesirable, and may say that they are single which, although accurate, may discount their cohabitee and five children. On the other hand, children may be included if they are thought to project an image of stability, even though they live a hundred miles away with the other parent. Considerable discrepancy between described and actual marital status was discovered by Goldstein's (1971) research.

Research indicates substantial incongruities between statements on the application form and other sources of information. Most disparities centred on qualifications, employment history, work description, salary and reasons for leaving. Goldstein (1971) compared information from application forms of prospective candidates with that from last employers and found that 57% of cases disagreed on previous employment and previous salary, both of which had been over-estimated by the applicant. Other differences occurred on marital status and reason for leaving. Discrepancies were widespread, with 63 applicants out of 94 (67%) disagreeing on two of these four categories. Cascio (1975) also found that age at marriage was incorrectly answered by one third of respondents. They either reported that they had never been married when they actually had been, or claimed that they were older at their time of marriage than was the case.

Qualifications

Qualifications are frequently enhanced, both in number and grades, whilst resits and failed examinations are omitted. Conversely, unemployed 'over-qualified' candidates may reduce the number and/or grades of qualifications in the belief that true statements would eliminate them from further selection stages.

Employment history

Employment history is also subject to massage. In Goldstein's (1971) survey, 17% of previous employers reported that applicants had never worked there, as they claimed. Duration of employment had the largest number of discrepancies (57%) and was consistently over-estimated by most candidates. Cascio's (1975) research revealed that half the respondents underestimated the number of full time jobs they had held before their current employment. Although inaccuracies may result from faulty recall, generally their purpose is to conceal periods of unemployment. This is easier for candidates if the form asks for employer history by year rather than years and months. Periods of unemployment may also be disguised by euphemistic terms such as being self employed.

Job titles, duties and responsibilities may be aggrandised. Long lists of minor tasks may make a simple job look important and the achievements of others may be described as belonging to the collective 'us'. Few or no achievements may be camouflaged by extensive descriptions of duties, if this is compatible with the actual wording of the question.

Salary

Salary is frequently manipulated, either in current or past employment, and Goldstein (1971) found that generally it was enhanced. Usually the objective is to keep the applicant in the job arena and/or to enlarge future earnings. An applicant seeking a job with a salary of £38k is confident in his ability to do the job well but feels that correctly stating his salary as £25k will disqualify him on the grounds that salary and the necessary experience are not commensurate. Therefore salary is inflated so that he can access a further selection stage and gain the opportunity to demonstrate his extensive and relevant experience. Alternatively, an advert stating 'salary in the region of £42k' implies potential negotiation and the applicant reasons that the company will try to employ someone at the lowest rate possible. Wishing to maximize financial benefit, he inflates his salary from £33k to £38k in order to strengthen his bargaining position and gain greater financial reward.

Applicants may sometimes believe that salary enhancement is justified. They feel that questions on salary do not indicate whether basic salary or total earnings are required, and so may give themselves the benefit of the doubt by including bonuses, commission and additional perks such as company cars which have financial implications. Some advisers to jobseekers consider such tactics to be realistic, justifiable and legitimate and so will advocate their adoption.

Sometimes applicants may reduce their salary. The out of work director may presume that meticulous salary details will deter selectors, who may wrongly assume that such applicants would not be serious contenders for lower paid positions.

Reasons for leaving

Some employers believe that reasons for leaving are indicators of future performance, but how truthful are such reasons? Employers are particularly keen to discover whether a person left of their own accord or was dismissed. This area may cause discomfort to applicants if they feel the truth would reflect badly on themselves. Consequently bland comments or more acceptable grounds have to be propounded, especially if it is fairly obvious that there is little differences between consecutive jobs.

Redundant staff may believe that potential employers will attribute redundancy to the candidate's behaviour or work performance rather than to economic considerations. In order to avoid any stigma, candidates may substitute other reasons for their departure.

Dismissal is more unequivocal. A candidate who has been fired for unsatisfactory conduct or dishonesty will be reluctant to disclose such unfavourable information, which could severely damage future employment prospects. Should he feel that his dismissal cannot be concealed, he may discount it by saying that he was sacked for some laudable reason such as refusing to comply with prejudicial practices. Goldstein's (1971) research found that in 63 cases which were comparable, 25% demonstrated inconsistencies, as employees said they had left because of low pay whilst employers maintained staff had been sacked because of violation of company rules.

Disagreements with colleagues or supervisors may have been genuine reasons for leaving or grounds for dismissal. Candidates may feel that employers would infer problems of social integration or 'troublemaking'. Consequently the candidate may feel justified in concealment, especially if the personality clash was attributed to the unreasonable behaviour of someone else rather than to personal failings.

Health

Answers to requests for medical information may be adjusted if candidates do not see their employment relevance. Ancient illnesses may be judged inapplicable and candidates may consider their complaint to be of minor importance, especially if well controlled by medication. Candidates with specific health conditions may believe from past experience that employers do not understand their condition. Concealment or minimization is therefore the easiest option.

Questions on absence for sickness can be problematic. People may have had considerable absence for genuine sickness and they may or may not wish to disclose this. Others may have worked in organizations with prescribed amounts of sick leave entitlement, which may have been used fully as 'unofficial holiday'. Sometimes staff have claimed 'sickness' when they were otherwise engaged, as in attending interviews. Consequently, a healthy employee with ten days' recorded sickness faces a dilemma. Acknowledging absence implies poor health; ignoring it could be tricky, especially if records are checked in references and indicate discrepancies with the application form. Candidates may have to judge which deception is most beneficial.

Impression management in open questions

Although impression management can be achieved through answers to closed questions, the most creative opportunities occur in response to open questions, exemplified in Figure 4.1. These may be relatively straightforward, though more complex questions may be asked on graduate application forms or those for senior positions. Candidates have free rein to portray themselves in the best light possible.

Leisure enables candidates to massage roles, involvement and responsibility. Questions give candidates scope to make themselves appear more interesting, outstanding or closer to the ideal candidate sought by the selector. Elevation from second team substitute to first team captain implies more than just sporting ability and could be of interest to a sports oriented company. Sometimes agendas are prepared in advance. Students may join clubs, but that is the limit of their involvement. Claiming membership is technically correct, but any implications of an active role or positions of responsibility are actually misleading.

Open questions on graduate application forms

Keenan (1983) identified three categories of open questions found on graduate application forms as:

• self appraisal, e.g. what do you have to offer us?

- choice of career, e.g. reasons or personal qualities needed to do job

- discussion of future career ambitions and aspirations.

General application forms

Describe your main hobbies and interests.

Why do you wish to work for Cherub Clothing?

Please use this space if you wish to add further information to support your application.

Graduate application forms

Explain what attracts you to the type of work for which you are applying and offer evidence of your suitability.

How do you think that Cherub Clothing can fulfil your ambitions?

What do you consider your most significant personal achievement to date?

What are your three weakest and strongest points?

What are the most important skills and qualities you need to develop over the next four years?

Describe how you see your career developing over the next four years.

Explain why you chose your course, and what attracts you to your chosen career.

Figure 4.1   Examples of open questions found on application forms

He believed that open questions provided opportunities to employ impression management and many of the 118 final year undergraduate respondents treated them accordingly. Keenan (1983) summarized that 'The types of questions asked on the majority of forms not only positively encourages this behaviour but may even discourage attempts to give authentic information.' He felt that some questions were 'more likely to test the applicant's powers of imagination and willingness to say what will please the recruiter rather than anything else', especially where it is easy to see what would be an 'acceptable' or obvious answer. Only one third of respondents strongly agreed with the statement 'I tried to be as honest as I could when completing the open end sections of the form.' The majority (62%) agreed that the best way to fill the form was to 'tell the employer what he wants to hear' and 45% of respondents said that

they were more concerned with impressing the company than with telling
them what they were really like as people.

The selector's use of discriminatory questions

According to the Equal Opportunities Commission (EOC) (1990) some
questions on application forms could be unlawful if they are asked only
of men (or women) and it can be shown that asking them constitutes 'less
favourable treatment'. Seeking information on married/single/divorced
status, the occupation of a woman's husband and the ages of children
could imply discrimination. This may undermine the candidates' confidence in being treated fairly. Similarly health information may contain
sexually discriminatory overtones.

CVS

The CV allows candidates almost complete latitude in presenting information to potential employers, and as such offers great opportunities for
deception. Regardless of whether it is being sent speculatively or in
response to an advertisement, the CV's most important function is to generate sufficient interest to produce an interview.

Much depends on the good impression made by the CV. Freedom of
design means that CVs reflect individuality and demonstrate an ability
to organize information and present it effectively. Consequently, some
candidates may wish to improve their skills in CV compilation so as to
maximize impact.

The compilation of CVs

Training and sources of help

Guidance and even training on CV preparation is widely available. Books
and computer packages boast that they can assist jobseekers in preparing
the perfect CV and job clubs may help the unemployed. Advice on writing CVs is routinely given to employees as part of redundancy counselling, though Fowler (1995) maintains that 'Career counsellors often
advise redundant staff to provide only a resumé of favourable career
information. Most outplacement advice emphasizes that CVs are marketing documents, not comprehensive factual inventories.' Candidates may
therefore be confused about the acceptable veracity of CVs, especially as

most guidance emphasizes two essential features:

• present yourself in the best or most flattering light

• prepare a CV that stands out in the crowd.

In Fletcher's (1992a) survey, the graduate interviewers (20%) who felt it was unfair for candidates to be helped in completion of application forms felt the same way about CVs.

Employers may be misled about the authorship of the CV. Candidates may compile their CVs unaided and type them personally or ask someone else to do so on their behalf. They may seek advice, undertake training or may employ a CV specialist for professional preparation of content and expert presentation of the CV. Employers may be deceived about whose efforts they are reviewing.

Style and content of CVs

A short personal profile at the head of the CV may be used to grab attention and make an immediate impact. If impressive, it can perhaps divert attention from subsequent information of a more mundane character. Such a profile, as illustrated in Figure 4.2, frequently incorporates cliches, is often subjective and usually cannot be verified.

Wallis N. Gromit
15, Huxtable Close, Eckerslyke

• an experienced inventor with tremendous imagination

• consistent achievements of superlative standards

• unrivalled, invaluable technical knowledge

Figure 4.2   A typical profile prefacing a CV

Deception in CVs

As CVs allow candidates to control the information they present, there is greater scope for creativity and consequently more opportunities for deception than in application forms. Qualifying phrases such as 'involved in', 'knowledge of' and 'exposed to' may be used to swell the importance of possibly mundane employment. Omissions may be easier to manipulate and difficult or sensitive areas can be avoided or at least handled imaginatively. Candidates can adopt euphemistic terms so that 'working overseas' may be an accurate description of time spent in Parkhurst Prison. Candidates may also use impression management techniques of indirect association with prominent people as a means of asserting a positive image. The case of Hugh Neil illustrates the flights of fantasy which can be presented in a CV.

Amount and nature of deception

Research has indicated that CV deception duplicates that found in application forms. An anonymous article (*Management Accounting*, 1995) reports a survey conducted by Robert Half and Accountemps which found that almost one third of employers felt that at least half of the candidates they saw were being economical with the truth in their CV, either omitting detrimental facts, exaggerating or lying outright. Level of education, length of time in the previous job, and type of responsibility were all frequently 'adjusted'.

Case Study 2
HUGH NEIL

Hugh Neil was deselected as Tory candidate for Hyndburn, Lancashire, when it was realized that the CV he submitted to the selection committee included bogus qualifications and false claims about his business interests and political background.

According to *The Times* (11 November 1996), his CV claimed, falsely, that he had:

- a doctorate in Business Administration from Harvard University

- acted as a consultant to the Polish Government

- been an adviser to the late Lord Joseph, Margaret Thatcher's mentor

- membership of the Bow Group, the Foreign Affairs Forum, and the Centre for Policy Studies

- was chairman of 'Britain's 19th largest building society', the Kenton and Middlesex. Neil's CV was never checked, though this would have shown that four years earlier he had been deselected

---

Cont'd

as candidate for Wallsend after his estate agency business col-
lapsed.

Neil did not reveal that he was an undischarged bankrupt and as
such was ineligible to be a member of parliament.

Party officials began to have doubts about him when he could
never be contacted at his office at Manchester Business School.
He did not have one. Win Frankland, the association chairman, said:
'He could have been an extremely good candidate but unfortunate-

THE SELECTOR'S DECEPTION IN SHORTLISTING

Many companies are overwhelmed and surprised by the sheer volume of
applications. Consequently, recourse may be made to arbitrary methods
of sifting such as opening only one of four mail sacks or ignoring any
application forms received after a certain time, regardless of the specified
closing date. Candidates are deceived by such practices.

Selectors have to process much information and it is difficult to balance a
variety of evidence which is differentially weighted. Sometimes sifting is
done intuitively; sometimes good methods are employed such as matching
personal attributes with essential criteria. However, methods may be administered inappropriately by inexperienced selectors or by people applying
different standards and interpretations of the scheme. Whilst sifting by one
person may appear more consistent, it may be more prone to personal bias.

Without a job description or personnel specification, sifting and shortlisting is likely to be difficult even when tackled professionally. An informal points system or biodata may be used which may be irrelevant to the
job. Selectors may sift negatively, seeking arbitrary information such as
the use of green ink as reasons for rejection.

Shortlisting may be based on race, gender or age and this can result in
outright lies being told to candidates who do not fit the profile envisaged
by the recruiter. It may also involve invalid assumptions by the employer
or agencies acting on their behalf. Jobs may be classed as 'men's work' or
'women's work'. A company needing someone with a caring disposition
may interpret this as meaning a woman and conversely a dirty job may
be considered unsuitable for a woman. Candidates are deceived if they
are rejected for invalid, unfair reasons such as 'a married woman with

young children would be unreliable'. This was judged to be discriminatory in the case of *Hurley* v. *Mustoe* (Employment Appeal Tribunal).

AGENCIES

The intermediary role of agencies means that they may mislead and be misled by both applicants and employers. As the relationship is triangular, each participant can disclaim responsibility by allocating blame to the other party.

Types of agencies, their functions and opportunities for deception

Employers use agencies because they wish to outsource part of their Personnel function or supplement other regular recruitment and selection methods. A perceived advantage is that agencies save management time because they conduct primary screening before candidates are sent to the organization. An examination of types of agencies follows, including their own particular opportunities for deception.

Job centres

Job centres fall under the auspices of the DfEE and focus on assisting unemployed people back into work. They are a free advertising channel for organizations and will recruit for firms, handle responses to adverts placed in the job centre or local press, supply jobseekers with information and may provide interview facilities. They operate on a local rather than national basis and rarely advertise higher management positions. Job centres are under some pressure to achieve placement targets and the government's introduction of the Jobseekers' Allowance may affect the ways and directions in which clients are guided towards employment.

Deception by job centres

Job centre staff may deceive employers and candidates by forwarding candidates who are unsuited to their particular vacancy. The following case, reported in the media (5 November 1996) illustrates this.

An unemployed, middle-aged mother was sent for an interview at a massage and escort agency and told she would have to take calls from men wanting to be 'male escorts'. Supplying details and prices of home massage services was also expected.

The woman was shocked and turned the job down on 'moral grounds', though she had been assured by the job centre that the job was 'above board'. She feared she might lose her Jobseekers' Allowance in consequence. A spokesman of the agency said that they would not take someone on unless they had liberal views and that had been made clear to the job centre. He is quoted as adding 'We were very disappointed that they sent someone who was clearly not suitable.' Another two applicants had also been unhappy about the job.

Recruitment agencies

Recruitment agencies are intermediaries between employers, who commission them to provide applicants for vacancies, and jobseekers. The agency keeps in touch with both parties and tries to match the two sets of requirements. Each party is unlikely to have an exclusive agreement or contract with any one agency alone.

Many recruitment agencies are extremely good, acting ethically, professionally and efficiently. Many belong to the Federation of Recruitment and Employment Services (FRES) which has its own code of practice. However, since deregulation, agencies are not required to be licensed and so can be run by anyone. As a result, some may possess a dubious reputation which can bring the business into disrepute. For example, it has been reported that Manchester Education Authority had to write to schools warning them that a teacher supply agency representative was on List 99, a list of teachers who may be suspected of child abuse.

Unlike job centres which are centrally controlled by government guidelines, recruitment agencies vary tremendously in size, scope, function and control. Many are small, individual bodies supplying both permanent and temporary staff and frequently specializing in one particular field, such as temporary clerical staff or haulage drivers.

Agencies operate by supplying clients with the CVs of jobseekers they have on their files. CVs may be amended to enhance presentation and utilize the agency's standardized format. CVs may also be stored on databases in order to give a rapid response. A rapid response is often critical as some employers award the placement fee to the agency which first submits a candidate's CV, so effectively encouraging a CV race. The ethics and professionalism of this practice have provoked discussion in professional personnel magazines.

Agencies exhibit considerable variation in roles. Some may be little more than a CV forwarder whilst others offer a comprehensive service. This may include shortlisting and interviewing applicants, administering work sample tests and psychometric tests to their jobseekers and sometimes validating qualifications and references.

The recruitment agency's deception of the employer

Agencies may mislead employers with or without the applicant's knowledge. They may interpret and implement organizational instructions in their own way, which can be potentially discriminatory if they have particular biases of which the employing organization is unaware. Agencies may disguise their own inefficiencies and biases by attributing them to the employer, so discrediting the organization and its impact on society.

Forwarding CVs and shortlisting

The pressure and haste to submit CVs may preclude prior discussion of the job with the candidate, and even in less rushed circumstances agencies may be careless and incompetent in their briefings. Consequently agencies may forward the CVs of unsuitable or uninterested candidates, so that the employer is therefore misled about the calibre and intentions of candidates.

An agency's shortlisting methods may not meet with the company's approval. CVs forwarded to the company may be accompanied by verbal or written comments on the physical attractiveness of candidates, e.g. 'lively redhead', or the existence of young children. Such practices themselves may be discriminatory and subject to legal redress.

Inconsistent treatment of candidates

Organizations committed to maintaining a positive public image may mistakenly believe that agencies treat candidates courteously and keep them informed of selection proceedings. Possibly because of inefficiency, lack of resources or bias, agencies may be inconsistent in fully briefing all candidates about the job, firm and selection procedures. Consequently, candidates may lack sufficient information to self select out of the process. Omitting information about further selection stages can be potentially damaging if it encompasses practice material for psychometric tests. A selector's assumption that all candidates possess this information may place uninformed candidates at a disadvantage.

Discrimination

Some agencies may consider discriminatory behaviour to be acceptable whilst other agencies may assert an ethical position then deceive employers by operating unfairly. The absence of a code of practice and an equal opportunities policy not only damages the employer directly, by discounting groups of suitable applicants, but also conveys an adverse image of the company if jobseekers attribute such behaviour to the employer instead of the agency. Other agencies may convince employers that they will conform to the organization's own code without any real intention of compliance.

The employer's deception of the recruitment agency

Briefing can be problematic. Some agencies complain of employers' reluctance to invest the time needed for proper briefing on vacancies and job requirements. This can create uncertainty and confusion of roles and responsibilities, possibly resulting in the omission of important checks which agency and employer presume are being conducted by the other. Agencies may succumb to pressure from the 'briefing' individual to behave unethically, so deceiving the company which may strongly condemn the employee's personal bias.

Employers may also deceive agencies by encouraging candidates to resign from agency books so that the payment of placement or retainer fees can be avoided. As in other areas, the employer–agency relationship is damaged and agencies may be less punctilious in future dealings with employers.

HEADHUNTERS

Headhunters, sometimes known as search and select agencies or consultants, are generally approached by employers, not jobseekers. They can economize on management time and have a reputation for discretion if organizations prefer to avoid broadcasting their vacancies to competitors. As headhunters tend to specialize in certain business sectors, their sound knowledge of the market value and availability of suitable candidates facilitates speedy recruitment.

The principle behind much headhunting is that the best candidates may already be employed, are not necessarily seeking alternative employment and so are unaware of other vacancies. Therefore headhunters proactively seek and identify candidates through direct, personal contact or via their extensive, detailed databases. They then 'sound out' potential candidates, interview, shortlist and submit written profiles to employers.

Deception of employers

Candidates may use headhunting or the subsequent job offer to obtain a counter offer from their current employer. If anticipated enticements of improved salary and/or other conditions materialize, the candidate may withdraw from the shortlist or offered position. Headhunters may be deceived about shortlisted candidates' motivation and intentions, so unintentionally misleading employers about candidates' realistic availability.

More active deception of employers may occur if headhunters follow hidden agendas for personal benefit. Their specialist knowledge and the limited availability of suitable potential candidates puts them in a strong position. It may be to the headhunter's advantage to fill one position in company A with an employee from company B if this creates a vacancy in company B which the headhunter will be asked to source. Hence a headhunter acting unethically may be able to instigate a merry-go-round of vacancies which he is commissioned to fill sequentially.

Headhunters may resemble agencies in discriminatory practice. Their more restricted, specialist spheres may increase their vulnerability to pressure from organizations, especially if they are briefed by high ranking people. A director seeking a marketing manager may make it clear that he wants a man in his mid-thirties, despite the fact that his organization has a strong commitment to equal opportunities in gender and age.

SUMMARY

Candidates, selectors and agencies appear to be pursuing a common goal but achievement of their individual objectives may be at the expense of other parties. Employers may be deceived by the accuracy of CVs and application forms, which are prone to impression management.

Candidates may take active steps to resemble the perceived ideal candidate. They may be economical with the truth, especially in regard to qualifications, experience and salary. Selectors may deceive candidates by questionable shortlisting methods.

Candidates may regard deceptive measures as acceptable and justified by the end result of obtaining an interview in which they can be genuine.

Interviews 5

The interview is one of the most popular selection methods and also one of the most criticized. As a social process, it is essentially an exercise in personal perception involving judgements of what is seen and heard. Information is exchanged and evaluated and decisions are reached. Each stage allows ample opportunity for deception, as interviewer and candidate try to influence the other's impressions.

Interviews are used almost universally (Robertson and Makin, 1986; Shackleton and Newell, 1991) and may be an almost ritualistic aspect of selection. Academics are concerned that interviews are not particularly good predictors of performance, with varying reliability and validity, though recent meta-analyses are more optimistic. This contrasts with practitioners' perceptions, as Industrial Society (1994) respondents rated them as the most effective selection method. The exchange of information between candidate and selector is the essence of the interview. However, it is subject to influences which operate before and during the process. Deception may operate in these preliminary stages, throughout the interview and in decision making.

Deception in the interview comes from several sources. Both candidate and interviewer may depend on uncorroborated statements which may be subject to exaggerations, omissions and falsification. Consequently decisions are often based on inappropriate judgements of incomplete, inaccurate data. Candidates may utilize impression management techniques to create favourable images and positive decisions. Faith in the professional content and conduct of the interview may be misplaced. Interviewers may deceive themselves and the organization about their interviewing abilities and Personnel staff may be misled or ignorant of the unethical conduct occurring in some interviews,

The chapter starts by providing background details on interviews, especially the traditional and structured formats. Preliminary influences on the interview are reviewed before progression to the core of the interview – the exchange of information. Impression management strategies used by candidates to influence interview outcome are highlighted. Decision making concludes the chapter.

BACKGROUND

The interview is a very flexible selection method and its versatility may outweigh its being a poor selection tool (Herriot, 1989b). It is multifunctional, adaptable in format and duration, and may involve one or many interviewers.

From the interviewer's perspective, the prime objective is to identify and select the most suitable candidate. The interview allows the selector to assess the candidate's knowledge, skills, experience and personality. She can then evaluate these qualities and decide whether the applicant not only can and will do the job, but will fit into the organization. Compatibility with prospective colleagues is crucial if working relations are to run smoothly. Essentially, the interviewer feels able to assess what the candidate is really like as a person.

The interview may serve other functions. The interviewer can clarify gaps or issues from the CV or application form, review the candidate's performance in tests or other selection methods and possibly discuss matters raised in references. It can also be used as a public relations tool to sell the company and promote a good image.

From the candidate's perspective, interviews offer the opportunity to convince the selector of personal suitability. They are also a two-way exchange of information. The interviewer's provision of details about the job and organization can facilitate the candidate's decision making, as can answers to candidate questions. Interviews may include some or all of these functions, and each function affords chances of deception.

Interviews exhibit other variables. Duration varies between five minutes and over two hours and applicants may have from one to five interviews. Many interviews are on a one to one basis, others involve two or three interviewers. Panel interviews may consist of 4–10 interviewers and appear more reliable and valid (Arvey and Campion, 1982). Interviewers are usually line managers and Personnel staff interviewing together or sequentially. Interview format affects the degree of formality and rapport which in turn affects the generation of discussion and its degree of frankness. The type of interview can be crucial.

Types of interviews

Most interviews are conducted 'face to face' but some use computer, telephone or video. The two basic types of interview are the traditional and structured interviews, and their salient characteristics are summarized in Figure 5.1.

Traditional interviews

The loosely structured traditional interview frequently resembles a social encounter, with heavy reliance on intuitive impressions. Its haphazard format encourages inconsistency. Interview content is frequently unrecorded or recalled impressionistically at the conclusion of individual or all interviews. The latter tends to favour the most recent candidates, who are more readily recalled than those interviewed earlier. Unstructured, ad hoc discussion of interviewees may occur, so hindering systematic comparisons of candidate performance and good decision making. The overall lack of clear procedure ensures that the traditional interview is a breeding ground for deception.

Structured interviews

Structured interviews focus on job related characteristics rather than personality and have developed rapidly since 1980. Structure permeates the interview and its components – questions, systematic recording and scoring of answers, and evaluations. Differences in focus have created contrasting approaches, especially in the *situational interview* (Latham and Saari, 1980) and *patterned behaviour interview* (Janz, 1989).

Structured interviews have better validity than traditional interviews and appear to be more robust, but this can be deceptive. Some interviewers mistakenly believe that a 'structured interview' is one in which there is any interview plan. This may be their own scheme or Rodgers seven-point plan, which may be misused and misinterpreted, especially in the 'physical make-up' component. Those who appreciate the concept correctly may delude themselves that they are conducting structured interviews when they are not. The situation may be compounded if Personnel staff believe they have improved interview procedures when actual progress is limited and less effective than presumed.

Interviewers may adhere to predetermined questions but fail to record answers or may misinterpret responses because they do not have the

TRADITIONAL	STRUCTURED
• Loosely structured	• Highly structured
• Emphasizes candidate characteristics	• Emphasizes job related behaviour
• Dynamic interchange – amendment of overall agenda	• Consistency predominates
• Sequence of questions often haphazard – ad hoc format	• All candidates asked identical questions or the same number of questions from a predetermined base
• Closed questions	• Open questions
• Limited information	• Encouragement of in-depth probing
• Answers jotted down	• Answers scored on checklists and rating scales
• Content frequently unrecorded	• Systematic recording
• Evaluations often subjective and impressionistic	• Structured evaluations
• Social encounter, encouraging stereotypes and bias	
	SITUATIONAL
	• Focuses on applicant's behaviour in a particular situation
	• Intentions seen as indicating behaviour
	• 'What would you do if ?'
	• Highly structured scoring guide with benchmark scales
	PATTERNED BEHAVIOUR
	• Focuses on applicant's past behaviour
	• Believed to be the best indication of future behaviour
	• 'What did you do when ?'
	• Responses rated according to subjective interviewer judgement

Figure 5.1   Comparison of the traditional and the structured interview

required key to provide systematic scoring. Latham and Saari (1984) found some misuse of the situational interview. Rather than record and score the answer to each question, some interviewers recorded nothing. They merely used the questions and scoring guide to help them form an overall impression of the applicant, then recorded a summary score, so showing that the method is not foolproof. They were effectively conducting traditional interviews. Latham and Saari concluded 'What one believes is taking place and what is actually taking place may not be highly correlated.' They had summed up one aspect of deception in a nutshell.

PREPARATION FOR INTERVIEWS

Interviewers and candidates exhibit various degrees of preparation. Without training or a good grasp of the job and relevant skill requirements, the interviewer's effectiveness is reduced. Questions may be inappropriate, so the requisite information will be unforthcoming, and ignorance may mislead candidates and portray an unprofessional image of the organization. Interviewers may also appear unfamiliar with candidate details, may muddle papers and even interview the wrong person for the wrong job.

Candidate nervousness about interviews is common and was reported by 80% of candidates (Fletcher, 1992a). This may prompt interviewees to undertake training to improve effective interview presentation. This frequently focuses on impression management techniques in verbal and non-verbal behaviour. Preparation of answers to expected questions may be incorporated though this was considered dishonest by 4% of candidates and 20% of interviewers in Fletcher's survey (1992a). Advice on appropriate dress and appearance, such as wearing a suit or removing nose rings, may be included. Frequently role plays and videoed mock interviews provide feedback and help. This is considered worthwhile because the interviewer's subjective judgements of the candidate's performance affect recommendations.

A frank exchange of information depends on rapport. Interviewers may fail to establish rapport through their poor introductions, an unorthodox questioning style and unusual behaviour. Rapport may also be hindered by unsuitable settings. Interviews held in open plan offices compromise confidentiality while phonecalls and personal interruptions distract both parties. Room layout may be a form of impression management to emphasize power differentials though often interviewees feel uncomfortable. In these circumstances frank discussion is constrained as the interviewee is not relaxed and is inhibited from performing well. This frustrates the purpose of the interview and the candidate feels a sense of unfairness in the method and result.

THE EXCHANGE OF INFORMATION IN THE INTERVIEW

Interviewer and candidate exchange information about each other through their words, behaviour and appearance. The interviewer's assessment of the candidate's motivation, skills, knowledge and personality is made through judgements of verbal and non-verbal behaviour. However, frankness of discussion and the accuracy, completeness and veracity of information may be determined by several influences summarized in Figure 5.2. It is in the candidate's interest to ensure that the information given produces the most favourable impression and this may be achieved at the expense of honesty or through the candidate's employment of impression management techniques.

Fletcher's (1992a) research showed a discrepancy between interviewer expectations of honesty and student behaviour. Almost all interviewers (97%) regarded honesty in interviews as essential but they would be disappointed, as 20% of students questioned said they were seldom or never completely honest during interviews. This reflects Keenan's (1980) findings, where about 25% of undergraduates involved in 'milkround' interviews admitted to being less than truthful in their replies to interviewers.

Impression management

In the interview situation candidates may try to influence the impressions of interviewers so that they adopt a favourable opinion of the candidate, manifested by a job offer. Tactics of impression management can take many forms, as shown in Figure 5.3, the most important of which are verbal statements and specific non-verbal behaviour.

Some candidates spontaneously practise impression management. They find it natural to embellish facts and exaggerate personal qualities. Others may find it difficult to make the most of themselves and may avail themselves of training courses which generally emphasize impression management techniques. Consequently it may be difficult to distinguish between impression management and non-impression management. The approaches adopted may include conscious or unconscious deception. Although unstructured interviews provide more scope for a wider vari-

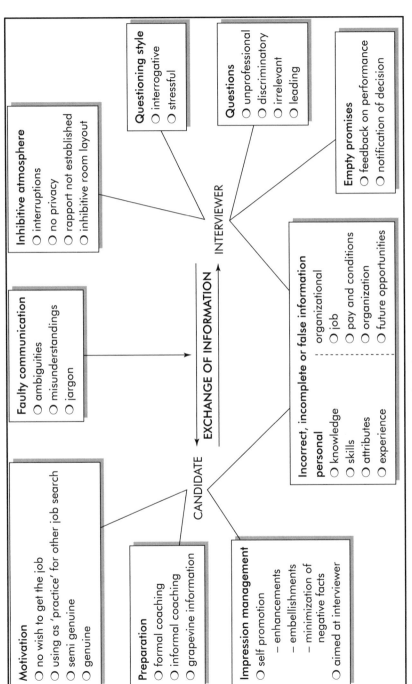

Figure 5.2 Influences on information exchange in the interview

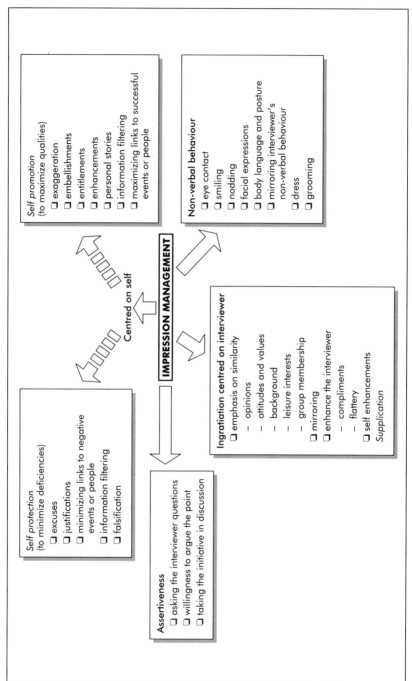

Figure 5.3 The candidate's use of impression management during the interview

ety of tactics, structured interviews also provide opportunities for the embellishment of past achievements and the imaginative narrative of future actions.

The interviewer's questions

Interviewers may spend little time obtaining information. Often they spend 70% of interview time talking at the candidate and giving information (Daniels and Otis, 1950). Candidates wishing to demonstrate their experience and abilities may feel thwarted by this or by interviewers who ask closed questions, cut off replies or discourage candidates from continuing. Confusion may occur if questions are ambiguous, hypothetical or laden with jargon, and the interviewer's rigid adherence to a checklist may resemble an interrogation.

The professionalism of the interviewer's questioning

Keenan (1980) questions the selector's proficiency and skills in interviewing. He argues that interviewers delegate assessment to candidates by frequently asking them to assess themselves. However, candidates' responses are likely to be misleading because of inaccurate self insight or a reluctance to disclose accurate information in the competitive selection atmosphere. Keenan (1980) felt that interviewers accepted candidates' statements at face value. They rarely probed candidates' weaknesses and did not investigate candidates' past behaviour. Consequently they frequently misinterpreted information and failed to uncover most candidates' weaknesses. Keenan concludes by questioning whether interviewers are failing to ask the right kind of questions.

Invasion of privacy

Candidates may feel that personal questions, which are not job relevant, are invasive and unfair. Fletcher's (1992) survey revealed that 12% of interviewers felt it was acceptable to ask candidates about their political beliefs, 30% about candidate's spouse and 27% about family background. Although slightly more candidates felt it was admissible to be questioned on these topics, the majority of interviewers believed such questioning was unsuitable. There was a discrepancy on questions on personal life, with 45% of interviewers feeling questions in this area were acceptable whereas only 27% of candidates agreed. Candidates appreciate the potential bias of such questions, but may feel powerless to resist answering them. This compounds their sense of inequity.

Discriminatory questions

Discriminatory questioning in interviews is often based on stereotyped assumptions about the applicant and may convey an impression of an underlying discrimination attitude or intent. For example, assumptions may be made about women's role in the home and family, and questioning focuses on women's domestic intentions and arrangements, such as implications about looking after children. The British Equal Opportunities Commission (1990) states that 'questions posed during interviews [should] relate *only* to the requirements of the job. Where it is necessary to discuss personal circumstances and their effect upon ability to do the job, this should be done in a neutral manner, equally applicable to all candidates.' Various industrial tribunals have found that asking applicants questions relating to their marital status, personal appearance, husband's nationality, marriage and family intentions were discriminatory.

Interviewers frequently precede unethical questions with qualifiers such as 'I know I shouldn't be asking this but . . . ' or 'We ask these questions of all candidates' to allay fears of discrimination. This does not make unethical questions acceptable. Stating that everyone faces the same questions may be untrue or is irrelevant if answers by different categories of candidates are treated unequally, which is obviously unfair.

Personnel staff face a dilemma if confronted by unethical questions posed in their presence. Staff may find it difficult to halt such questioning, explain why questions are inappropriate and advise interviewers to disregard answers. Private reminders may be more discreet but possibly less forceful. Forgetfulness or joking responses may be offered as excuses, but both may be used to disguise potentially offensive behaviour. Other panel members may find it hard to ignore recently heard information, especially if it has attracted attention and coincides with their personal stereotypical views.

The candidate's response

Faith in candidates' responses and their veracity is one of the fundamental weaknesses of the interview and an area of potential deception. Candidates describe their successes but may omit the contributions of others or unsuccessful activities. There is no guarantee that candidates would do what they say they would do and speed of thought and response in interviews does not necessarily correlate with effective action. Marchington and Wilkinson, (1996) state succinctly that some people are very 'good at articulating their achievements and plans but poor at putting these into effect, whereas others may do the job well but not act in a very convincing way at the interview'. Consequently, the interviewer is deceived.

Unintentional deception

Verbal communication contains inherent faults through misperceptions and misinterpretations and there is considerable scope for misunderstandings. Some candidates may reply incorrectly because of this, especially if questions are convoluted or loaded with jargon. The candidate's quandary is whether to offer a potentially absurd answer which could effectively disqualify him, or display incomprehension through seeking clarification. Similarly, hypothetical questions may be difficult to answer if they are beyond the candidate's experience. The interviewer may believe hypothetical responses to be factually correct, and this can be problematic in situational interviews used for graduate applicants or school leavers.

As most candidates find interviews a daunting experience, nervousness may contribute to mistakes which deceive the interviewer unintentionally. Details of past qualifications or events that happened a long time ago may not be recalled easily, especially if memory is faulty or a person finds it easier to remember some aspects of information better than others.

The interviewer may contribute to the candidate's unwitting deception. The interviewer's behaviour, communication style and inability to establish rapport affects the candidate's perceptions of the interviewer and his own performance. For example, the absence of empathy may hinder the candidate's ability to think clearly about what he wishes to say, particularly if he feels inhibited or even threatened by the interviewer. Interviewers who display minimal eye contact tend to inhibit candidates and produce restricted or shorter responses. Candidates perceive interviewers differently, and sex of interviewer may influence topics of discussion and limit potential disagreement. Consequently, the curtailment or brevity of interviewees' answers may cause salient facts to be omitted inadvertently.

Optimistic answers

Candidates may overestimate their ability or aptitude for undertaking particular work or learning new skills. Tasks which appear superficially simple may be far more taxing than initially anticipated. An applicant who says he can easily transfer from one computer system to another may discover that this is easier said than done.

Sometimes candidates genuinely believe in their proposed actions, but these may involve others who may not share their commitment and enthusiasm. Undertaking a job involving considerable overnight absence from home may reverberate on family relationships, so engulfing others in the consequences. Consequently a candidate may accept the job and then withdraw after family discussion, or commence work and subsequently resign when practical problems emerge.

Half truths and ambiguous replies

Occasionally candidates may feel forced to give answers which do not accurately reflect their own opinions and experiences. Leading questions engender particular responses, and unusual or honest replies could damage job aspirations, especially if past experience has proved that declarations of unfavourable information may be penalised. Similarly, closed questions may force a 'yes' or 'no' answer. Neither response mirrors the truth accurately without further elaboration, which may appear inappropriate. A candidate who is asked whether he has used specific equipment may have to respond negatively, even though he considers he has had valid experience from use of similar instruments.

Applicants may avoid telling lies by inviting the interviewer to make false inferences. The candidate arriving late may explain that a lorry had overturned on the motorway. The interviewer concludes that this caused the delay, but is misled, because the candidate omitted to add that the incident occurred on the other carriageway and caused him no inconvenience whatsoever.

Candidates may deliberately formulate ambiguous answers to questions they feel are unfair. A candidate asked 'Do you have any children?' replied by saying 'I am childfree', which the interviewer could interpret as a childless state or the absence of any dependent children.

Dishonesty

There are many opportunities and reasons for deliberate misrepresentation in interviews. Lies may be told to perpetuate existing falsehoods, conceal unfavourable information, present the image the candidate has identified as necessary to fit the job and organizational requirements or to make the candidate appear outstanding.

Factual distortion

Complete fabrication of facts such as educational qualifications, skills, employment history, salary and experience may be undertaken to match the candidate with the ideal employee sought by the selector. Educational qualifications may be enhanced by numbers and grades, though some candidates may play down their expertise, believing that their overqualification will cause rejection whilst others may invent qualifications completely from scratch.

Weiss and Dawis (1960) checked the replies of interviewees with their former employers and other factual sources. The accuracy of replies depended on the subject area of the question, but even in those areas of greatest accuracy, such as job title and pay, over one fifth of candidates gave misleading replies. Invalid information was also found on questions related to previous education and length of employment.

Some candidates massage their background to bring it closer to that of the perceived typical candidate sought by the organization. Claimed membership of a professional society was significantly related to the interviewer's overall impression, personal liking and chances for further consideration in the interview (Campion, 1978). Candidates' opinions, intentions and expectations may be false, they may name drop when they do not know the person well or may generally make themselves more interesting. Achievements may be exaggerated and their whole personality may be misrepresented

Candidates may prevaricate for various reasons, frequently to sustain incorrect information supplied in a CV or application form. Some individuals may intend to rectify this at the interview, but if this proves more difficult than anticipated, they feel forced to maintain their original story. Other candidates do not have such sensibilities. They believe that they would be unsuccessful if the truth were told, and judge that the revelation of dishonesty may itself be reason for disqualification. Having started the deception, they are committed to maintaining it, with or without compunction.

Factual questions on non-job related topics may provoke lies which the candidate feels are justified. He may consider questions on biographical details such as marital status to be an invasion of privacy, illegal or unethical.

Concealment of unfavourable information

Most candidates are not eager to divulge unfavourable information. They prefer to omit or minimize perceived negative features which may or may not be job related, and if they have previously experienced stigma they have usually formulated strategies to conceal their background. If not questioned directly, candidates may justify omissions, reasoning that they could not be expected to volunteer potentially negative information.

Sometimes candidates may consciously decide to wait until the interview stage to disclose adverse details such as a previous criminal record or health issues. They may believe that the information is highly confidential and best disclosed in person, or that details will be more palatable once the interviewer has met the candidate, and hopefully formed positive impressions which may counteract the negative tidings. These good intentions may be difficult to implement and the candidate may deceive by default.

Candidates may resort to deception if there is no clear channel of communication or they feel at a disadvantage. Candidates may misconstrue questions or jump to conclusions. Nervousness may contribute to feelings of insecurity and candidates may be offended by questions which are unjustified, impertinent or asked discourteously. If candidates feel threatened they may become defensive, and abandoning the truth may be the easiest option.

The candidate's influence on the interview

Use of impression management in responses

There are two main types of verbal impression management methods: first, an assertive approach, in which the candidate proactively constructs a positive image second; defensive techniques produced reactively as a damage limitation exercise.

In interviews, greatest use is made of proactive techniques. Self promotion occurs through deliberate misrepresentation of job qualifications and positive self descriptions. Declarations of being confident, competent, hardworking and energetic were the qualities most frequently mentioned in Stevens and Kristof's (1995) research into real life interviews. These extend to descriptions of future plans or past accomplishments and their impact is enhanced through elaboration. The technique aims to demonstrate knowledge, expertise, skills, abilities and fit with the organization. It is done to elicit specific character attributions such as competence or respect and can be used to highlight leadership skills.

This assertive approach utilizes three other strategies. The candidate may claim responsibility for positive events (entitlements). He may profess that events for which he was responsible, or their value, are more positive than initially appears (enhancements) whilst accompanied by descriptions of how obstacles were overcome in the pursuit of goals. A third assertive technique of ingratiation, designed to evoke personal liking, was used comparatively rarely in the interview. When it did occur, it focused on the job and organization, not the interviewer (Stevens and Kristof, 1995).

In addition, personal stories were used to construct attractive images through descriptions of past behaviour and events (Stevens and Kristof, 1995). They were often told in response to interviewers' questions and are especially pertinent in the patterned behaviour interview.

Defensive, reactive strategies aim to minimize negative attributions resulting from one's behaviour. They consist of 'repairing one's image when it has been damaged, either by one's own behaviour, e.g. being late, or by information that surfaces during the interaction, i.e. being fired from a previous job'. These avoidance strategies consist of disclaimers. They involve excuses for the negative behaviour, such as being fired because of downsizing, or justifications that the behaviour is not as bad as it appears such as being fired because of rejecting the sexual advances of a superior.

The effects of impression management

It can be argued that impression management interferes with the interviewer's evaluation and decision process, so reducing interview validity. In this way an interviewee's impression management is a potential source of error in interview judgement, which may or may not be recognized as such.

Consequently, interviewers may base their evaluations on impression management skills – which may or may not be related to job performance. In this way the use of impression management may contribute to errors that are already there. On the other hand, impression management success may predict future performance if social interaction – the ability to get on well with others and create a good impression – is a skill which is required by the organization or by the job. Organizations recruiting sales staff may be impressed by a candidate's ability to sell himself and may also be pleased by a modification of behaviour to fit in with a given situation. Employers of cashiers may not view such creativity in a favourable light.

According to Stevens and Kristof (1995) self presentation strategies influenced interviewers and significantly predicted interviewers' evaluations. However, there may be a divergence between applicant and interviewer perceptions of impression management. An applicant may think that he has used these techniques excessively whilst the interviewer considers the amount and nature of impression management were par for the course.

Other strategies

Although the interviewer controls the interview, the proactive candidate can adopt a few tactics to redress the perceived imbalance of power and secure favourable decisions.

Applicants who talk a lot are more likely to be selected (Tullar, 1989) though it is uncertain whether this is because applicants who talk more improve their chances or because interviewers encourage candidates they like to say more. Long replies may deflect the interviewer's attention from the candidate's avoidance of unwelcome questions or those which would necessitate divulgence of unfavourable information. Applicants may blind the interviewer with science in areas in which the candidate detects the interviewer's unfamiliarity or ignorance. The length of their answers may determine how many questions are asked, and so they can exert some control on the interview.

Research indicates that candidates can impress the interviewer by discussing factors of achievement, personal growth and doing jobs well, rather than issues of money, working conditions and company policy (Harlan, Kerr and Kerr, 1977) which candidates may choose to underplay. This tends to maximize the likelihood of a job offer, but could be deceptive as salary is usually an extremely important factor.

Information given by interviewers

Interviewers give information which may be incomplete or incorrect, especially if interviewers know little about the vacancy beyond their wish to fill it rapidly. The job itself may be painted in glowing colours in order to enhance its attraction. Basic factual information on terms and conditions such as pay, hours and holidays may be manipulated. Similarly promotion prospects and organizational culture may be presented euphemistically. False expectations may be raised about training while career development opportunities may be exaggerated, so that the psychological contract is based on dangerously shifting foundations. Tenopyr and Oeltjen (1982) concluded that interviewers were often not credible sources of information.

Expected information may be unforthcoming, so placing the candidate in a predicament. He may hesitate to raise salary matters, for fear of appearing mercenary, whilst seeking clarification may be attributed to obtuseness or inability to assimilate facts. There may be little or no opportunity for questions or the interviewer's behaviour may be inhibitive. If questions are asked, interviewers may avoid direct answers and resort to vague generalizations. Such deception restricts the candidate's information and creates false premises for subsequent decision making.

BEHAVIOUR IN INTERVIEWS

Behaviour is a source of information in interviews. Both parties may use body language as cues to personality, interest and assertiveness and as behaviour can be manipulated, it is a source of possible deceit. The interviewer's deliberate actions and tactics may also be unprofessional and unethical.

The role of the interviewer

The interviewers's communication style and non-verbal behaviour can set the whole tone of the interview and affect the candidate's perceptions of the interviewer. This may be done quite openly, as in the following example.

> Brenda, a newly qualified graduate, travelled nearly two hundred miles for an interview in a male dominated industry. The interviewer entered the interview room and said that he did not wish to conduct the interview but had been saddled with it, had many better things to do with his time and could only spare fifteen minutes. He also did not see the point of the exercise since there were very few girls in the industry and that was as it should be.

The interviewer's behaviour is a key influence on the candidate's responses. Body language may express apparent boredom, indifference and inattention, suggesting that the interviewee is not getting a fair hearing. Taking copious notes reduces eye contact, may inhibit rapport and reduces the flow of candidate conversation, so adversely affecting the likelihood of job offers.

The expected professionalism of the interview may be compromised if the interviewer adopts unethical tactics. In Fletcher's (1992a) research, 15% of interviewers said it was ethically acceptable to tape record an interview without the candidate's knowledge. Questioned on the use of stress tactics, 13% of interviewers revealed that they often used them, 27% did sometimes, 27% rarely and 33% never used them. The interviewer's assumption of threatening or aggressive conduct, an excessively interrogative style or displayed disapproval of some of the candidate's answers may become so marked and unacceptable that it is effectively unfair and unethical.

Candidates' perceptions of interviewer behaviour

Applicants judge the organization and job on the basis of what they are told and how they are treated and this influences their decisions to accept or reject job offers. Salient features were perceptions of the interviewer's personality and non-verbal behaviour (Schmitt and Coyle, 1976) and characteristics such as personableness, competency and the degree to which an interviewer is believed to listen (Harn and Thornton, 1985). Consequently it is possible that interviewers themselves may 'lose' the best candidates through their own behaviour. Failure or inability to appreciate this means both they and the organization are deceived.

The candidate's behaviour

Interviewers' expectations of candidate behaviour

Interviewers ascribe a certain role to candidates, but this reveals considerable inconsistencies. The candidate has to draw attention to his good qualities while remaining modest and submissive. He may need to show qualities of decisiveness and forcefulness without using these powers on the selection board (Torrington and Hall, 1987). The perceived role for the candidate may be at variance with the prospective job role. Candidates who appreciate these subtleties and the significance of behaviour may manipulate their own accordingly.

In Herriot and Rothwell's (1981) study, interviewers expected candidates to spend more time talking about themselves whilst candidates expected interviewers to spend more time talking about the job and organization. The less candidates talked about themselves, the less likely they were seen as suitable for the job, as they were not following the expected norms of interview behaviour but had adopted 'out-of-role' behaviour. However, as these rules are not clear, explicit or universal, either party may perceive the other as a rule breaker. They may therefore feel cheated and draw unfavourable conclusions.

The candidate's use of non-verbal impression management

Candidates may adapt their appearance and actions in order to make a good impression and sway interviewers' judgements. Candidates may modify self presentation to match interviewer preferences and influence decisions. Dress, appearance, demeanour and composure offer obvious scope for emphasizing similarities between the interviewer and interviewee. This can be effective in increasing the interviewer's liking of the candidate, as people tend to like others who are similar to themselves. This impression management may portray a desired image which does not necessarily reflect the candidate's real personality and may be part of a more proactive deception.

Anderson and Shackleton (1990) reported that non-verbal behaviour influenced interviewers' impressions of a candidate's personality and subsequent appointment decisions. A candidate with more eye contact and more positive facial expressions was rated as more interesting, strong and relaxed and was more likely to be accepted. Interviewers may also make inferences from the candidate's non-verbal behaviour to his verbal skills and may not view the two as independent. As non-verbal behaviour can be manipulated, candidates may adopt such tactics deliberately.

DECISION MAKING IN INTERVIEWS

The relationship between decision making and deception is complex. Interviewers may deceive themselves and the organization about their abilities. As decisions may be governed by impressions, rather than job related ability, and are subject to errors, their fairness and efficiency may be questioned.

The key issues impinging on decision making are summarized as:

- decision making may be subject to questionable influences, as shown in Figure 5.4

- decision making confirms the importance of impressions

  - first impressions are based on early sight of the application form and candidate and seldom altered

  - interviewers are swayed by their personal liking of the candidate

  - negative evidence or unexpected behaviour may provide reasons to reject

- decision making is subject to error and illusion through use of stereotypes and frequent sex bias.

From this summary, the following conclusions may be drawn:

- Impression management techniques appear to be successful. Applicants who make a favourable impression, emphasize their similarity to the interviewer and conceal negative information are more likely to be appointed.

- Interviewers' confidence in their ability to evaluate information and reach unbiased decisions is frequently misplaced. Overall judgements based on general impressions are more inadequate and open to prejudice than analytical judgments based on facts.

- Candidates may question the fairness of interview decisions, especially towards minority groups, and procedures may be challenged as discriminatory. Stereotypes favour false assumptions and early decision making means interviewers lack fully informed, objective opinions about the candidate.

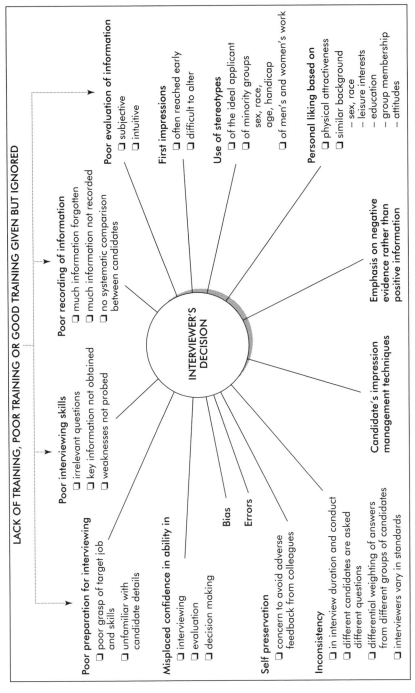

Figure 5.4 Questionable influences on the interviewer's decision

OUTCOMES OF INTERVIEWS

There may be a difference between immediate and final outcomes of interviews. A candidate may accept the job during the interview and then decline it or fail to turn up for work, so deceiving interviewer and organization. The candidate's initial reaction may be euphoria in actually being offered employment. However, subsequent reflection may dampen jubilation and acceptance of the job offer may not be translated into reality. Alternatively, the candidate knowingly deceives when accepting the job. She may lack the social skills, conviction and courage to turn it down immediately, especially in view of professing sincere interest in the job only a little while earlier. The easier option is to accept and then withdraw subsequently.

Interviewers often appoint inappropriate candidates because of rapid decisions based on impressions, stereotypes and the candidate's similarity to themselves. This can strengthen the organization's status quo and encourage cloning. Both features may be contrary to the company's best interests whilst inhibiting cultural diversity and the expansion of equal opportunities. Interviewers' self interest and preoccupation with negative information may dictate safe choices which prevent the organization from maximizing the potential opportunities for growth offered by selection. Candidates, Personnel and the organization may be deceived by the absence of professionalism found in many interviews. Interviewers' behaviour and questioning may be suspect, and those expecting decisions to be made on job related qualities may be surprised that physical appearance may be considered more important.

Women with exactly the same or similar credentials as men get fewer job offers, although this is moderated by the type of job applied for (Arvey and Faley, 1988; Reilly and Chao, 1982) but more recent work has found some evidence in favour of women (Harris, 1989). Associated variables included type of job and associated stereotypical views, attractiveness and applicant competence or qualification. If these were included, gender had little effect.

SUMMARY

Interview diversity is matched by a variety of deception practised by interviewer and candidate. Both parties may manipulate the truth in the exchange of information. Candidates may provide inaccurate, unreliable and invalid information, especially in the traditional interview though it is not totally excluded from those with more structure. The interviewer may also provide misleading details about the job and organization, so establishing a flawed psychological contract.

The interviewer's decision making may be based on false premises orchestrated by the candidate. Impression management can be effective and training of candidates may encourage its use.

As much deception in interviews is related to their subjectivity, it is not surprising that more objective methods are sought. Structured interviews are one result. However, many selectors wish to use other techniques to supplement the interview and have turned to psychometric tests as a solution.

Psychometric tests   6

Psychometric tests are an increasingly popular selection method but they are by no means deception-proof. Smith and Abrahamsen (1992) estimated that ability tests were used in about 18% of appointments and that personality questionnaires were used to select people for about 20% of posts. Baker and Cooper (1995) reported that 58.5% of their 217 organizations had used tests for at least some posts. Increasing test use may be attributed to perceived greater objectivity and less inaccuracy than other selection methods such as interviews. It is paralleled by a growth in the number of tests and product range.

Psychometric tests are a distinctive method of selection that yields stark, quantitative scores. Consequently many issues such as relevance and administration are extremely important, as tests are complex instruments. Many are inherently sound, but Personnel staff may unwittingly mislead the organization and candidates by utilizing tests of dubious quality or by using fair tests inappropriately and unfairly (Feltham and Smith, 1993). Candidates may attempt to deceive selectors by test preparation or by impression management in personality questionnaires. However, unlike most other selection methods, some personality questionnaires actually incorporate countermeasures to identify possible dissimulation.

This chapter falls into two parts – the tests themselves and the ways in which they are used. Initially the background of tests, their common features and specific types of tests are described. The susceptibility of tests to deception – previewed in Figure 6.1 – is examined and strategies of combating socially desirable responses in personality questionnaires are highlighted. The perspective then shifts to the human aspect. Possible deception arising through the Personnel department and candidates is explored, with particular emphasis on practice effects in ability tests and faking of personality questionnaires.

BACKGROUND

Psychometric tests try to measure and analyse basic human characteris-

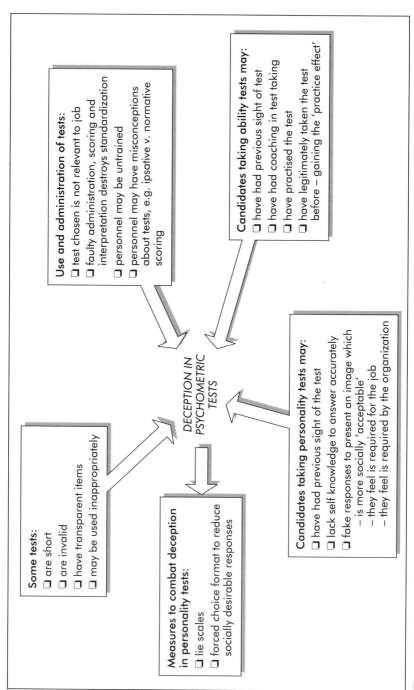

Use and administration of tests:
□ test chosen is not relevant to job
□ faulty administration, scoring and interpretation destroys standardization
□ personnel may be untrained
□ personnel may have misconceptions about tests, e.g. ipsative v. normative scoring

Candidates taking ability tests may:
□ have had previous sight of test
□ have had coaching in test taking
□ have practised the test
□ have legitimately taken the test before – gaining the 'practice effect'

DECEPTION IN PSYCHOMETRIC TESTS

Some tests:
□ are short
□ are invalid
□ have transparent items
□ may be used inappropriately

Measures to combat deception in personality tests:
□ lie scales
□ forced choice format to reduce socially desirable responses

Candidates taking personality tests may:
□ have had previous sight of the test
□ lack self knowledge to answer accurately
□ fake responses to present an image which
  – is more socially 'acceptable'
  – they feel is required for the job
  – they feel is required by the organization

Figure 6.1 Deception in psychometric tests

tics. They evoke carefully formulated samples of behaviour in a systematic and standardized manner. Results are compared with those of a representative sample of an appropriate population (Smith and Robertson, 1993).

In work settings, tests are used mainly for selection and development and are of three main types. First, ability tests can measure both cognitive ability and more specific abilities such as dexterity. Second, personality questionnaires analyse behaviour such as conscientiousness and extroversion. Third, interest tests are concerned with people's interests in things such as outdoor activities or medical activities. Robertson (1994) reported a validity of up to 0.22 for cognitive ability tests (corrected validity was 0.53) and up to 0.33 for various scales of personality inventories. In recruitment some companies use ability tests as definitive judgements, so that a candidate may have to reach a specified score in intelligence or numeracy to remain in the selection process. However, reliance on one particular measure does not receive universal approval. Newell and Shackleton, (1993) comment that 'tests, especially personality tests, have been designed in order to stimulate more penetrating discussion with a person about their capabilities and preferences rather than as some purely objective measure of "*the* person". That is, tests should not be used as an objective determinant of success (or failure) but as a basis for the further exploration of strengths and weaknesses.'

Tests are also used internally. This may occur in development settings such as assessment centres, or in restructuring situations where tests can help to identify new skills for redeployment. The background often contains possibilities of promotion or dismissal, and sometimes those who do not achieve a high score are made redundant. Unison, the public sector union, maintains that testing, especially using personality questionnaires, was insulting when the result could mean test takers lost their jobs (Pickard, 1996).

COMMON CHARACTERISTICS OF TESTS

To achieve test objectivity and consistency, it is important to maintain standardized administration and interpret scores through the use of norms. Subsequent feedback of results to test takers is recommended by the British Psychological Society (BPS). These characteristics are summarized in Figure 6.2 which also outlines their potential for errors and deception.

Tests may be administered by Personnel staff, their assistants, outside consultants, occupational psychologists or by computer. In a good test it is essential that *everyone* undertakes an identical task, with identical instructions, timing, scoring and test-taking conditions. As instructions are often read verbatim from a test manual or card, test administrators may seem aloof and formal. However, from a technical point of view, as long as everyone is treated with equal formality, no harm is done.

Standardization may be less than perfect. Individual administrators, disliking the formality of instructions, may adopt a friendlier approach. However, research by Bartram, Ashley, and Wright (1995) has demonstrated the 'importance of getting test instructions right', as minor alterations or additions to standard instructions can affect a person's score quite dramatically. In these cases, standardization between people, time and place is destroyed.

The test administrator's role is very important. Creating a suitable atmosphere and setting candidates at ease encourages them to voice any concerns in practice sessions. Candidates who feel unable to ask questions may feel confused or resentful, and consequently not produce their best performance. This may account for the very low acceptability or face validity of psychological testing (Silvester and Brown, 1993). Administrators remain influential during test completion. Leaning over candidates may increase anxiety and some administrators occasionally provide extra assistance to candidates taking physical ability tests. Such activities may threaten standardization and produce misleading results.

TYPES OF TEST AND THEIR OPENNESS TO DECEPTION

The main types of tests used in selection are ability tests and personality questionnaires. Ability tests, which may be strictly timed, divide into two main types: tests of mental ability and those of more specific abilities such as dexterity.

Mental ability tests

Mental ability tests measure three types of ability – attainment, intelligence, and more specific aptitudes. Tests of attainment measure a person's level of knowledge or skill at the time of test administration, e.g. a test of spelling. A wider group includes tests of general intelligence, e.g. AH4, Ravens Progressive Matrices or Wechsler's Adult Intelligence Scale (WAIS). Intelligence testing may be quite controversial but despite all

COMMON CHARACTERISTICS   OPENNESS TO DECEPTION

Standardization

All participants are treated equally in respect of:
- everyone is given identical tasks of equivalent difficulty
- everyone is given identical instructions – often read 'verbatim' from a test manual or card
- everyone is given the same time limits if time is an important factor
- everyone's answers are scored identically
- everyone completes the test in similar settings that are equivalent to a quiet office or examination room that has few distractions

- Breaches in one or more aspects of standardization
- Poorly written administration instructions may mislead test users and test takers (Rees, 1996)
- Individual administrators may adopt a friendlier approach to set candidates at ease
- Timing may vary if stop watches are not used – a one minute inaccuracy can be vital in some ability tests

Norms

Tables of scores obtained from a representative sample of an appropriate population (the norm group). Sometimes a choice of norms is available, e.g. for men or women or for people of differing educational attainment. Interpretation of test results is achieved by 'raw scores' with norms.

- Choice of an inappropriate norm group may mislead, though this may be minimized if the effect is systematic
- Some criticism of tests using American norms or ones considered out of date

Feedback

BPS guidelines state that 'ownership of [test results] must rest jointly with tester and testee. This is an important ethical point here . . . [about] the need for the opportunity to be arranged for at least a debriefing . . . When it is possible to extend feedback to counselling proper, so much the better.'

Newell and Shackleton (1993) found that only 33% of organizations studied 'always' gave feedback and discussed results with test takers. Employers are less likely to provide feedback to external candidates (56%) compared to those from inside the organization (86%) (Baker and Cooper, 1995).

Figure 6.2 Common characteristics of tests and their openness to deception

their imperfections, there is a mountain of evidence that intelligence tests are the best *single* predictor of how well a person will do in a job (Gottfredson, 1986; Hunter and Schmidt, 1989), especially in complex jobs. The third category of tests focuses on tests of particular aptitudes or abilities such as numerical reasoning and verbal reasoning, which are popular in graduate selection. This group also includes spatial reasoning and tests for clerical checking which measure speed and accuracy and may be presented as a battery of tests.

General concerns about mental ability tests

Some tests may not measure what they purport to measure, which would appear to be in itself deceptive. Tests of numeracy may be embedded in verbal explanations which may be inappropriate. Consequently candidates whose first language is not English may be penalised, even though verbal ability is not the focus of the test.

This impinges on wider issues. In some ability tests, lower mean scores have been observed for some groups, especially ethnic minorities, than for others and this has caused unease about indirect, unfair, discrimination. In some instances employers have withdrawn tests after finding ethnic differences in test performance, as in London Underground's use of tests for selection of middle management (CRE, 1990). However, from a scientific and legal viewpoint, a lower average score for one group or another is not conclusive proof of bias.

The scores from timed ability tests should ideally represent the maximum score allowed by the candidates' true ability. Selectors may be deceiving themselves if they think this always occurs. A candidate's score may be raised by coaching and practice, may be an underestimate because of anxiety or may be affected by test-taking strategies.

Test-taking strategies in ability tests often focus on a trade-off between speed and accuracy, possibly involving time management and guessing. The naive candidate, unversed in test-taking strategies, could produce a test score which underestimates his ability, rather than reflecting it accurately. Strategy is also an important variable in differences in test-taking performance between ethnic groups (Fletcher and Wood, 1993). A study at British Rail revealed that Asians and whites adopted different test-taking strategies. Asians preferred to work slowly and accurately on aptitude tests, avoiding guessing, but quickly on safety tests so they made more mistakes. In both cases their adopted strategies put them at a disadvantage, though this may not have been recognized.

Physical ability tests

Physical ability tests, sometimes called sensory motor tests, are often used to select people for craft and operative jobs. They usually measure people's ability to make things or operate machinery. A typical example is the handtool dexterity test, pictured in Figure 6.3. It is used for jobs that require hand co-ordination and the use of basic tools such as spanners, and can be used to select trainees for jobs in engineering and auto servicing. The test is very simple. The applicant is asked to unscrew the nuts, washers and bolts from one side of the frame and reassemble them on the other side of the frame. They are given a standard set of spanners, pliers and screwdrivers and their total score is the time taken.

Physical ability tests are liable to the same breaches of standardization as other tests. In theory, the advantage of pre-knowledge can be negated by good instructions and a short practice session, though an experienced candidate is likely to retain some advantage over a complete novice.

Figure 6.3 The handtool dexterity test

Personality questionnaires

Personality questionnaires have been designed to assess an individual's capabilities and preferences. They vary in type and scoring methods, but since they rely upon self report answers they offer more scope for deception than ability tests.

Types of personality questionnaire

The majority of personality questionnaires focus on the whole personality and include Cattell's 16PF and the Californian Psychological Inventory (CPI). The number of personality characteristics varies but may include extroversion, anxiety, conscientiousness, agreeableness and openness to experience. Not all traits may be relevant to the employment situation, though assessors may find it hard to ignore them once they have been revealed. The Saville and Holdsworth Occupational Personality Questionnaire (OPQ) differs from others because it has been specifically developed for an occupational setting.

There is also quite a wide use of other, mainly personality orientated questionnaires which have been designed to measure more specific attributes such as customer orientation or sales aptitude. Others may be more focused on motivation and teamworking. Questionnaires may be ipsative or normative in their scoring, and this has important consequences for subsequent interpretation.

Normative scoring questionnaires

Scores on a normative scale are independent and can usually be treated as measures of different qualities. A given question has a number of options as below:

New ideas fascinate me:
a   yes   **b**   occasionally   **c**   no

A normative scale allows comparisons between people. They also allow use of a non-committal middle response and are open to social desirability.

Ipsative scoring questionnaires

In ipsative tests one answer affects more than one scale. For example:

In the following pair, which word would be the *most* accurate description of you:

1a   experimenting   **1b**   calm

If you answer A to question one, your score on being experimenting goes up but at the same time your score for being calm would probably go down. A clear signal that a test is ipsative is that everyone has the same total when the scores for all the scales are totalled. Tests which ask the candidate to rank various qualities are also examples of ipsative tests, as in the following example:

Here is a list of the ways that people behave at meetings. Rank them according to how often you adopt these behaviours:

BEHAVIOUR	RANK
Someone who chairs the meeting	
Someone who plants new ideas	
Someone who monitors progress	
Someone who takes care of others	
Someone who finishes things off	

Ipsative tests help to identify an individual's relative strengths. They cannot be used to compare people so cannot be used directly in selection, though they can be used to improve the quality of interview or assessment decisions. Assessors who are unaware of the properties of ipsative tests may use them incorrectly, so deceiving themselves and others.

Personality tests in selection

The role of ipsative personality questionnaires in selection is part of a wider debate about the value of personality questionnaires and their accuracy in predicting job performance (Kinder and Robertson, 1995). Several attacks on personality questionnaires by Blinkhorn and Johnson (1990, 1991) have focused on their apparent low validity and exaggerated value. They appear to represent a minority view. Recent research provides reassurance on the usefulness of personality questionnaires, but recommends a focused approach, accompanied by 'an understanding of how the individual scales relate to job performance' which in turn can be facilitated by job analysis (Kinder and Robertson, 1995).

The susceptibility of personality questionnaires to faking may limit their usefulness in selection. As the questionnaires are self report measures, the candidate's willingness to be honest is crucial. Questions are frequently transparent, enabling candidates to give the socially desirable answer (Lewis, 1985) and selectors may be deceived.

Attempts to reduce the opportunities for faking

The prospect of faking concerns test producers and they have devoted considerable time and effort to combating it. The main outcomes have been the development of forced choice questions and lie scales.

Forced choice questions

Questions have been designed so that all alternatives look equally good or equally bad, ensuring that answers are equated for social desirability. As there are few clues about which is the best answer, honesty appears the only option. This design is seen most frequently in forced choice questions, usually encountered in personality questionnaires that are ipsative, for example:

> In each of the following pairs, which word would be the *most* accurate description of you:
>
> **2a** active   **2b** respectful
> **3a** honest   **3b** sociable

The basic formula can be varied in many ways. People may be asked to choose the alternative that is least like themselves, or the questions can use negative qualities, as in the following examples:

> Here are three words. Underline the one that is *least* like you:
>
> **4a** honest   **4b** respectful   **4c** thoughtful
>
> Here are three words. Underline the one which would be the *most* accurate description of you:
>
> **5a** deceitful   **5b** stupid   **5c** inconsiderate

Nevertheless, giving an honest answer to these types of questions can be surprisingly difficult. It is not at all impossible for all the alternatives to be equally applicable. Some candidates may be equally honest and sociable; they cannot answer question three without distorting the truth in some way.

Lie scales

The other way that test developers have sought to minimize the element of deception in personality questionnaires is to use lie scales. These may be called lie scales, as in the Eysenck Personality Questionnaire (EPI), or given slightly different titles, e.g. the 16PF test's Motivational Distortion scale. Most people think that lie scales are based on the consistency of the answers given to questions which are repeated throughout a test. In fact, few lie scales are based on this principle. Instead, they are based either on the probability of giving a series of unlikely answers or by counting the number of socially desirable answers given to certain questions.

Lie scales based on unlikely answers

These scales will contain a series of questions where more than about 95% of the population will answer in a certain way. Examples of these questions and unusual answers might be:

STATEMENT	UNLIKELY ANSWER
I never lose my temper	True
I never exceed speed limits	True
I sometimes forget to repay small favours	False
I am sometimes late for meetings	False
There are times when I am irritable towards other people	False

Firm conclusions about truthfulness cannot be drawn from just one of these questions. However, it is possible to calculate that the chances of truthfully giving an unusual answer to three questions is about one in ten thousand and therefore it would seem that one would be likely to be correct in concluding that some answers are lies. This conclusion would be generalized on the basis that a candidate who is prepared to lie to one question would be prepared to lie to other questions.

Unfortunately lie scales based on unusual answers have two major problems. First, the questions in the lie scales are easy to spot and the required answer is easy to determine. Second, it is hard to produce questions where there are clear 'minority' answers. Often it is necessary to ask about family and personal life in order to obtain suitable questions. At best, this means that candidates feel the questions are unnecessarily unfair and prying – with the consequence that candidates reciprocate and give unfair answers. At worst, it means that some candidates will be upset because the questions revive unpleasant memories or sadness.

Lie scales based on socially desirable answers

The second method of constructing lie scales requires considerable research. First, a question is given to a sample of people under neutral circumstances where there is no incentive to deceive or give untruthful answers. Then after a delay of about a month, the question is re-administered under conditions where there is an incentive to create a good impression. The two sets of answers are compared on a question by question basis. Those questions where the sample has consistently tended to change its answers are identified. These questions are then collated to form a lie scale. Anyone who answers these question in the pattern of the second administration will obtain a high score on the lie scale.

Some concerns about lie scales

As the use of lie scales has become more widespread and as experience in their use has accumulated, a number of concerns have grown (see for example Seisdedos, 1993).

First, it has been observed that certain types of people tend to produce high scores. Often they are the people who would be classed as 'pillars of society', who clearly aspire to high personal standards and who occupy responsible and trustworthy jobs, such as civil servants, church ministers and bank managers. It would seem that these groups either have been deceptive on a gigantic and systematic scale or that the lie scales are themselves deceptively measuring something else and then branding it as lying or deception. An inspection of the questions used in lie scales suggests that these scales are measuring a mixture of conscientiousness and sociability. Consequently, if lie scales are used to screen people they could be screening out precisely those people whom organizations would want to do some of the most responsible jobs.

The second concern is partly philosophical and partly practical. Pragmatists are blasé about the possibility of deception in personality tests. They reason that if the applicant is clever enough to turn on the 'correct' personality for the purposes of passing a test, they will be clever enough to turn on the 'correct' personality when it is demanded by the job. Indeed the complete pragmatist would contend that anyone who could *not* deceive personality questionnaires would be unsuitable for some jobs in, say, sales, politics or espionage. The philosophically inclined are more subtle. They maintain that dissimulation is a personality trait in its own right that may or may not be useful. In order to distort a personality profile, a person must first have the ability to work out the type of behaviour which is needed in certain situations. There must then be the willingness and ability to produce the desired behaviour consistently. To some extent, it could be claimed that lie scales are measuring the motivation to 'fit in' to a given environment by identifying the appropriate social requirements and then meeting them.

Interest tests

Interest tests, such as the Rothwell-Miller Interest Blank and a range of Saville and Holdsworth interest questionnaires, are used to identify those aspects of jobs that give individuals mental enjoyment. Interests might be relevant to selection because if something provides mental enjoyment, people will work harder at that kind of activity, so creating general success.

However, interest tests are used relatively infrequently in selecting employees because they are very transparent and easy to fake. A typical interest test will ask an applicant whether they like, are indifferent to or dislike a range of activities such as:

6. explaining to people the
   benefits of objects   Like/Indifferent/Dislike
7. working with animals   Like/Indifferent/Dislike
8. persuading people to
   try new ideas   Like/Indifferent/Dislike

An applicant for, say, a sales job will find it easy to work out that they should answer 'Like' to questions six and eight. Longstaffe, as long ago as 1948, showed that people could fake their replies to the Kuder Interest profile to a very large extent.

A further reason why interest tests are seldom used in selection is that interests are much less stable than personality or abilities. Interests can change quite rapidly. Indeed a job can provide so much activity in an area that interest can be sated and motivation is lost.

Having examined the psychometric tools used in selection and some of their weaknesses, the chapter now turns to the people involved in their use. Test publishers, Personnel staff and candidates approach tests from different standpoints, especially in regard to technical knowledge, experience, motivation and attitudes. Personnel staff and publishers may disagree on their relative rights and responsibilities, each 'blaming' the other for apparent inadequacies. The Personnel department may feel that if they purchase tests they have the right to believe that the publisher has validated the test for the specific use intended by the organization. Publishers may feel this is an abdication of responsibility. They claim that 'in the last analysis, the end user must bear the final responsibilities for the results of using a test in a particular way . . . test developers and publishers . . . have only the dubious privilege of receiving the blame for others' misuse of their instrument' (Feltham, Baron and Smith, 1994). In this debate, the candidate may assume the role of 'piggy in the middle'.

THE ROLE OF THE PERSONNEL DEPARTMENT

Whilst tests themselves have the perceived advantage of objectivity, this objectivity can be damaged by human influence, especially in the choice of tests, their administration, scoring and interpretation. This may result in inadvertent deception of the Personnel department, organization and candidates.

The quality of tests

Test users may deceive themselves about the quality of some tests, or may be misled, unwittingly or otherwise, by some test publishers. There is no independent control of technical standards and some tests may be technically poor, short and lack validity.

Not all tests are valid predictors of job performance (Fletcher, 1993). Concern has been expressed about 'the use of largely invalidated "quick and dirty tests" which claim wider generisability than the data available warrants' (Brindle and Ridgeway, 1995). Purchasers of these tests may be unaware of their defects and may be misled into believing that they are sound products.

Similarly test norms may be produced on the basis of small samples. Statistics based on small samples may be very volatile. As a result, some norms which have not been extensively researched and validated may be used to inflate the apparent quality of tests.

The choice of tests

Choosing a test necessitates care and knowledge, but Bartram (1991) suggests that some test purchasers lack the knowledge to critically evaluate test material. Rees (1996) identified a number of common misunderstandings on technical matters among test users and Fletcher (1989) suggests that other test users may use ipsative and normative questionnaires interchangeably, without appreciating the differences.

Careful choice of test is crucial. Unless a test is clearly job related there is likely to be suspicion, controversy and misunderstanding, especially among test takers. Candidates are frustrated by tests which are apparently impersonal and irrelevant, especially if rejection decisions are based only on test scores. Test choice should be based on job analysis so that there is demonstrable relevance to occupational criteria. In their survey of employers, Baker and Cooper (1995), found that 15% did not actively check that tests were appropriate for the required qualities they wished to measure. Without such checks, it may be difficult to prove that any predictor is measuring job relevant attributes and this can lead to complaints of indirect discrimination.

Having identified key attributes for testing, further decisions have to be made on their specific characteristics and the appropriate level. For example, numeracy is a key requirement of many jobs but may range from routine arithmetic to complex problem solving. Choosing a problem-solving test for a job involving routine arithmetic not only fails to measure the required characteristic, but produces results which may be irrelevant to the position.

The value and reputation of tests is jeopardized by untrained staff. In their guidance for test users (1989) the BPS state 'the use of psychological tests by people not trained in their administration, evaluation and interpretation is inefficient. It may result in serious injustice to the victims of such usage. It may also be dangerous to the individual, to the organization on whose behalf the testing is being carried out or both.' The BPS guidelines are fully supported by reputable suppliers of tests and the Institute of Personnel and Development (IPD) code on occupational testing.

The administration and interpretation of tests

Choosing well known tests does not necessarily result in valid test use. An organization can take a well designed test and use it inappropriately or ineptly, and then make invalid inferences from the scores. Personnel departments may therefore deceive themselves, candidates and the organization because the objectivity of using tests in selection has generated a false confidence. The handling, administration and interpretation of tests may cause inadvertent deception by destroying the scientific basis on which psychometric tests rest. Test users may use arbitrary and inappropriate cut off scores, which can result in unfairness. Brindle and Ridgeway (1995) report varying standards of test use and naive interpretation of test data by managers who may be inadequately trained. Misconceptions over scores can result in over-interpretation of small score differences on personality questionnaires. Interview panels may draw false conclusions about tests if they receive information from a third party, unqualified in test use, who fails to understand them (Pickard, 1996).

THE ROLE OF THE CANDIDATE

Tests are mistrusted and even feared by some candidates. Their concerns may centre on the stress of the test-taking situation, the tests themselves and possible invasion of privacy. To candidates, tests may appear as scientific measures with incomprehensible methods of scoring and interpretation. Their very standardization and objectivity gives candidates the feeling that they cannot influence or control the results as much as they can influence the results of, say, interviews. Whether or not these feelings are justified, they exacerbate the feelings of unfairness felt by most rejected candidates.

Although test taking is advocated by the BPS as a co-operative experience, this may be demonstrably untrue in selection. Test takers frequently are not in a position to exert the rights implicit in the BPS and IPD codes of practice. They may be impotent in a process that offers them little choice.

The candidate's knowledge of testing and test-taking strategies

If candidates are not forewarned that they will be asked to complete tests, they may not give their best performance because they are unprepared and resentful. Totally inexperienced candidates face an unfamiliar task which they do not know how to tackle. In ability tests they may not know whether incorrect answers are penalized. In personality inventories they may be unsure of whether extreme answers are better than those in the middle of the road and some are severe on themselves while others are lenient. Test-taking skills may be as necessary as having the skills the test measures (Wood and Baron, 1992).

The candidates' preparation for tests

Ideally everyone completing a test should have the same level of experience. This aspect of standardization is difficult to achieve. Some candidates have much greater test-taking experience than others. Selectors sometimes complain that candidates have done the same tests before, especially in ability tests, so that their own test results may be of less value. Some ways in which candidates prepare for tests can be deceptive, as can their concealment of such preparation.

Test-taking orientation

Test-taking orientation usually involves familiarization with psychometric tests and guidance in the principles of test taking and test-taking skills. It is available through books and interactive methods. Graduates may have access to university seminars or the public can attend commercial courses. Some employers themselves run schemes which are designed to eliminate differences in test sophistication. As these methods are differentially available through cost and employment position, standardization is difficult to achieve. Some organizations attempt to redress this situation by providing practice leaflets, which is useful if they are sent to all applicants.

Coaching or practice for ability tests

Candidates may wish to gain practice in order to improve their speed, accuracy and overall scores. Sometimes this may consist of practice on the items contained in the publishers' practice leaflets. Sometimes candidates may be provided with sample tests and test-taking strategies on courses. Candidates may revive forgotten skills or undertake intensive instruction on items similar to those included in tests. Up to a point, coaching or drilling can improve test scores. This would lower test validity, as the candidate's score could rise without a corresponding rise in level of job performance. Consequently organizations are misled about the candidate's apparent suitability.

Taking the same test twice – the 'practice effect'

The most effective preparation a candidate can make for ability testing is to take the same or similar test on one or more occasion. This familiarizes candidates with the format of test and answer sheets, whilst previewing the atmosphere of timed test-taking conditions. Candidates may even remember some answers or the ways of working out specific problems (Baron, 1991). This strategy can be successful with ability tests, but with other tests it can rebound unsuccessfully, as organizations may use the same test to measure different characteristics. People who rehearse what they think are the correct answers may, in fact, distort what would be a 'natural' and required profile into an unsuccessful one.

The 'practice effect' may occur legitimately, as when graduates apply to a number of organizations which use the same test (Hunter et al., 1990). In Silvester and Brown's (1993) research on graduate recruitment, 74% of 737 students in the survey had been asked to complete aptitude tests, 57% being asked to take an aptitude test more than once and 40% said they completed the same test on more than one occasion.

The 'practice effect' can also arise in an illegitimate way when candidates gain unauthorized access to tests. This can occur when ambitious candidates try to discover the name and nature of any tests that are used. Some applicants will then try to obtain copies of the tests and perfect their answers. Theoretically attempts to obtain copies of tests should be unsuccessful, since tests are only sold to qualified users and on condition that their confidentiality is safeguarded. Direct requests for copies should be politely but sympathetically refused, but other more devious routes exist.

Tests may become more readily available through leakages in security, especially if tests are, wrongly, sent by mail to unqualified users. This may occur when firms are considering using management consultants to install a selection system in their organization and request a copy of the test for Director approval. Although this improper request should be politely refused, some consultants may comply out of ignorance or an avaricious fear of losing the contract. Once the test is despatched, all security may be lost and the test may be photocopied, circulated round other staff or stored insecurely.

Other devious means of obtaining tests are described in John's case.

> John discovered that a prospective employer was using a well known personality measure and ability tests. He sought out a vocational guidance organization that used the same tests and obtained some practice and feedback by pretending to want vocational guidance. He was pleased with his astuteness. Unfortunately, when John arrived at the organization he was presented with the alternative version of the personality test and higher levels of ability testing than he had practised.

Practice effects cause several problems in selection. Hunter, Keys, Wynns and Corcoran (1990) describe recruiters' concerns that candidates who have taken tests previously 'may benefit from their prior experience and thus have an unfair advantage over other candidates'. Research indicates that practice improves performance, and often score improvements will be large enough to affect decisions made by selectors (Adams, 1991). Scores continue to increase with further administrations, and practice effects may be greater if consecutive administrations are close together (Anastasi, 1988). Practice effects cast doubt on the predictive validity of tests and Hunter et al. (1990) believe it could introduce unfairness into the selection procedure.

Recruiters may wish to establish whether candidates have taken specific tests before. However they may be deliberately misled by individuals who conceal their previous test experience in order to appear as more favourable candidates or to avoid any consequent action by selectors. Even if selectors are aware of a candidate's previous experience of that test, their action is limited. They cannot reduce the scores of 'practised' candidates because practice effects are not constant over individuals and other candidates may have had practice but chosen to conceal it.

Organisations' reactions to 'practice effect'

Selectors who would prefer to eliminate opportunities for practice have few available options, since there seems no way of developing tests that are not subject to practice effects. Hunter et al. (1990) suggested that selectors may wish to use tests which are not extensively used by others. Alternatively, a small group of organizations could sponsor test development projects, and then have exclusive access to test materials.

Other organizations favour a more proactive approach. They acknowledge the benefits of practice and may introduce formal practice sessions. Practice effects are greatest for naive subjects (Jensen, 1980) and can reduce unfair discrimination. Practice improves scores for ethnic minorities and possibly disadvantaged, groups, such as the educationally disadvantaged, who improve more than the majority group through coaching in test taking. Practice makes the test fairer and more valid as a test of ability (Kellett, 1991) and is recommended by the CRE. Organization practice sessions would be advantageous because candidates would be provided with equivalent familiarity with tests and have greater awareness of test-taking strategies. British Rail introduced practice test materials which were examples of mini tests and candidates were guided through these, and the correct answers were provided and explained. A general familiarization process and basic hints for the tests and test-taking strategy were also included. The pass rates of Afro-Caribbean and Asian candidates increased markedly more than those of the white majority as a result of practice (Callen and Geary, 1994).

As might be expected, such actions do not receive universal approval. If practice test sessions are conducted within an organization, external applicants may be disadvantaged. If they occur before the actual test session, additional demands may be placed on candidates, especially if they are participating in a lengthy and demanding selection procedure.

Candidate's behaviour when taking tests

When taking tests, some candidates may adopt unorthodox means of test completion. In physical ability tests they may devise unconventional strategies, enabling them to work faster and increase their scores. Such results may be deceptive if the candidates' methods cannot be transferred to a work situation, because, for example, they could compromise safety regulations. Candidates may fake personality inventories or cheat in ability tests by copying others' answers. They may make mistakes in marking answer forms by working across the page instead of downwards, which inadvertently deceives selectors about performance.

Faking of personality questionnaires

The susceptibility of personality questionnaires to faking has been discussed. Although faking usually involves impression management, self deception may also occur (Paulhaus, 1989). Barrick and Mount (1996) found both types of response distortion on scales of conscientiousness and emotional stability amongst two applicant samples.

Impression management features a dual approach – enhancing perceived positive personality features and underplaying perceived negative features.

There is little doubt that when people make a conscious effort, they can alter their scores on personality tests. In a typical study a group of students are given a personality test under neutral conditions where there was no incentive to distort their scores. The students are asked to complete the test a second time about a month later, but are instructed to fake good and change the answers in order to maximize their chances of obtaining a job. There are usually significant changes in the direction that would be expected: among other things students give answers that are more extrovert (Borislow, 1958; Jacobs and Barron, 1968; Radcliffe, 1966; Strickler, 1969 and Wiggins, 1966). Dunnette et al. (1962) suggest that about one in seven applicants fakes the replies.

Fortunately for the advocatesof personality tests, there is considerable evidence that faking on personality tests has little effect on their effectiveness in selection. As long ago as 1983, Nevid concluded that the issue of social desirability was 'a methodical dead horse'. More recently, Hough, Eaton, Dunnette, Kamp and McCloy (1990) found that the validities of personality scales are not destroyed even for individuals who are responding in an overly desirable manner. Furthermore, they conclude that applicants' responses to personality scales do not indicate distortion. After reviewing and re-analysing previous studies, Ones, Viswesvaran and Reiss (1996) arrive at similar conclusions. The crucial analysis involved 14 studies and 9966 subjects and showed that socially desirable responses had an insignificant effect on the validities of personality tests. Indeed they unequivocally conclude that worries about social desirability in the use of personality tests for selection is 'the red herring'.

The implications of this ability to fake the answers to personality tests are not at all clear. While studies in artificial settings using students show that personality tests can be faked, studies in natural settings suggest that the level of faking is in fact much lower. Rimland (1962) offers evidence that faking is more likely to consist of shading the truth rather than committing downright lies.

Deception by candidates after taking tests

External candidates who have received their results may use them selectively to impress other employers. Similarly internal employees may leak their best scores to their boss or other important decision makers in the organization.

SUMMARY

Tests themselves are complex. Their objectivity can facilitate fairer selection but test use involves decisions on choice of test and perceived relevance to the job. Confidence in tests can be misplaced, as tests vary in usefulness, validity and reliability and not all achieve their stated purpose. Flawed tests, sound measures chosen for irrelevant purposes or used inappropriately and faulty standardization can deceive the organization and bring tests into disrepute which is not always deserved. Deception may stem from the use of tests, rather than the tests themselves.

Use of tests involves test publishers, Personnel staff, test administrators and candidates. Each has open and hidden agendas and may deceive other participants and the organization, whether wittingly or unwittingly. Publishers may over-emphasize the advantages of poorly constructed tests and Personnel staff may use tests unethically or inefficiently. Candidates may try to gain previous sight of tests and so improve their scores. They may fake personality questionnaires to put themselves in a good light, though this may be detected by lie scales.

Companies may incorporate psychometric tests into other selection procedures, such as assessment centres.

Other methods   7

Practical tasks, assessment centres, biodata and graphology are other methods used in the selection process. They are much less popular than the classic trio and enjoy differing degrees of effectiveness, ranging from the high reputation of practical tests to the negatively rated graphology. Practical tasks are not a homogenous category but encompass disparate tests such as work samples, written reports and presentations which may be given to entrants for manual or non-manual work. Sometimes several tasks are combined in an assessment centre and administered on a group basis rather than individually.

Robertson and Kandola (1982) believed that applicants considered work samples to be fairer, more appropriate and more enjoyable than aptitude tests. On the whole, opportunities for candidate deception appear minimal, though there are some exceptions. However there is much greater scope for unwitting deception by the employer in test construction, administration and scoring. The role of the person giving the work sample is crucial and can be instrumental in unwitting or more deliberate deception.

Assessment centres are much more complex. Organizations may be deceived by placing so much faith in them, since their validity can be prejudiced by poor construction and scoring problems. Both biodata (the collection of biographical data), and graphology may be subject to candidate faking and more deliberate deception may be employed in biodata. Organizations may conceal their use of these methods, so deceiving applicants, and technical concerns may limit their effectiveness.

This chapter deals with each method in turn, initially describing its background before considering possible deception. Although the methods differ considerably, there are certain common sources of deception. Figure 7.1 shows that these centre on the construction, administration and interpretation of the methods themselves and the roles of the evaluator, candidate and organization.

WORK SAMPLES

The use of these practical tasks and others by Industrial Society Survey (1994) respondents is summarized in Table 7.1. According to respondents, practical tasks were rated as the most effective selection method, in joint position with interviews, closely followed by presentations and then by written reports.

Type of job	Percentage of respondents using methods in selection		
	Presentations	Written reports	Practical tests/tasks
Senior managers	45	23	13
Other managers	35	14	14
Administrative/clerical	2	3	40
Professional/technical	23	11	28
Manual	1	1	28

Table 7.1 Proportions of Industrial Society Survey respondents using practical selection methods for types of job
Source: Industrial Society Survey (1994)

Work samples are miniaturized replicas of jobs and should contain the crucial elements of those jobs in terms of behaviour and conditions (Wood, 1994). Asher and Sciarrino (1974) argued that work samples should be realistic, with point to point correspondence between the behaviour in the test (predictors) and the actual work behaviour required in the job (criteria). The more the test resembles the job, the greater the faith in the assessment of candidate effectiveness. Some would argue that work samples provide a realistic alternative to psychometric testing.

Construction of tests

The first concern about work sample tests is their proper construction by careful job analysis, ensuring that they accurately represent the job's required skills, materials, tools and environment. High job specificity is essential, even within a particular class of job, e.g. a cook in a small cafe will probably differ from a cook in an enormous hospital in terms of

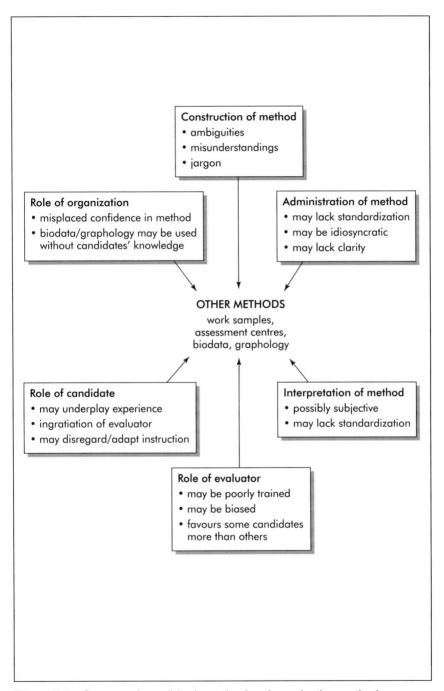

Figure 7.1 Sources of possible deception in other selection methods

equipment and processes. This specificity may not be possible for reasons of practicality (large machinery), economy (cost of breakages and wastage) and possible danger to the applicant or others. Candidates may be deceived if the job specificity is inaccurate or not maintained to keep pace with changes in job characteristics. Not only does this destroy validity, but the candidate who performs well on the work sample may feel a misplaced confidence which evaporates when faced with real work conditions, especially if they are significantly different from those experienced in the test.

According to Wood (1994) the degree of fidelity in the test varies from 'task to task, job to job and instrument to instrument'. Tests measure an isolated part of work and ignore surrounding activities, and this may can be more disadvantageous in some jobs than in others. For example, a work sample involving assembly of parts on a conveyor belt may accurately reflect the whole task whereas a test measuring computer skills does not mirror the full content of work of a magazine editor and may therefore be misrepresentative.

Role of the evaluator

The tester may wittingly or unwittingly distort the results through errors in administration and scoring. This may reflect evaluators' liking some candidates more than others or the introduction of an element of sex or racial bias. Problematic scoring or evaluating behaviour rather then describing it may allow common errors to occur. Consequently results can be misleading.

Some tests are also unstandardized, subjectively scored and fairly uninformative, so that selectors' faith in this selection method may be misplaced. The typing test is usually a poor work sample for these reasons.

Deception in work samples

The main types of work sample tests are shown in Table 7.2 and all are susceptible to deception.

Skills based work samples

As these measure skills already acquired in particular jobs, the situational familiarity to candidates means tasks are generally acceptable. However in

---

Skills based work samples

☐   measure skills already acquired in particular jobs

☐   *motor tests*
     physical manipulation of objects, e.g. tests in typing, bricklaying, sewing and operating lathes

☐   *verbal tests*
     problem solving exercises with a language or people orientation
     – pencil and paper tests of existing job knowledge
     – individual, situational decision making tasks, e.g. in-tray exercises
     – group discussion/decision making

Trainability tests

☐   assess inexperienced candidate's suitability for training

---

Table 7.2   Types of work sample

some motor work sample tests candidates may adapt tasks in the light of their own experience rather than follow the strictly determined procedures of the test. This increases speed and efficiency but can be misleading.

Presentations and written reports

It could be argued that presentations and written reports are both work simulation exercises and verbal in content. Presentations may be given as an adjunct to an interview or as part of an assessment centre. Frequently they are on work related topics and involve the candidate in research and a short presentation to managers followed by questions. Skills of communication, time management, appropriateness of content for the audience, persuasion and the ability to handle queries can be assessed. Written reports have a similar format but there may be a greater emphasis on technical knowledge which is more easily absorbed through longer scrutiny of written material.

Both methods provide candidates with opportunities to submit work which is not their own and does not truly reflect their abilities and attributes. Assistance with research can enhance content whilst professional preparation of overhead transparencies and other visual aids may boost candidate performance and minimize the impact of poor content. Coaching in presentation skills or prior practice to similar audiences may also maximize favourable impressions.

Job knowledge tests

These tests cover a minimum of two areas – the required technical knowledge of how to perform a job and the knowledge of processes and judgemental criteria needed to perform the job effectively – and can mislead selectors about applicant abilities. Hartigan and Wigdor (1989) studied the General Aptitude Test Battery and discovered a significant gap between scores and work skills. Applicants who lacked formal education, were inexperienced in paper and pencil tests and had language difficulties tended to be rated lowly in intellectual ability, though many could demonstrate job relevant skills in 'hands on' work simulations.

Individual/situational decision making

This type of job simulation investigates the candidate's ability to make decisions similar to those found in the job. It can include psychomotor simulators, e.g. for pilots or air traffic controllers, in-tray exercises and hypothetical discussions such as a prospective retail store manager being asked how she would deal with a shopper who has just pulled out a knife on a fellow customer.

The in-tray is widely used to investigate managerial ability. The tray contains letters, memos, faxes and other written material and the participant has a given time limit in which to resolve particular problems usually involving data, procedures and personnel. Decisions have to be made, actions suggested and both have to be communicated to others in a written manner. The exercise simulates the pressures of decision making, problem solving, prioritization and dealing with people which are common in busy offices.

Group discussions/decision making

This is used almost entirely to assess managerial potential and typically occurs in assessment centres. Applicants are grouped together to discuss particular topics, and each individual's performance is assessed on the basis of personal contribution. It is described more fully in the section on assessment centres.

Trainability tests

Trainability tests are used comparatively rarely, despite their validity and success as realistic job previews. In terms of deception, candidates can understate their initial experience in order to appear to make more progress than warranted by the training period. Trainability tests are 'particularly vulnerable to distortion to the tester' (Downs, 1989).

ASSESSMENT CENTRES

An assessment centre is not a place but a complex process of assessing a group of individuals by a team of judges using a number of methods (Feltham, 1989). It usually involves groups of 6–12 candidates who are assessed by line managers, senior managers and/or psychologists on a ratio of one assessor to two participants. The methods generally include written exercises, individual and group exercises plus presentations and the event lasts for 2–3 days or as long as a week.

The main purpose of assessment centres is to identify managerial or leadership potential. This includes selecting external candidates, usually graduates or identifying internal staff for promotion and development. Interestingly, Industrial Society Survey (1994) respondents indicated some use for non-managerial jobs, with 3% of respondents using the method for administrative/clerical jobs, 10% for professional/technical jobs and 1% for manual jobs.

Assessment centres are now believed to be one of the most valid approaches to selection and identification of long term potential, with a validity of about 0.4. Industrial Society respondents rated them as the third most effective method after the joint leaders of interviews and practical tests/tasks. Their popularity is growing. However, faith in assessment centres may be misplaced. Criticisms of the construction of assessment centres, scoring procedures and the assessors' conference may mean that selectors and organizations are deceiving themselves about their effectiveness. Participants may also contribute to deception.

Background
The design of an assessment centre

An assessment centre involves the evaluation and rating of participants on a number of dimensions or competencies which are indicated in a series of exercises. Scoring is recorded on a matrix as illustrated in Figure 7.2.

The *dimensions* are qualities felt to indicate future job performance such

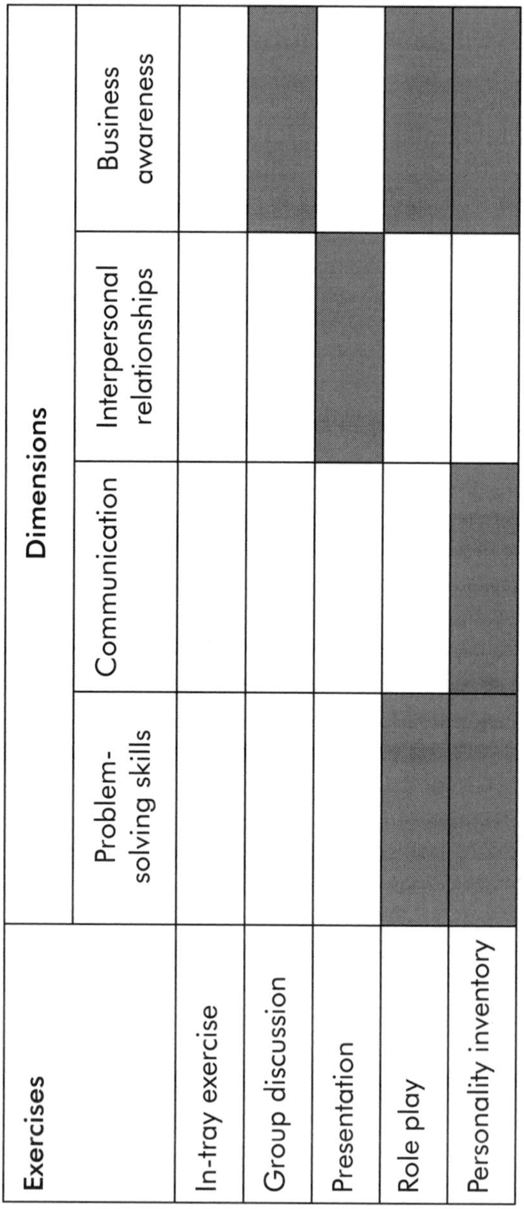

Exercises	Dimensions			
	Problem-solving skills	Communication	Interpersonal relationships	Business awareness
In-tray exercise				
Group discussion				■
Presentation			■	
Role play	■			■
Personality inventory	■	■		■

Figure 7.2 Typical exercises and dimensions in an assessment centre

as supervisory skills, interpersonal sensitivity, leadership and organization. There can be 4 to over 20 dimensions, chosen from published catalogues and various generic competency frameworks, or they can be developed on the basis of job analysis.

Exercises to measure the dimensions are used in a comprehensive and integrated manner. A minimum of two qualitatively different methods of assessing each dimension is required, so that interpersonal skills might be assessed in both group discussion and role play interviews. Ideally exercises should be simulations based on the specific position to be filled and at least one should be a work sample – typically an in-tray exercise in managerial assessment. The usual types of exercise are outlined below, and individual choice depends on the vacancy and the organization.

1. Written exercises, e.g. reports, in-tray and psychometric tests of ability, aptitudes and personality.

2. A presentation.

3. One to one exercises, usually involving a role play. These may take the form of a disciplinary interview in which the candidate deals with a poorly performing employee whose role is standardized and played by a trained assessor under the scrutiny of an observing assessor.

4. Group exercises, including group discussion and team exercises. Candidates may have designated roles or unassigned positions, as in leaderless groups. As candidates are assessed in the context of other candidates, group dynamics develop and facilitate assessments of interpersonal skills, leadership potential, ability to compromise and to get on with and influence colleagues. Problem solving and planning may also be measured. These exercises are therefore opportunities for observation and evaluation of job related behaviour, as candidates argue from past experience and apply themselves to a new problem.

5. Interviews.

There is a system where assessors rotate amongst candidates to observe and evaluate their performance and assess the dimensions. They use scoring procedures based upon what the participant should do in each exercise. Assessors may record examples of specific behaviour and give a rating after each exercise and at the assessment centre's conclusion. Sometimes rating of dimensions is left until the close of the assessment event, when all information has been collected. At the end of the assessment centre assessors confer and produce an overall score for each participant.

Deception in assessment centres

Assessors may deceive themselves and candidates about the aims, objectives and measuring methods used in assessment centres. Assessment centre construction and choice of its components may be questionable, whilst the actions and evaluations of assessors may also be deceptive. Participants may present a false image of themselves.

Each selection method used in an assessment centre is open to abuse. For example, a personality inventory is as susceptible to candidate faking within the context of an assessment centre as elsewhere. Similarly, ability tests can lose standardization through administrative errors and manipulation by candidates.

The assessment centre itself

The 'assessment centre' title may be a misnomer for a motley group of exercises and tests which lack structure and integration. In some cases organizations may confuse participants about the purpose of the assessment centre, either deliberately or unintentionally. Internal candidates may believe they are attending a development centre and later discover that the process has been used to measure participants, and the unsuccessful may effectively be made redundant.

Construction of assessment centre

Potential catastrophe looms through lack of forward planning needed to construct assessment centres and scant attention to determining the criteria at the job analysis stage. Dimensions have to be job related and clear guidance on the criteria to be applied is crucial, preferably illustrated with examples of relevant job behaviour that might be observed during the assessment centre. Without this, the assessment centre framework can disintegrate, as assessors disagree about the aspects of performance which they think are important. Similarly, exercise design and assessor training may not receive the deserved attention. The result is 'many low quality assessment centres – cheap and hastily assembled with little or no professional input – have negligible validity. There is a large number of such assessment centres' (Feltham, 1989). It may be argued that low quality assessment centres lower the 'average' validity to 0.4 from the 0.6 achieved by institutions who give considerable care to the design and implementation of assessment centres.

Dimensions

The number of dimensions may be misleading. They imply that decision making is complex and multifaceted whereas in reality the number of source dimensions underlying assessment judgements is much smaller. Sackett and Hakel (1979) found that although assessors were instructed to use all dimensions, the overall assessment rating could be predicted accurately from a subset of only three – leadership, organization and planning, and decision making.

Dimensions may be interpreted incorrectly as measures of stable and enduring personality traits. Ratings of the same dimension may vary considerably across different exercises as skilled performance tends to be specific to particular kinds of tasks and information, e.g. interpersonal skills in a team task will not necessarily transfer to effective interpersonal skills in one to one counselling. Conclusions about individuals are likely to be more valid if related to tasks and situations than if related only to dimensions.

Exercises

There can be similar problems with exercises. Assessment centre validity rests on their job relevance but has to be balanced by the need to avoid specific prior knowledge. This is especially important in group discussions involving external candidates. Internal candidates of differing status could also be disadvantaged by disparate experience of particular situations. Simulated tasks should reflect real life job situations that correspond to the level of the job, but designers may make tasks too difficult or too easy.

The candidates

Candidate authenticity

The length of assessment centres engenders the view that assessors get to know the 'real person', as there is a belief that candidates cannot successfully adopt and maintain a false image over considerable time. This may not be true and can be a dangerous premise if it creates a false sense of security among assessors. Candidates may be able to maintain an uncharacteristic persona or emphasize specific attributes judged to be required by the ideal applicant.

Assessment centres themselves challenge this view of candidate authenticity. Participants are frequently expected to role play in the one to one exercise and presumably those with histrionic ability can sustain their talents. Interestingly, when the assessment centres were initially developed in the USA they demonstrated unique properties in regarding systematic lying as a virtue (Cook, 1995). Psychologists advised the Office of Strategic Services, forerunner to the Central Intelligence Agency, how to select agents to be dropped behind enemy lines, collect intelligence and return it. Nine dimensions of effective spying were identified and each candidate was required to 'maintain cover' during the assessment, pretending to be someone else, including 'to have been born where he wasn't, to have been educated in institutions other than those he attended, to have been engaged in work or a profession not his own, and to live now in a place that was not his true residence' (Mackinnon, 1977).

Leadership is a pivotal quality sought in assessment centres. Several researchers have commented on the difficulty of its accurate measurement (Lowry, 1995) especially in an assessment centre where the required long term commitment and motivation cannot be demonstrated. The candidate who appreciates its importance may be able to feign the outward trappings without the fundamental underlying requisite qualities (Brannick et al., 1989; Lowry, 1995).

Impression management may not be confined solely to the actual exercises of the assessment centre. Since assessors and candidates are frequently in offsite residential accommodation there are opportunities for social interaction. Factors such as physical attractiveness, which were influential in the interview situation, may be similarly potent. The broader social context widens the scope for impression management. There may be opportunities for ingratiation and self enhancement, especially if targeted at key decision makers or those judged to be sympathetic. This may be facilitated if there is already a degree of assessor/candidate acquaintance, which is in any event a constraint on validity.

Assessors may be deceived if they assume that participants are strangers to one another. Some candidates may already be acquainted, especially if they are within the same organization or from the same university, which may help some candidates to more readily portray their desired image. Alliances formed during the course of the assessment centre can be beneficial to candidates.

Training of candidates

As with other methods, candidates, especially graduates, may have gained experience from their attendance at previous assessment centres and benefitted from available feedback. Unemployed graduates may have had additional training, with a particular emphasis on group exercises, through the Careers Service and/or Training and Enterprise Councils (TECs).

Internal candidates may benefit from the grapevine discussion of assessment centres. Assessees may pass on information, perhaps as strategy suggestions and specific hints on how to tackle exercises (Sackett, Burris and Ryan, 1989). This may bestow 'inside knowledge' which is believed to be possessed by others, would help performance and could give an unfair advantage to some candidates. Other studies have shown that coaching in specific exercises such as the leaderless group discussion and the in-tray can be effective.

Both graduates and internal candidates may have contacts who are able and willing to provide instruction in role plays, presentations and other exercises. For political reasons the internal candidate may be assisted and even coached by the sponsoring manager who submitted his name, so that the manager's judgement is applauded when the candidate performs well.

Role of assessors

Individual differences

The impersonality of exercises, especially role play interviews or presentations, may be thwarted by inconsistency of assessor input. The personality and seniority of the role playing assessor may have differential effects on the candidate's behaviour. A graduate enacting the role of a manager dealing with a poorly performing employee may respond differently if this part is played by the regional director rather than a line manager. For internal candidates such encounters can be daunting.

Assessors of differential seniority may have individual hidden agendas which may interfere with fair evaluations. A senior manager paired with a junior colleague may dominate joint decision making, especially if the junior assessor avoids disagreement for reasons of self interest, career preservation, inexperience or fear. If several assessors are involved, as in resolving disagreements in ratings of group exercises, expediency may override other considerations, producing compromise ratings which satisfy no-one.

Assessors have different expectations of behaviour and standards of performance, and may even disagree about the traits they consider important. Such differences can influence their assessments and scoring, especially if the scores are weighted between the various exercises. Some research suggests that all-male groups of assessors are more lenient in their rating of female candidates than mixed-gender groups of assessors.

Assessors' conference

The 'wash-up session', in which scores are combined or collated, occurs at the end of the assessment centre. Although it aims to utilize fresh memories, assessors may feel jaded and reluctant to contribute the necessary time and attention and there may be some pressure for rapid completion. In this context, individual differences between assessors may become increasingly important.

A consensus of assessors can be reached in two ways. If decisions are reached through discussion alone, social influences may be manifest. Debate may be swayed unduly by an extremely talkative personality, especially if forcefulness and seniority are involved, as these attributes exert considerable influence and others are likely to conform (Sackett and Wilson, 1982). The end result may be negative, with social pressures to adjust ratings rather than agree on true scores. Distortion may become especially pronounced.

Alternatively, final scores may be mechanically generated. This produces the same results as a conference, is equally valid and saves a lot of management time (Pynes et al., 1988). Such scoring would probably be at the expense of subjective discussion and such exclusion could be beneficial. However, it is counterintuitive and likely to be rejected by many involved, and without line managers agreeing to act as assessors assessment centres lose much of their credibility.

Assessors may also mislead in their handling of data. On the one hand, a wealth of information is available but it may not be processed efficiently. Conversely missing data may cause problems as their absence may cause assessors to give a poor overall rating (Jagacinski, 1991).

Inconsistency of assessment centres

As in all selection methods, consistency is important but may not be present. Some pairings of assessors may be more lenient than others, especially if there is still a vestige of disagreement over what the dimensions are actually meant to be measuring. Also the assessment centre cannot be replicated accurately, if there are a series of centres, because different candidates will create different group dynamics, just as a different group of assessors are likely to have a different emphasis in their evaluations.

An associated reservation about assessment centre validity stems from the interdependence of individuals in group exercises. The rating of one person's behaviour depends, to an extent, on the performance of others in the group, so that a fairly dominant person in a group of extremely dominant people may look weak and ineffective by comparison. Similarly a candidate performing poorly in an otherwise good group received lower ratings than a poor candidate in a generally poor group (Gaugler and Rudolph, 1992). Assessor ratings were more accurate when candidates differ a lot, suggesting that assessors compare candidates with each other rather than an external high standard.

Reservations about assessment centre validity

Cook (1995) voices further concerns which could affect validity. These focus on criterion contamination and 'face fits' criterion, both of which could damage the organization's and candidates' beliefs about what is really occurring in the assessment centre.

Criterion contamination can be a blatant self fulfilling prophecy whereby highly rated internal participants are promoted or given more challenging tasks so that they 'develop more'. 'Face fits' criteria are important and assessment centres may judge these rather than actual effectiveness. It is argued that assessment centres predict higher management ratings of management potential better than predictions of actual job performance (Cohen, Moses and Byham, 1974).

Other researchers, such as Schmitt, Schneider and Cohen (1990) found validity was moderated by type of assessor, the centre's administrative arrangements and prior assessor participant contact. Validity deteriorates by slipshod practice or if assessment centres become a fad. Consequently, managers may be deluding themselves about assessment centre validity and should not overstate their value and objectivity. Assessment centres may be a way of legitimizing organizational activities and are often a convenient fall back for managers, allowing them to confirm or reject personal prejudices (Rowe, 1994). Assessment centres also had a high false negative rate – 46% 'unacceptable candidates' nevertheless succeeded as first line managers.

Critics of assessment centres say they are an elaborate charade, which has several implications for deception. They believe that assessment centres perpetuate the status quo, pick managers whose 'face fits' and fill the organization with carbon copies of top management if not with sycophants.

BIOGRAPHICAL DATA (BIODATA)

Biodata are used to predict various important aspects of work performance and potential, and their links with successful job performance are used in selection decisions (Asher, 1972; Drakely, 1989). Based on the premise that past behaviour forecasts future actions, biodata are a systematic method of gaining information about past events and presenting a factually based view of a person's life.

Biodata can be very useful for screening out unsuitable applicants prior to undertaking in-depth selection procedures. It is used most frequently for selecting sales staff and least often for managerial occupations, with Robertson and Makin (1986) reporting that 5% of major British companies used biodata for managerial selection. The mean validity of biodata across a range of criteria was 0.24 from 99 studies (Drakely, 1989).

Biodata material

Biodata seek two types of information – hard and soft data. Biodata generally centre on hard, verifiable, objective factual information such as age, number of dependants and number of years in education. It is frequently supplemented by less objective, soft information covering more abstract matters and personal qualities. These include value judgements, aspirations, motivations, attitudes and expectations, e.g. asking whether an applicant would enjoy conducting scientific experiments.

'Hard' biodata questions differ from those on personality inventories and examples are given in Figure 7.3. They seek precise and definite information, most of which could be supplied by someone who knows the candidate well, and may need more time and consideration than those found on personality inventories which often require immediate, instinctive responses. Questions are frequently in multiple-choice format and answers are objectively scored by machine scoring or direct computer entry. Scoring usually involves a system of weights and the total score is used for selection purposes. The biodata may be classified into background, commitment and achievement biodata.

Methods of collecting biodata

Application forms and biographical questionnaires are the main source of biographical information, though they differ in the amount and type of information collected. All application forms provide some basic biographical data, such as gender and previous employment history. In contrast, biographical questionnaires are specifically designed to collect a detailed life history and therefore are much more comprehensive, frequently containing over 100 questions.

In what type of establishment did you study for your A levels? Answer for the last establishment attended.

Comprehensive school

Grammar school

Independent school

Sixth-form college

How many brothers and sisters do you have?

0　1　2　3　4　5　6+

How many are older than you?

0　1　2　3　4　5　6+

Which of the following categories best describes the newspapers you generally read?

Financial Times/Economist

Times/Independent/Telegraph/Guardian

Daily Mail/Daily Express

Other

Figure 7.3　Examples of biodata questions

Biographical data can be collected in other ways, including retrospective life experience essays, employers' references and educational information from school or university reports. Structured interviews can be used, as long as responses are recorded without too much interpretation by interviewers (Drakeley, 1989).

Deception by candidates

Two sorts of deception may occur in the supply of biodata. Firstly, faulty memory may mean that candidates reply incorrectly, or they may be more calculated in their deceit. The major discrepancies on application forms (Cascio, 1975; Goldstein, 1971) mentioned in Chapter 4 suggest that substantial falsification may occur if these are the source of biodata.

Secondly, biodata are easy to fake. The apparent transparency of some items may stimulate deliberate manipulation if the candidate wishes to project a socially desirable image which will impress the selector. Candidates may feel some justification in faking if they feel that questions are intrusive, e.g. 'Were your father and mother married when you were born?' They may also feel less committed to the truth since biodata often lack face validity. Robertson and Smith (1989) found applicants greatly disliked biodata inventories and thought them both inaccurate and unfair, partly because they seemed arbitrary.

Faking has been found in research. Moore (1942) revealed that recruits to the American army in the First World War gave very unreliable accounts of their skills and only 6% who claimed a trade really knew it. Klein and Owens (1965) studied fakeability of biodata used to predict research creativity and found it was successful. Students could double their chance of 'passing' one component and increase their pass rate on a second. A laboratory study of college students (Schrader and Osburn, 1977) reported that students under 'fake' conditions were able to score significantly higher than students under 'honest' conditions. Similarly, Kluger, Reilly and Russell (1991) reported the socially desirable responses of subjects pretending to be job applicants which shifted their scores considerably when a simple linear score is used but not when more complex scoring systems are used.

Although proponents suggest biodata are unfakeable because they can be independently verified, the sophisticated candidate will surmise that few organizations have the inclination, time and money to pursue positive vetting. Verification of hard data is feasible but soft data, especially self-evaluation, cannot be corroborated and are easier to fake.

Deception by organizations
The nature of questions

Questions may seem intrusive, personal and potentially offensive. Asking a candidate whether she felt homesick when away from home as a child may appear an irrelevant and unfair way of deciding whether a person should be selected. Questions are also problematic if answers are beyond usual British experience. For example, a candidate educated abroad would find it difficult to answer the question 'How many GCSEs did you pass?'

Biodata questions may be a possible source of discrimination, as candidates may be rejected on the basis of their gender, age or race. As such factors may not be related to specific job competencies, they may be illegal if used for personnel selection (Mitchell and Klimoski, 1982). They also appear unfair because they are beyond the candidates' control. Cook (1995) argues that class is a pervasive feature in biodata questionnaires, and that biodata appear to be a selection system process which 'looks both capriciously arbitrary, and blatantly biased in favour of middle-class applicants'.

Technical concerns

The organization may deceive itself about the effectiveness of the process. Biodata should not be used unless validity has been established from a good validation sample and validity is likely to shrink on cross validation. Biodata also seem to have less validity for jobs with general requirements. Much depends on the insight used by the author and interpreter, and Hunter and Hunter (1984) argue that 'suitability' may really mean that the applicant's 'face fits' which might or might not indicate that the applicant is more effective.

GRAPHOLOGY

Graphologists infer personality classifications or behaviour predictions from handwriting, though there are no well defined rules or evidence for making such inferences (Ben-Shakar, 1989). As graphologists seek spontaneous writing, often provided by brief autobiographical accounts, contamination may occur through interpreting content rather than actual handwriting.

Both candidates and organizations can practise deceit. Candidates can deliberately alter their handwriting and students who were asked to produce the handwriting of methodical and original people were reliably judged as such (Loewenthal, 1975). Alternatively candidates may use the pen picture to create a favourable image. Organizations may deceive by concealing their use of graphology as a selection method. Cooper and Robertson (1995) report that the Head of the International Graphoanalysis Society believes that 3% of UK companies, many in *The Times* Top 1000, currently use graphology for selection purposes, though many try to keep the fact confidential. Using graphology without the applicant's knowledge can be criticized as unethical and evidence suggests that such situations could encourage unsuccessful applicants to pursue legal challenges as they would appear to have a very strong case (Cooper and Robertson, 1995).

Graphology has little scientific support and trained graphologists were no better than non-trained (Ben-Shakar et al. 1986). Candidates dislike it and consider it an invasion of privacy (Kravitz, Stinson and Chavez, 1996). The British Psychological Society's (1993) report concluded that 'graphology is not a viable means of assessing a person's character or abilities'. It would therefore seem so poor in predicting applicants' job performance that selectors may be deceiving themselves about its usefulness, reliability and validity.

SUMMARY

Graphology emerges as the least effective of these methods. However, although work samples, assessment centres and biodata are more valid, they are by no means deception proof. As in other selection methods, candidates may attempt various forms of impression management and organizations may deceive themselves about the robustness of their processes.

References 8

References form one of the most paradoxical aspects of selection – despite extensive use, they are widely regarded as being ineffective. Surveys consistently report heavy use of references (Industrial Society, 1994; Robertson and Makin, 1986;) whilst Clark (1993) discovered that 87.8% of executive recruitment consultancies used them. The popularity of references may stem from tradition, cheapness and the belief that they may reduce applicant tendencies of lying or exaggeration.

Practitioners and academic researchers agree that references have little to commend them. Industrial Society respondents rated references as only marginally positive whilst studies into their psychometric properties showed disappointing reliability and low validity that is rarely above 0.2, ranging from the unacceptable to the mediocre (Muchinsky, 1976). Despite their perceived inadequacies, references can be very important to applicants, as job offers are often subject to satisfactory references, so candidates may be tempted to actively ensure they come up to expectations. A second paradox is therefore evident. References, which are themselves checks on deception, can be used deceptively.

In this chapter a preliminary analysis is made of differences in reference format, content and means of obtaining information, as these may impinge on reference validity and contribute to various sources of deception. Deception and errors experienced in the process can then be explored. Unwitting or deliberate misrepresentation on the part of the referee, the candidate or the two working in collusion may occur. Sometimes deception may be compounded by Personnel practices. The role of external agencies involved in reference submission and/or checking candidates concludes the chapter.

BACKGROUND

References are a means of gaining an independent assessment of a candidate by a third party. They are based on the twin premises that past behaviour is a good predictor of future performance and that the best source of information about an individual's past behaviour is someone familiar with that person.

Most selectors only meet applicants within the context of selection interviews. Their encounter is brief, rather artificial and the applicant's aim is to make a favourable impression. The candidate's statements are uncorroborated. In contrast, the referee's lengthier observations of the applicant in natural circumstances should facilitate accurate, realistic judgements about the applicant's abilities, work related conduct, previous job performance and character. The referee is therefore in a position to verify information supplied by the applicant, report on behaviours and provide evaluations.

Not all organizations seek such comprehensive information and some may restrict requests to verifying self reports of work history. Beason and Belt (1976) found 82% of employers verified some information from the application form, with 18% verifying all material. Although factually objective information is presumably less prone to error, many employers value assessments related to personality traits, e.g. co-operation (Peres and Garcia, 1962; Sleight and Bell, 1954). Such subjective evaluations tend to be about general matters, including behaviours, e.g. honesty or work experience, e.g. timekeeping, and are prone to inaccuracy.

The choice of referee

Having established the type of information the organization wishes to acquire, selectors have to identify the most appropriate sources. Whilst employers invariably determine the number of referees – usually two – individual choice of specific referees frequently rests with the candidate, so facilitating subsequent deception. Generally the names of referees may be requested on the application form or sought at interview or in the offer letter.

Current employers are the most popular group of referees because prospective employers consider them to be the best assessors of candidates' work performance. However, for those embarking on the job market for the first time, such as school leavers or recently qualified graduates, academic or character references may be substituted.

The purpose and time at which references are requested

In Britain most employed people do not broadcast their job seeking activities to current employers until they are reasonably certain of having acquired alternative work. In this way they avoid possible recriminations and a questioning of their commitment to the current organization (Hyde, 1982). Because of this tradition, general UK practice is to make job offers subject to satisfactory references which are sought after selection, though this practice is not universal.

There is a close correlation between the timing of reference requests and their purpose. American research by Beason and Belt (1976) showed that 13% of references were requested prior to selection, 69% of references were taken up after selection but before hiring and 18% after appointment.

References sought before selection can be used in shortlisting and decision making, as they can help to identify the best qualified people and predict future work performance and candidate suitability for the job. Of the Industrial Society's 428 respondents, 26% identified references as a method usually used for shortlisting candidates for interview. Opponents of obtaining references at this stage maintain that if candidates were informed of this procedure, the applicant pool might be reduced and good candidates might refrain from applying.

References taken after appointment appear more of a formality and final safeguard to ensure there are no reasons for not employing the individual, such as unreliability, violent tendencies or previous dishonesty. Respondents questioned by Beason and Belt (1976) used references in the belief that they might uncover some negative information about an applicant (21%), so confirming the desire to eliminate potentially problematic applicants. Such references are likely to check on a candidate's suitability, usually in terms of honesty, co-operation and social adjustment. They often ask 'Do you know of any reason why we should not employ him or her?'

Companies may use references for different purposes. In Nash and Carroll's research (1970) respondents wished to check information and also used them as a means to predict success in new jobs. Other respondents questioned by Beason and Belt (1976) used references to get additional information about the candidate (30%) and to verify the information provided by applicant (48%), presumably from other sources such as the interview or application form. Factual checks may be supplemented or replaced by character references, especially if the applicant lacks previous work experience.

There may be legal reasons for using references. Mandatory checks may be required in certain fields such as work with children. In the USA references can serve as a defence that a company did all it reasonably could to prevent possible tragedies or disasters by enquiring about prospective employees.

Manner of obtaining reference information

References are usually obtained in writing or by telephone. The methods represent differing degrees of selector control, and influence the nature, format and structure of the reference. They also vary in speed, cost and the demands imposed on the referee.

Written references

A written reference request may range from a brief letter to a more complex pre-prepared form. Often the letter is an open ended request and content, volume and value of information is left to the referee's discretion. Sometimes topics may be suggested to guide the referee on identified attributes, behaviours or job experiences.

Alternatives to the letter comprise checklists, an open ended question–answer format, a form including closed questions, rating scales on various dimensions, or a forced choice design to measure specific attributes. Answers may be confined to spaces next to the form, written elsewhere, or recorded as numbers or ticks on a five or seven point scale. The request may be despatched by itself or with a letter briefly stating which position the candidate is applying for, sometimes described in such generalized terms as to be virtually unrecognizable.

More time may be needed to obtain a written reference, unless a fax is used, plus more effort and possibly thought from the referee, who may have to assemble and check material before committing it to paper. The documentary nature of evidence has legal implications and there would appear to be little scope for misunderstandings.

Phone references

Phone references range from a brief general chat to phone interviews, in which the selector follows a pre-determined format of questions. They may be preferred in the belief that referees will be more frank in speech than on paper. However, being 'off the cuff' allows bias and personal feelings, especially if conversations preclude thoroughness and checking. Though the actual phone calls are speedy, they may be more time and resource consuming overall.

Dobson (1989) maintains that the phone interviewer can supply information about the target job, assess the weight that should be given to replies, probe for supporting evidence of judgements, determine what opportunity the referee has had to observe relevant behaviours and assess the referee's motives. The interaction and dynamism of phone references increases their appeal.

References are used for various reasons, in various ways, by various people. This multiplicity influences the effectiveness of references, presents different opportunities for errors and deception and may affect the nature of duplicity.

DECEPTION

The abuse of references is complex, as Figure 8.1 illustrates, and can occur in every stage of the reference procedure. However it focuses on two areas – the reference process and the compilation of the reference itself. The referee, candidate and source of the request, whether agency or Personnel department, generally work independently and the procedure provides many opportunities for errors and deception, which may be exacerbated by Personnel practices. Deception may be unwitting or deliberate and because of the complexity, vagaries and expectations of the reference process it may be impossible to distinguish which is which – a situation which the unscrupulous candidate may use to advantage.

Deception in the reference process

The reference process incorporates three areas of potential abuse – choice of referee, despatch and receipt of reference requests and the processing and checking of completed references by the Personnel department.

Nomination of the referee

A candidate who wishes to deceive may manipulate the nomination of referee. This may be done to ensure the provision of a favourable reference or to prevent a detrimental one. Prospective employers usually stipulate a reference from a current employer and this may cause the employed candidate considerable concern.

Employees may not wish their current employers to learn of their proposed departure. They may be anxious, justifiably or otherwise, about the potential quality and fairness of the reference. Their unease may stem

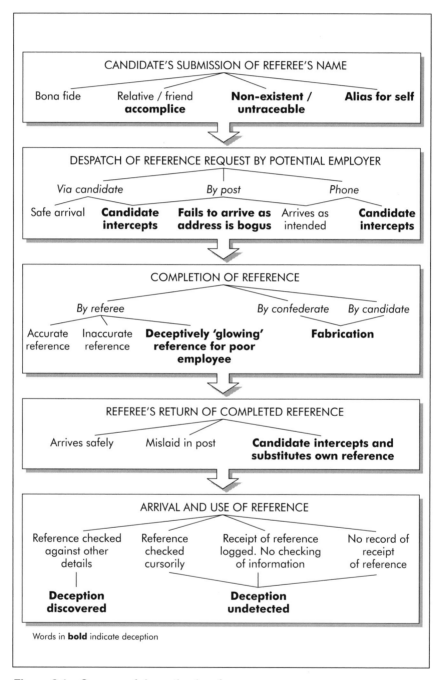

Figure 8.1   Sources of deception in references

from past experience, organizational culture or personality clashes with referees. In large organizations reference completion may be removed to the more distant and impersonal confines of the Personnel department or may necessitate delegation to a line manager felt to harbour a personal grudge. Alternatively, candidates may wish to avoid justifiably negative references which reveal inadequate work performance, disciplinary action and detrimental facts such as theft or damaging aspersions on the candidate's character.

The candidate may deal with this situation by mixing fact and fiction. Instead of nominating the expected referee he may substitute the name of a sympathetic line manager or someone else of seniority and imply that this person is the designated employer. Having established the circumvention, the reference procedure then continues in the expected manner. The candidate may regard this as a perfectly legitimate procedure and may even justify it on the grounds that the nominated person is in a better position to supply the reference than the actual employer.

Past employers offer more scope. A genuine referee may be nominated by a candidate in the certainty that the referee cannot be located, so nullifying the reference. The referee is known to have 'disappeared' through departure from the company or staff restructuring, or the company no longer exists because of mergers or bankruptcies. Should enquiries be made, there is no evidence of deception since the person is known to exist. In more extreme circumstances, a candidate may invent a completely false work history. Careful choice of defunct companies and citation of fictitious individuals ensures referees are completely untraceable.

Sometimes inappropriate referees are nominated. Inexperienced candidates may unwittingly deceive the organization by selecting relatives or friends who are generally considered to be unsuitable because of their pronounced leniency (Mosel and Goheen, 1959). Candidates may select such referees through ignorance, limited choice or genuine belief that the chosen referee appears to satisfy the stated criterion of knowing the candidate well over a long period of time. A more cynical and deliberate nomination of acquaintances may arise to ensure reference content reaches the desired standards.

Despatch and receipt of references

Reference requests produce a typical response rate of 35–56% (Carroll and Nash, 1972; Mosel and Goheen, 1959) unless the organization makes a concerted attempt to follow up with phone or face to face interviews.

Possible explanations for this situation are that the request never reaches the referee, the referee does not complete the request or the completed request does not reach the requesting organization. Candidate deception and interception of reference requests are possibilities, but may remain undetected if other alternatives appear more feasible.

First, a reference request may fail because it never reaches the referee. For example, the nominated referee has 'disappeared', his organization may no longer exist or mistakes in addresses thwart delivery. Whilst such situations may be genuine, devious applicants may deliberately manoeuvre them to advantage.

Second, the low response rate may be due to the referee's non-completion of the request for reasons of disinclination, inexperience or organizational policy. Disinclination may stem from past experience, time pressures, dislike of the candidate or from the candidate's nomination of a referee without first seeking permission. Alternatively, referees may feel uncomfortable about supplying a poor reference and ignore the request, so deceiving by default. Inexperience in reference compilation and indecision caused by vaguely worded requests may create uncertainty. A poorly worded request may persuade referees that their reply would be of such little value that it is not worth the time and effort involved.

Decisions not to respond to reference requests may have been determined by individuals or collective professional agreement, and this may be communicated to the company. The UK National Association of Head Teachers advises its members to refuse to give references when a job offer has already been made, and many universities have individually adopted this policy.

Lastly the completed reference, despatched in good faith, fails to arrive. Disregarding the vagaries of the postal service, this may stem from the referee's uncertainty over where or to whom it should be sent.

Interception by the candidate

On the other hand, low response rates may be one angle of deliberate deception. Candidates may deflect references from reaching the referee or may intercept completed references before they are despatched. This is a feasible option for candidates who have nominated their current employer as a referee and both parties are working in the same organization. The situation is facilitated by open access to incoming mail awaiting collection in pigeon holes, or to outgoing mail assembled centrally. The interception of telephone calls may be more problematic, though possible if the candidate has been able to supply an extension number to which he has sole access.

Candidates may adopt this procedure to delay or suppress potentially damaging information. They may reason that stalling tactics will allow the selection process to advance to a stage where emphasis on references diminishes. The candidate may believe that if enough time elapses, the absence of a reference will be overlooked or frustrate Personnel staff to the point whereby it is forgotten or ignored indefinitely.

The organization's handling of references

Personnel staff may unwittingly allow deceptive practices to remain undetected. Administrative procedures, especially a poor logging system, may mean that the return of references is not monitored efficiently. Missing references may not be pursued because of the difficulty, expense and time requirements, especially if the reference procedure is perceived to be of little importance.

In some organizations receipt of references may be given higher priority checking them. Checks may be cursory, especially if undertaken by junior, untrained staff who accept the given information at face value, particularly if a glowing reference is provided. Lack of experience in 'reading between the lines' may mean that the ambiguity and possible coded intent of phrases such as 'If you need any further information please phone me' are overlooked. References may be viewed in isolation, without recourse to information available from application forms or other sources, so that potential discrepancies remain undetected, as illustrated below.

> Theresa applied for a position as a solicitor with a large company. On the application form she stated her current salary as £23,500 and on that basis negotiated a starting salary of £28,000. A reference request was despatched, completed and returned and this detailed her current salary as £19,500. The reference was checked for completeness but as it was viewed in isolation the discrepancy was not detected. Six months later a performance appraisal necessitated reference to Theresa's personnel records and a casual glance by Theresa's mentor revealed the financial information. As the mentor had been privy to the salary negotiations he readily appreciated the significance of the statement. Theresa was dismissed.

The role of Personnel staff may be more active. Pressure to appoint rapidly may result in waiving organizational policy, especially if the selector has complete faith in her judgement of character and the candidate's qualifications, experience and general background appear highly credible. Similarly organization policy may be contravened by seeking references after the person has been appointed or started work. Again such practices are more likely to occur in organizations where references are judged to be a formality rather than an essential part of the selection process.

Deception in the reference

Much research has been conducted on the psychological basis of reference reports, especially on the processes of person perception, the ways in which referees and recipients of references form impressions of candidates and the factors likely to impinge on the accuracy of these opinions.

The construction of a reference involves several stages (Dobson, 1989). Having received the request, the referee has to identify correctly the information that is required, assemble and evaluate it and write the reference in terms of the information requested. The assessor then interprets the report, decides its significance and the weight that should be attached to it. Dobson (1989) concludes that 'In fact it is difficult to envisage a measuring device that is more open to error and abuse. A reference is characterized by the passage of information between two people who will never meet, on an applicant who will never know what was written'.

A fundamental concern about references centres on the referee's motives, accuracy and the context in which references are completed. These are related to the referee's attitudes to the candidate, the reference procedure in general and the particular organization seeking the reference. Referees are in a position to deceive the requesting organization unwittingly, through errors in identifying the candidate, genuine mistakes about the applicant and misunderstandings or uncertainty about the reference requirements. Alternatively, some referees may deliberately deceive, either for personal motives or through collusion with the candidate.

The referee's misunderstandings about the information required

Referees' varying experience of reference construction and a lack of guidance on the information desired by the organization, may cause bewilderment, especially when referees are faced with a vague request for information to be given in an undetermined manner. Not knowing the type, depth and detail of information required, the referee may provide irrelevant, superficial information whilst inadvertently withholding pertinent details desired by the organization but not actively specified.

The situation may be made worse if potential employers fail to provide adequate background information. Job titles may be omitted, given generically or described in vague terms which are open to several interpretations. Alternatively, candidates who are changing career directions may target jobs which are unfamiliar to referees. If the required attributes are very different to those characterizing the candidate's current employment, the referee may be baffled about how to compile the reference and unsure of what information she is meant to supply. Sparse or absent detail of required personal qualities may contribute to the confusion. Potentially more damaging is the referee's misplaced confidence in her comprehension of the intricacies of the new job. In both circumstances the reference produced is likely to be inaccurate, so limiting reliability and validity.

The referee's difficulty in compiling the reference

Assembling the information

The referee's gathering of information may be problematic and can have repercussions on the quality, authenticity and validity of the subsequent reference. Referees have two possible sources of information on candidates and their work performance – personal knowledge and/or written records. As documents such as performance appraisals or examination reports require more time to access, collate and assimilate, greater dependence may be placed on knowledge or memory.

Referees may have limited acquaintance with candidates if their seniority has restricted direct contact with the individual or if either person has only been in the organization for a short time. Mistakes of identity particularly arise in large organizations, and organizations with a rapid turnover of casual staff. Here the reference causes unwitting deception, if it does not relate to the individual for whom it is sought, as illustrated below.

> Lois, a production manager in a large textile firm was requested to provide a reference for Ms A. Jones who left the company five years previously. Consulting her

records she identified Andrea Jones and Anne Jones. Confusion reigned when she also recalled Ann Sally Jones who had always been known as Sally at work. Discarding Sally as unlikely, Lois focused her attention on Andrea and Anne. She recalled hearing that Ann had moved in with George Jarvis, but could not remember whether she had changed her name to Jarvis. Lois decided to plump for Andrea, though was not totally convinced she had got the right person. She then realized that it does not matter very much in any case, as she had always muddled Andrea and Anne because they were quite similar in appearance though not character. Lois felt disgruntled. This conjecture had taken some time, she was very busy, she was not receiving much thanks for her task and she had never liked Andrea or Anne. She decided she would write a non-committal reference that could apply to either of them and blamed the requesting organization for not being more specific.

If referees lack a very good knowledge of candidates, they have an inadequate basis for judgement and therefore evaluations suffer (Blum and Naylor, 1968). In these circumstances two options may be available. The first is to depend on the opinions of others. This can be unsatisfactory, since other people may be unguarded and inaccurate as they do not have the ultimate responsibility for compiling the report. Referees may have to interpret or possibly decode their phraseology, which may be influenced by hidden agendas. If referees accept comments at face value, are rushed and/or disinclined to check facts and so concoct references carelessly, incorrect information may be provided about applicants. This not only deceives the requesting organization but may defame the applicant, as exemplified by Spring, an employee of Guardian Assurance, who was described as dishonest, accused of misselling and giving poor advice to clients. His actions to remedy the situation are described in Chapter 11.

The referee's second choice is to rely heavily on implicit theories of personality where first impressions tend to be given more weight than later impressions. Consequently, if referees possess little information on the applicant, or the information is ambiguous, references are likely to reveal more about the personality of the referee than that of the applicant (Mischel, 1968).

Sometimes referees may be incapable of obtaining accurate assessments of work related talents (Blum and Naylor, 1968) even when they know the candidate. There may have been few opportunities to see the candidate in the work situation and referees may have little first hand experience of the job currently undertaken by candidates, its characteristics and the incumbents' ability to do it. In such circumstances referees may find it difficult, if not impossible, to judge candidates' suitability for work in a particular job.

Limited care may be taken in assembling the information if the reference is perceived to be of little worth or the organization is seen as being dishonest about the value of the reference, as indicated in Mary's case.

> Having received a request to provide a reference for Ben, the son of a close colleague, Mary spent considerable time and effort on constructing her response, especially as the request stated that employment decisions could not be made until receipt of the reference. Wishing to check details of employment history, she phoned Ben and was taken aback to discover that he had been working in the job for the past three weeks. Mary felt she had been misled about the immediacy and importance attached to the reference. She completed the remaining sections with scant time and attention and decided that in future reference requests would be dealt with summarily.

Evaluating the information

Although referees may possess information, they may not be good judges of character and may find it difficult to assess and weigh the significance of evidence. This becomes more pronounced if the information is inconsistent, ambiguous or based on observations made in the distant past, when again dependence on implicit personality theory may occur. Referees have considerable discretion about the amount of information proffered and the results may be highly subjective and open to error and abuse.

Presenting the information

Even when candidates are correctly identified and well known to referees, errors, mistakes or misimpressions can still occur in reference compilation. Although these arise in providing general information, more specific difficulties are encountered when trying to measure personality traits. Referees may find it difficult to compose accurate and meaningful references, which may result in misleading the recipient about candidate characteristics.

Biases of leniency and halo effect influence all human judgements and are commonly experienced in formulating references. Leniency is reported to be a major problem (Nash and Carroll, 1970) and stems from two sources. First, wherever possible, applicants will hand pick a referee whom they think will supply a good reference, and this is regarded as a problem of pre-selection (Myers and Errett, 1959). Second, referees will generally provide the most favourable possible assessment of the individual. They give candidates the benefit of the doubt by saying only positive things and not being critical or pointing out failings (Moore, 1942). Cronbach (1955) found referees were reluctant to give poor ratings. Positive references may reflect both the referees's sense of fair play, especially as they can identify with candidates in this respect, and social norms which dictate that the provision of a bad reference is unacceptable.

Other errors may cause unwitting deception. The halo effect is especially likely to happen when the referee relies on memory and tends to rate different traits similarly, rather than independently. Consequently, an applicant judged to be well above average on conscientiousness is likely to be seen as well above average on other qualities such as ability and co-operation, whether or not this is true. In other cases the bias of central tendency (Cronbach, 1995) also contributes to inaccuracy as some referees may use the middle points of rating scales and avoid the extremes, so describing candidates as middle of the road rather than outstandingly good or bad.

Errors may be compounded by two other tendencies, the first of which is the referee's use of generalized trait descriptions rather than descriptions of specific behaviour (Peres and Garcia, 1962). The second factor is the referees' doubts of their ability to write accurate assessments, especially if they feel uncomfortable about their communication skills. Consequently organizations face difficulties in comparing references given by different referees, each of whom is affected by personal attitudes and values.

Some referees may wish to safeguard their own position. The skilled reference writer may damn with faint praise or employ coded language which may or may not be correctly decoded by the recipient. They may use phrases which have a variety of interpretations such as:

'Works well under pressure'	completed a three month project in just four days
'Computer literate'	knows how to switch on a computer and access Minesweeper

| *'Imaginative'* | never gave the same excuse twice for absent work |

On the other hand, referees may be able to construct accurate and truthful references but refrain from doing so because of company policy. This restricts the amount of information the company is prepared to divulge, though considerable information may be expected from others. Company policy may also decree disclosure of references to current employees, so prompting the construction of insipid, generally unhelpful references. If the employee perceives any faintly negative connotations, pressure may be applied to improve the content. This may be a type of collusion. Ignorant of these procedures, organizations may misconstrue the brevity of references or their blandness. Alternatively, companies requesting references may inform referees that these will be shown to candidates. This may cause consternation to referees who may have to adapt their procedures accordingly.

The references considered so far have involved unwitting deception by the referee. Most references compromise referees who may feel obliged to be 'economical with the truth'. Consequently the borderline between unintentional and deliberate deception is a gradation, often depending on the scale and gravity of mistakes and errors in reference construction. Other factors may be influential.

A candidate seeking a reference from a doctor may be charged for the service, so raising ethical issues of professional disinterest, integrity and location of loyalty. The candidate may believe that the exchange of money 'buys' the reference, and this may be a move towards the deliberate deception described in the following section.

Deliberate deception

Deception may be deliberately engineered by the referee, acting alone or in collusion with the candidate, or by a confederate of the applicant. The candidate may intercept a genuine reference request and substitute a forged reference, pose as the referee or create a completely fictitious referee and supply appropriate information.

The role of the referee

The assumption that all referees wish to give accurate references can be challenged. Employers may have hidden agendas which generate questionable motives in reference compilation. Complete fabrication may result and remain undetected as the parties do not meet and, unlike other selection methods, there is little control exercised over the accuracy of reports.

In 1968 Blum and Naylor proposed that some employers may write overly positive evaluations of marginally performing employees to get rid of the person by making her look highly attractive. Such workers may be incompetent, outspoken, perceived as troublemakers or may have a clash of personality with their employer. Conversely, a valued worker may be depicted negatively in order to be rejected by the target organization and retained in current employment. The referee's motives may be altruistic, if the candidate is regarded as an irreplaceable asset to the firm, or selfish. The departure of a valuable employee could cause the referee personal inconvenience, an increased work load and the hassle and costs of recruitment, induction and training of a new employee which the referee may prefer to avoid.

Sometimes, enhanced references may be provided to fulfil promises or terms in sacking or redundancy situations. Liking for the candidate will produce a longer, and presumably more favourable, reference than for a disliked candidate or one with whom the referee has some personality clash which may colour judgements negatively.

Collusion between the candidate and referee

The actual nomination of referees may include an element of collusion, but pronounced complicity may develop from further contact between the two parties. Candidates may approach referees and supply key information for inclusion in references, the truth of which may be difficult to verify. Similarly, referees may check details with candidates or agree on which particular facets of employment or character should be emphasized.

This indicates that the job descriptions supplied to referees are either absent or inadequate. It may also imply that referees lack real or up to date knowledge of candidates, so defeating the whole purpose of the reference. In other circumstances candidates may control the content of references by working with referees who complete references from candidates' suggestions or dictation.

Deception by the candidate

Candidates may occasionally write their own references, using one of two strategies. They may intercept reference requests sent to genuinely nominated referees at genuine addresses. Subsequently forged references are substituted. This is more likely to occur if the nominated referee and candidate are in the same organization with equal access to the mail, phone or fax. Whilst the seeking company may be reassured of the validity of a reference given on the company's headed notepaper, especially if it is authenticated by the official stamp, companies should be aware that both commodities, especially paper, can be stolen from the organization with relative ease. Sometimes referees are asked to enclose the completed reference in a sealed envelope which is forwarded with the application form. This gives an easy opportunity to applicants who wish to substitute more favourable references.

The second strategy involves candidates' inventing a fictitious referee, whose address is one to which the candidate has access, e.g. at a friend's house. Candidates or confederates pose as referees and construct references which are complete fabrications. Use of confederates means that handwriting cannot be matched with the applicant's.

An alternative scenario is the occasional connivance at such deception by referees. Referees may tell candidates to complete their own references, using the justification of speeding up the selection process.

THE ROLE OF OTHER AGENCIES IN OBTAINING REFERENCES

Organizations do not always instigate the reference procedure themselves. Agencies and headhunters used to recruit staff may be asked to obtain references. Sometimes organizations may use the services of professional vetting agencies or other bodies to verify applicant details. Not all such measures are successful and employers may be deceived about the scope and effectiveness of these services.

Recruitment agencies and headhunters

Organizations may expect and entrust agencies supplying temporary staff to check references on their behalf, though the stringency of agency methods may be at variance with their own. Sometimes there may be confusion on roles and ultimate responsibility. This may enable candidates to elude both systems, as in the following case study, based on a report in *The Times*.

Case Study 3
THE SCREENING OF TEMPORARY TEACHERS

Local education authorities are legally obliged to check the criminal records of all teachers and the Department for Education's List 99, which contains the names of teachers who may be suspected of child abuse.

However, teachers on the list may sidestep screening checks by joining agencies which supply teachers to schools on a temporary basis, as some corner cutting agencies can avoid the screening checks if they hire teachers on a self employed basis.

A survey by the National Association of Schoolmasters and Union of Women Teachers found that one in four head teachers did not know whether security checks had been made on supply teachers sent to them by agencies. In one instance, a teacher who had been sacked and placed on List 99, was sent back to a primary school by an agency.

The Union called for regulations to require the checks, which it claimed were routinely ignored by some agencies. Screening was said to be often overlooked for the hundreds of supply teachers from Australia and New Zealand on agency books.

Headhunters may take up all references before submitting a shortlist. This has its own problems. Prospective shortlisted people may dislike this vetting, since they have not yet been offered jobs. Consequently, 'reference checking' may consist of little more than informal enquiries through social contacts.

Commercial bodies

Occasionally organizations may employ independent agencies to vet prospective candidates. Investigative agencies may offer a comprehensive service but the reality may fall short of expectations. Proposed status checks on CV information, such as verification of addresses, academic records and previous employer history may be limited by the time available. Checks on other information such as credit ratings and even political affiliations may be available, but are rarely job relevant. Although some agencies imply that they can check criminal records, such information cannot usually be obtained in the private sector, despite the agencies' hints at informal access to police files by employees who are ex-police staff. Positive vetting involves considerable checking and a status check may cost £400. It can be prone to inaccuracies such as mistaken identities, arising from checks on the wrong people with similar names.

SUMMARY

References are a problematic selection procedure and afford many opportunities for deception. Candidates, referees and Personnel staff may contribute, unwittingly or deliberately, to the deceit. The independent assessment of candidates by a third party is both the strength and weakness of references. Assessors and referees are unlikely to meet, and communication between the two is prone to interceptions and inaccuracies. Employers may deceive the requesting organization in order to retain quality staff and offload poor performers. Some referees may collude with candidates whilst candidates themselves may forge or intercept references.

Organizations appear to appreciate the system's inadequacies and this may contribute to the half hearted procedures adopted by some Personnel departments, so limiting the detection of deception.

The consequences of deception 9

The tangled web woven by candidates and selectors practising deception enmeshes both parties in unforseen ways. Personnel and applicants readily recognize the more immediate effects of deception on themselves but appear less willing to appreciate its impact on others. There seems little awareness of society's interest in selection and its pressure for policy or legislative change to rectify apparent inequity and malpractice.

Whilst some may dismiss deception as inconsequential, few Personnel managers escape its results. Changing work conditions compel the selection and retention of quality staff, as organizations cannot prosper without their skills and talents. If applicants deceive selectors about their abilities, experience and attributes, results can be devastating. Few companies can afford the luxury of poor selection.

Applicants may suffer in practical, financial and possibly psychological terms if they are deceived by organizations. Unsuccessful applicants' sense of unfairness may prompt recourse to tribunals. Successful candidates' unmet expectations may cause disillusionment, rapid exit from the company and further recruitment.

This chapter examines consequences in four areas – the deception of the organization, deception of the candidate and deception by third parties. The final section focuses on the effects of deception on society and its responses. Three case studies are included to illustrate the complexity of deception's consequences.

DECEPTION OF THE ORGANIZATION

An organization which is deceived by candidates and third parties may suffer both internally and externally. Probably the most widespread consequence is the appointment of an unsuitable applicant who has succeeded through deception. Workplace unsuitability has many manifestations, which are illustrated in Figure 9.1. These may damage the organization, its employees, clients and customers in financial and

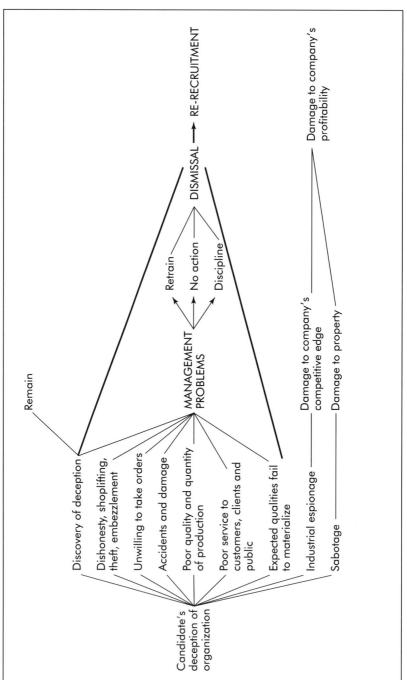

Figure 9.1 Consequences of the candidate's deception of the organization

behavioural ways which may worry society. Organizational reactions to deception may reverberate on the deceiver, the organization and future selection activities.

Internal organizational consequences of the candidate's deception

Staff turnover

The successful deceptive candidate may leave before the organization has recouped its investment in induction and training. Companies with prestigious training programmes may suffer if trained workers are poached by competitors who find it more economical to reap the rewards of others' training schemes rather than establish their own.

Turnover is costly. As selection has not produced the desired results, it has to be repeated, incurring further time, money and effort. Rapid turnover can create staff shortages, with increased pressure on remaining employees to work harder and/or longer. This may foster stress or companies may be forced into making overtime payments to achieve productivity deadlines.

Productivity

The deceitful candidate's false claims of skills and experience may translate into inability to do the job or reach the required speed and standards. Quality and output levels suffer. Cook (1995) believes such lost productivity can be quantified – 'good workers do twice as much work as poor workers . . . the difference in value between a good worker and a poor one is roughly equal to the salary they're paid.' Colleagues also suffer through lost team bonuses.

Similarly, a professed aptitude to learn new skills may not materialize, resulting in an inept worker who is incapable of absorbing training. Inability to follow instructions, clumsiness and incompetence may damage equipment, breach health and safety regulations and cause workplace accidents resulting in compensation claims.

Interpersonal relationships with colleagues and managers

Productive employees may be unsuitable in other ways. The apparently 'ideal' candidate may transpire to be unco-operative with workmates, difficult to supervise or at odds with the general organizational culture. The over-qualified person who minimized his qualifications completes tasks effortlessly but quickly becomes bored with routine, may be reluctant to take orders and confronts managers.

The candidate's apparent charm may effectively conceal unpleasant characteristics which emerge subsequently. An employee's violent tendencies, bullying, racism or the sexual harassment of others can cause potentially serious problems for colleagues and the organization, possibly resulting in litigation.

Emergence of dishonesty

Unpleasant behaviour may produce more tangible outcomes. Employees may join established patterns of cheating at work or may initiate their own scams. Organizations are deprived of materials, finished goods and profit through theft, white collar crime, computer hacking and embezzlement. Employee shoplifting and fraud are increasing problems. A survey by Ernst & Young revealed that more than 40% of the participating 126 UK businesses had experienced more than five incidents of fraud, of which 75% were committed by employees (*Personnel Today*, 4 June 1996).

Occasionally applicants have embarked on deception for espionage, aimed at theft of company secrets and piracy of proprietary information. Large computer companies, specialists in information technology and the pharmaceutical industry are prime targets. Knowledge of advertising campaigns and strategic plans is considered valuable, especially in industries such as detergents and confectionery where marketing effort is a large part of the total product sold (Cornwall, 1987). Information need not be so specific. A rival or predator may be interested in more general details such as accounts, customer and supplier lists, research and development projects plus new product details.

The candidate's expected qualities fail to materialize

Sometimes, especially in graduate recruitment, candidates are appointed specifically because selection identified personal potential or certain required qualities. If these fail to materialize, the new employee does not make the expected contributions to future success in operational areas, initiative, creativity, team building, management and leadership. If the appointment concerned senior management or board directors, organizational viability may be threatened.

Employees who appreciate the situation may remain untroubled and happily continue to underperform until the organization takes action. Alternatively they may feel out of their depth, subject to pressure from peers or superiors and so become prey to stress.

Discovery of ineligibility

So far this chapter has considered employees who were deemed unsuitable for reasons of skill or personal qualities. However, the organization may select a model employee who apparently satisfies all criteria, only to discover afterwards that the candidate was never eligible for appointment.

Ineligibility may be temporary or permanent, arising on legal grounds or for breached professional codes of practice which result in suspension or disbarment. The skilled haulage driver may be ineligible because of a twelve month disqualification from driving. Nurses and doctors may be struck off official registers and solicitors may be suspended from the Law Society. Candidates may not have the required immigration status to work in Britain.

The organization may be prosecuted if it has not fulfilled its responsibilities in checking applicants' credentials thoroughly. Employment of an illegal immigrant carries a maximum fine of £5,000. The disqualified driver is guilty of motoring offences and the employer may be held legally liable. Sometimes the repercussions of employing inappropriate people extend beyond the organization to its clients and customers, and these wider consequences of deception are considered next.

Recriminations, retraining and re-recruitment

Organizations usually take some action over unsuitable employees. A particularly catastrophic appointment may prompt cries of 'How did he come to be appointed?' or more scathingly 'Who appointed her?' The internal inquiry may cause recriminations between Personnel and line managers, with doubts being cast on the competence and professionalism of each. Selectors may be disciplined for carelessness or inefficiency. A subsequent review and amendment of selection procedures may follow, possibly incorporating additional and compulsory training for all involved.

Where an employee has apparently engaged in illegal or unethical activities, the organization's accusation has to be substantiated by firm proof. If there is doubt about the culprit's identity, an investigation may create distrust, unpleasantness and anxiety, especially for innocent staff who become embroiled.

Subsequent actions can include retraining the poor performer, disciplining a dishonest worker, dismissal or the instigation of civil or criminal procedures. Choice may depend on resources, ethical considerations and the organization's attitudes to publicity. Such activities are time consuming, costly and are not guaranteed to be successful.

Re-recruitment demands further time, effort and expense in replacing dismissed staff or those individuals who have been wrongly selected and choose to leave soon after starting work. If turnover is rapid, repeated advertising may be interpreted as signifying organizational difficulties.

Legal implications

An organization may prosecute an employee who deceived to gain employment, as in the case of Alison Durbar who was given one year's probation and ordered to pay £2,000 costs, as described in Chapter 1. It may also be prosecuted itself if it appears to have colluded at the deception or is held responsible for its outcomes. Since court proceedings are conducted publicly, media coverage may broadcast events to a wide audience. The resultant publicity may expose the organization as being inefficient and gullible if it can be deceived so easily. Alternatively legal action may be applauded by those seeking to bring more openness into selection.

External consequences of the candidate's deception of the organization

Candidates who mislead selectors about their personal qualities have immediate, obvious effects on customer service and satisfaction. The offhand sales assistant or rude receptionist rapidly reduces repeat business. Similarly the dishonest supermarket checkout operator may cheat the store and short change customers. Unscrupulous insurance agents may persuade clients to take out pension schemes which are not in their best interests. Complaints rise, business falls, an organization's good reputation evaporates.

Serious though such incidents are, they pale into comparative insignificance when the organization's clients are vulnerable people who are entitled to expect that staff are trustworthy and professional. In these instances the masquerading employee may cause physical, psychological or emotional damage to others. Children, the elderly and the sick form the largest group of potential victims.

The media highlight cases of child abuse by care workers, though less sensational cases do not always receive national coverage. The press quote instances of registered residential homes for the elderly being run by business and nursing staff with previous convictions for assault, sexual indecency and theft. In some cases convictions are not disclosed on the application form because there is no requirement to do so. In other instances organizations have not conducted background checks. The successful adoption of aliases circumvents superficial enquiries which could reveal details of previous unacceptable, inappropriate behaviour.

CONSEQUENCES OF THE ORGANIZATION'S DECEPTION OF THE CANDIDATE

Deception by the organization has repercussions for both unsuccessful and successful candidates, whether they are external applicants wishing to enter the organization or internal staff seeking promotion. As Figure 9.2 shows, these can become quite complex and form part of the wider consequences of deception.

The unsuccessful external candidate

Practical, emotional and psychological effects

An applicant may experience a catalogue of disasters if the selection process and methods are perceived to have been deceptive. At the practical level, failure to reimburse expenditure incurred through travelling and subsistence costs may cause hardship to the unemployed. Employed individuals may resent the time spent on the selection procedure if it has to be deducted from holiday entitlement.

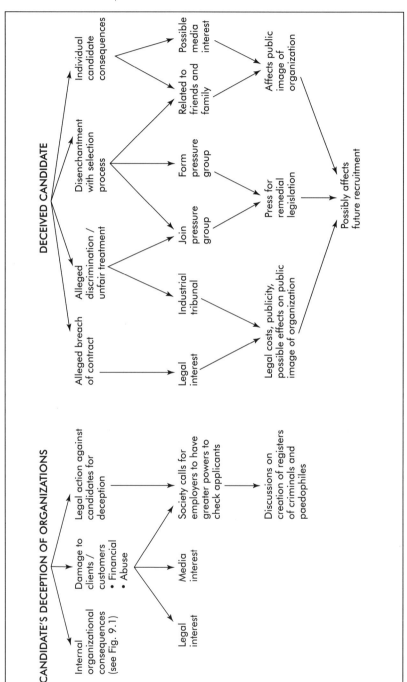

Figure 9.2 The wider consequences of deception in selection

At an emotional level, frustration and resentment may fan a sense of injustice. Perceptions of being used as a pawn in an organizational game may generate anger and subsequent cynicism, directed towards selection or the Personnel department. The commonly reiterated phrase 'Personnel don't come clean with you' indicates disenchantment. Perceptive candidates detect discrepancies between the company's espoused policy that 'people are our greatest asset' and the treatment evident in selection. This may be pinpointed by candidates who, rightly or wrongly, feel they have been given dishonest reasons for their rejection. Damaging psychological consequences, lowered self esteem and ill health may occur in these circumstances.

The public relations aspect

Retailers believe that a negative sales encounter will be recounted to a minimum of nine people and for most people selection is a much more significant event. The disappointed candidate is likely to relay bad experiences of selection and a perceived sense of unfairness to family, friends and acquaintances. As candidates and their associates are customers, clients and suppliers of organizations, companies may develop unenviable reputations as poor employers.

Undergraduates are particularly likely to share their experiences with fellow students. A survey by N.B.Selection Ltd (reported in the *Interviewer*, 24 May 1996) found that over 75% of the sampled 570 final year undergraduates felt that unprofessional handling of any aspect of selection would have a lasting impression on their perception of the company. As undergraduates may have a wide choice of companies, some may see the opportunity to eliminate firms as advantageous. However, organizations may miss out on good candidates because of a bad reputation in selection.

A candidate who feels deceived by blatant bias may seek redress through industrial tribunals. This reaction to deception is described in the following chapter. Attendant publicity may similarly dent the organizational image.

The unsuccessful internal candidate

Internal candidates, who failed to gain promotion because of deception, share some of the reactions of unsuccessful, external candidates.

However, these may be compounded by their established position within the organization. They may be less likely to disclose perceived injustice, either because they fear accusations of 'sour grapes' or for political self preservation. However, superiors and peers are likely to note their apparent 'failure' and may genuinely sympathize or utter hypocritical platitudes.

Alienation of the unsuccessful candidate

Anxious candidates may develop strong emotional reactions which affect self esteem, job satisfaction and work attitudes. They can become alienated, demotivated and lose their commitment to the job, their colleagues and the organization. In turn they consider leaving the company and may actively seek other positions. If this option appears unrealistic or doomed to failure, they may feel trapped within the organization. Consequently work performance and health decline whilst resentment, stress and absence flourish.

Failure to properly explain the selection process and its consequences can have disastrous effects on internal candidates and the wider organization. This may be heightened if selection methods lack face validity and job relevance or subsequent feedback is poor, inaccurate or non-existent. The Levi's case study illustrates the ramifications of poor communication in preparation for an assessment centre.

The successful candidate

External candidates may succeed in being appointed whilst internal candidates achieve promotion. Their subsequent discovery of deception by the organization may occur in various ways, at different times and with disparate results.

Failed practical expectations

The first day at work may convince the individual that all is not as anticipated. Tasks may be less demanding, more physically tiring or take place in conditions which are much dirtier, noisier or unpleasant than described during selection. Alternatively, the job is more demanding than expected, pressure is greater and compounded by insufficient help from managers, understaffing and inadequate resources which were glossed over at inter-

> ## Case Study 4
> ### LEVI'S
>
> Having decided to change its marketing strategy, Levi's put all UK sales staff through an assessment centre in 1994 to select staff for expanded customer service roles. The exercise had repercussions for participants, assessors, the rest of the company and customers alike.
>
> Levi's later acknowledged that the exercise had not been an unqualified success and identified ways of improving the assessment process. Several of these focused on communication which was recognized to have created some unfortunate results:
>
> • Neither the significance of the assessment centre nor its consequences was explained fully to candidates. As a result, some participants were too casual in their approach. Half of the participants were successful, the rest were made redundant.
>
> • The reasons for the assessment process were not communicated. Consequently the rest of the company became anxious once they heard of it and the exercise proved controversial.
>
> Other consequences followed. Changes in the sales team reverberated on customers as many service tasks were neglected, to the annoyance of customers. It was also acknowledged that the company gave insufficient support to managerial assessors and a need to 'debrief and heal' the assessors was recognized by the UK general manager. Possibly the most significant consequence was the firm's positive approach to identifying and remedying shortcomings in selection.

view. The disillusioned employee leaves as soon as possible, so increasing staff turnover and the inherent costs of further recruitment.

Sometimes discovery of deception coincides with the arrival of payment, which may not match expectations. A well documented example of the latter is the case of casual student labour employed at Burger King. The case study, collated from media reports, is described in its entirety, since a single incident escalated into a virtual campaign attracting public, union and media support.

Case Study 5
BURGER KING

Michael Griffiths, 17, a trainee teacher, believed he had been employed by Burger King for £3.10 an hour. He then discovered that when business was quiet staff were asked to clock off and take unpaid breaks. Some days he received less than £1 and he never got a full five hours' pay. After three weeks he left and spoke out about the situation.

Today newspaper reported the events on its front page and the company attracted heavy criticism. The campaign was joined by Labour and unions who highlighted 'exploitation' of young staff. John Monks, the TUC General Secretary, condemned Burger King for using 'virtual slave labour'.

Eventually, in December 1995, Burger King gave £106,000 compensation to 900 workers who were told to take unpaid breaks, average back pay being £118. It scrapped its compulsory clocking off and affirmed its 'commitment to equitable employment practices.' Mr Griffiths received £98 back pay and said he was pleased on his own account and for current workers who couldn't speak out because they were still employed at Burger King.

Burger King blamed 'misuse of scheduling' for the dispute. It would not say how many of its 350 outlets operated the clocking off procedure or whether any of its staff or franchise holders had been disciplined.

The issue resulted in a high price in compensation and questionable publicity.

Breakdown of the psychological contract

Not all organizational deception is discovered as quickly. More time may elapse if deception surrounds the psychological contract and the candidate's expectations of the organization. The job's intellectual demands, complexity and responsibilities may have been exaggerated and training opportunities, promotion and salary progression may have been overstated. Empty promises, subsequent disappointment and the conflicting, complex reactions experienced by a high flying candidate who felt severely misled by a company are illustrated in Case Study 6.

Successful internal candidates may be similarly disillusioned. Staff who have been identified as fast track employees may eventually discover that such opportunities are a mirage. Selection, although itself above board, may be seen as part of a wider organizational deception.

In both situations there may be feelings of incomprehension and powerlessness, stress, lowered productivity and decreased commitment to an organization which has not honoured its side of the agreement. Research has found that the candidate's reaction to selection processes may affect motivation, commitment, willingness to recommend the organization to others and more thoughts about quitting the job (Mabey and Isles, 1991 and Robertson et al.). Organizational climate can also be impaired (Kravitz, Stinson and Chavez, 1996) and morale may suffer. Some disenchanted candidates may feel justified in pursuing retribution through unethical behaviour such as sabotage, or offering valuable company specific business knowledge and experience to business competitors in return for employment.

Cloning

Occasionally companies may suffer if selectors recruit in their own image. Cloning, whilst superficially successful, maintains the cultural status quo. This prevents organizations from recruiting innovative individuals whose fresh ideas could revitalize moribund operations. It also limits the expansion of equal opportunities policies.

A re-assessment of selection strategies

Candidates and selectors who have experienced deception may reassess their selection strategies and modify future behaviour. This may include adopting tactics of dubious honesty and a suspicious approach to subsequent selection procedures which creates a vicious circle of mistrust. A 'chicken and egg' situation evolves in which each party claims that their deceit is a response to the actions of the other.

Case Study 6
ANITA

Anita, a young, ambitious law graduate, started work in a prestigious firm of solicitors, rapidly gaining considerable experience and several promotions. She moved to a manufacturing company and soon became head of the legal department. Her meteoric rise to fame and fortune was particularly gratifying because of her youth and she was the first woman to hold such a position. Anita enjoyed the work, and intellectual challenge. Her valuable contribution was recognized by a place on the board.

She was then approached by a headhunter to work for another company. The job entailed establishing a similar in-house legal department and sounded very exciting. Although there was little financial advantage, the challenge appeared irresistible and Anita took the job.

Almost immediately she experienced misgivings about the position and the organization. Her office was not ready and her nomadic existence made it difficult to hold meetings or formulate plans. The promised budget failed to materialize, she could not establish herself and felt constantly fobbed off. Anita undertook mundane work, had no responsibility and was not exercising her skills and intellect.

Anita began to blame herself. She believed that adopting the right approach would persuade board members to give her the promised latitude. Her attempts were futile and Anita tackled her sense of failure by constant work in a vain attempt to prove herself. She was unhappy and displayed symptoms of stress and depression necessitating a visit to the company's medical adviser.

Anger and disappointment replaced stress. Anita had sacrificed much to gain a job which failed to match expectations. She felt that she had ruined her career, as the manufacturing company would not re-employ her and her current employment could be seen as a retrograde step, despite the title and salary. Her attempts to redress the situation failed and Anita questioned the existence of the job for which she had been recruited. She eventually had to raise the possibility of proceeding with actions concerning misrepresentation and breach of contract. She was paid one year's salary and kept the company car.

Today Anita still feels bitter and resentful. She had sought satisfaction in a 'better' job with greater potential and challenge. Instead, she undertook routine work well below her capabilities. Anita would not have left her previous employment if she had known the true situation.

DECEPTION OF CANDIDATES AND ORGANIZATIONS BY THIRD PARTIES

Deception practised by agencies, headhunters and referees may impede the efficiency and ethical conduct of selection. The consequences are felt by both candidates and organizations.

Agencies

The unethical or inefficient activities of some agencies may reflect on organizations, especially if illegal discrimination is involved. The selector's time may be wasted if agencies forward CVs without the candidate's consent, send CVs of uninterested candidates or mislead candidates who arrive at interview with unrealistic expectations of the job's content, conditions and opportunities.

Inefficiency has other repercussions. Inadvertent despatch of a candidate's CV to his current employer alerts a manager to the employee's search for other work, and may prompt a review of the applicant's apparent commitment. This creates awkwardness and embarrassment for the candidate, who occasionally may actually lose the current job. If agencies do not undertake the expected checks, unsuitable people may slip through the net, with the potential to damage the organization, its staff and customers.

Candidates' and organizations' discovery of such events may result in changing agencies or investigating agency procedure and applying pressure for better practice.

Headhunters

Headhunting affects candidates and their current employers. Candidates who are approached by headhunters but subsequently abandoned as serious contenders may be unaware of their comparative merit and consequently may have an inflated opinion of their abilities. They may become dissatisfied with their current employment and seek alternative positions – moves which may not be in their best interests.

Alternatively, the headhunted candidate's approach to the current employer may be apparently successful. Research (reported in the *Interviewer*, 16 August 1996) indicates that 80% of headhunted staff receive a counteroffer. Firms may subsequently regard the headhunted employee in a different light, questioning her loyalty and so causing potential damage to the previous employer–employee relationship. Further reflection may lead to a reconsideration of promises made as part of the counteroffer, and other salary increases may be waived because a raise has already been awarded. Firms may also deceive themselves about the effectiveness of the counteroffer, as many previously headhunted employees still tend to leave their job within six months.

Referees

Referees may deceive both candidates and employers by providing questionable references. Repercussions are complex. Employers may withdraw job offers on the basis of information received. This destroys a candidate's aspirations and can be devastating if the candidate has already handed in notice to his current employer who may be reluctant to re-employ him.

A candidate who believes the reference was inaccurate may seek redress from the referee for compiling an allegedly careless or damaging reference. This can result in legalities such as in *Spring* v. *Guardian Assurance*, described in Chapter 11. Recompense may be sought and a computer graduate was awarded £25,000 compensation when she challenged the former Polytechnic of Wales after an unfavourable reference led to the withdrawal of a job offer.

Consequently, employers may re-evaluate their reference procedure, and suggested improvements are included in Chapter 10. They are likely to be less candid in the references they furnish and may limit themselves to verifiable factual material rather than supplying opinions which could be disputed.

WIDER SOCIETY

Deception by candidate, organization or third party impacts on wider society through media coverage of specific events or the general activities of pressure groups. Closer scrutiny of the fairness of selection may result from changes in social climate, a growing awareness of social equity and society's readier recourse to litigation as a remedy for perceived injustice.

Interest in deception

Media interest

Media interest is one of the consequences of deception and sometimes the media may adopt a moral standpoint, verging on a crusade for change. Individuals caught in the public spotlight achieve a notoriety they would presumably have preferred to avoid, and which may hinder their future jobseeking. Companies may gain adverse publicity which damages public opinion, custom and future recruitment. The focus of media attention may encourage organizations to conduct internal inquiries, review their procedures and instigate tighter checks on staff.

The law

There is a legal interest in deception. Laws of contract, employment, criminal law or the discrimination legislation may all be relevant. The latter involves acts covering Equal Pay (1970), Sex Discrimination (1975), Race Relations (1976) and Disability Discrimination (1996), all of which exist to eliminate discriminatory practice and have a focus on selection.

Consequently, aggrieved employers, employees and unsuccessful candidates who feel deceived by other parties may seek compensation and vindication through legal action. Employers may also be prosecuted under the Asylum and Immigration Act, 1996. Legalities involve more than court appearances and may result in adverse publicity, penalties, legal costs and payment of compensation.

The role of interested parties

Individuals who perceive general shortcomings in the selection system may group together to address a perceived social injustice and press for change. Employers and applicants may act simultaneously. For example, ageism is addressed by the Employers' Forum on Age and the Campaign Against Age Discrimination in Employment (CAADE), and both include selection practices within their wider remit.

Professional interest groups such as trade unions, professional associations and those involved in selection may have a common interest in raising standards and professionalism, and bodies such as IPD, the CRE and EOC produce guides outlining good practice. Practising professionals may adopt a narrower perspective, highlighting poor practice and protecting themselves against subsequent harm.

The recruitment industry has debated the creation of CV Concern, a pressure group formed to eliminate the CV race which was felt to be damaging the industry. The agency consultant first submitting a CV to an employer is financially rewarded for the introduction of the candidate.

Supporters of CV Concern wish to ban the practice, which they feel fosters unprofessionalism. They regard the primacy of duty to the candidate, and believe that consultation before despatch of CVs is essential, even if slower submissions result in lost rewards. The group's opponents maintain that the system is encouraged by the client and tends to be reasonably equitable.

The professional concern of teachers is manifested through union pronouncements over unsuitable staff and the possibility of sexual abusers having access to school children, described in Case Study 3 (Chapter 8). The National Association of Schoolmasters and Union of Women Teachers called for tight new regulations to stop agency teachers on a government blacklist from sidestepping screening checks which it claimed were routinely ignored by some agencies.

Proposed action to reduce deception

Employers may find it difficult to identify unsuitable candidates who conceal unfavourable personal information. This is especially pertinent where vulnerable people may be subject to the activities of potentially dangerous staff. There is also concern about the employment of many ex-criminals in security firms or as 'bouncers'. This has increased the call for change and stimulated government proposals to establish vetting bodies.

Under Home Office proposals, employers operating in sensitive areas could be given access to the criminal records of job applicants. A junior Home Office minister was reported as saying 'we believe a system of pre-employment checks is needed that is more accessible and more open, and will meet the needs of employers and other organizations who need to employ people in positions of trust.'

Proposals centre on extending the categories of employers able to access criminal records to cover jobs such as doctors, lottery ticket sellers and people seeking employment with children. However, all employers should be entitled to ask an applicant to present a criminal conviction certificate, obtainable from the proposed criminal records agency. Different levels of employment would be entitled to different levels of information.

The proposals were criticized by penal reform groups and probation staff associations. They argue that offenders will be increasingly excluded from employment, so being doubly punished when they are already experiencing discrimination in the workforce. There are also concerns that an employer may gain knowledge of some convictions which were irrelevant to the particular job. A register of convicted paedophiles has been introduced under the Sex Offenders Act 1997.

SUMMARY

Deception may be discovered directly but frequently it emerges from the doubts and suspicions raised through unsatisfactory productivity, ineffective interpersonal relationships and poor treatment of clients and customers. Candidates may experience the profound practical, financial and psychological repercussions of deception. Organizations may sustain damaged reputations, falling profits and increased staff turnover. Vulnerable people may suffer and society may press for remedial action from the government and employers.

Discovery of deception usually involves a re-assessment of selection by candidates and organizations and both parties may attempt to strengthen their selection strategy.

What can be done about deception? 10

The final three chapters explore ways of tackling deception. Several perspectives and strategies are examined but the predominant emphasis is on proactivity. Reducing the opportunities for deception and one's susceptibility to it appear preferable to reactivity. This chapter provides an overview on addressing deception whilst the following chapters concentrate on maximizing and checking verifiable information provided by candidates. Combating deception by improving selection methods, especially application forms, interviews and references, occupies the penultimate chapter. The concluding chapter covers other checks on candidate claims and authenticity, including integrity tests.

This chapter focuses on what can be done about deception. It starts by assessing the need to tackle deception and then suggests proactive strategies available to applicants and organizations. These include reviewing and re-assessing their present position and improving the exchange of information between both parties. The next section outlines the candidates' and selectors' reactive options after discovering deception. Finally the chapter considers a re-evaluation of deception and alternative perspectives. It is suggested that deceit is not always negative and that some impression management techniques can be used positively.

IS IT WORTH TACKLING DECEPTION?

Tackling deception takes time, skill and effort. Applicants, selectors and organizations may wonder whether this is justified and their decisions may be influenced by:

- attitudes to deception, fairness and ethics
- views on the extent of deception
- assessment of personal skills in selection and detecting deception.

If organizations wish to select the best candidate and act fairly, they may want to tackle deception. If they are less scrupulous, deception may seem irrelevant. Selectors may be ambivalent. They may believe that selection involves some deception and impression management but wish to reserve this behaviour for themselves and are less tolerant of it in candidates.

Ethical considerations prescribe that selection should centre on ability to do the job and job relevant criteria. Appointing people for other reasons opens the door to bias and unfair practice. The interviewer's 'I thought she/he would fit in' may mask personal prejudice. Ideally organizations wish to recruit the best candidates, rather than the best impression managers, unless that characteristic is considered job relevant.

The extent of deception is problematic. Personnel may assume it is either too widespread or too rare to warrant countermeasures. Deception appears widespread. As described earlier, research has revealed deception in submitted verifiable information in application forms, CVs and interviews. Faking of personality questionnaires and the practice effect in ability tests may cause selectors some concern about assessment results. Impression management techniques pervade selection and culminate in interviews.

Research shows that impression management is frequently successful and interviewers' susceptibility to it may be greater than imagined. Interviewers' are often influenced by irrelevant information and their liking of the skilled impression manager may make rejection difficult. Gilmore and Ferris (1989) showed that interviewer perceptions were swayed more by a candidate's skilful impression management, e.g. smiles and compliments, than by information about actual qualifications.

Interviewers may be underestimating the amount of deception and overestimating their powers of detection. Anderson (1991) found that positive facial expressions affected interviewers' assessments of motivation and the degree of candidates' eye contact influenced selector's impressions of strength of character and competence. He concluded that links between non-verbal behaviour and personality would appear to be inaccurate, especially as candidates can easily control their facial expressions. He cites Ekman and Friesen's (1974) study in which 'observers seeing just the face of the deceiver were unable to judge deception attempts accurately and consistently'. Anderson and Shackleton (1991) concluded that 'impression management by the interviewee, either in the form of deception or ingratiation . . . represents a potent source of error in interview judgements which may or may not be recognized as such by the recruiter.'

MINIMIZATION OF DECEPTION

Proactive strategies adopted by candidates and organizations aim to increase the accuracy, honesty and completeness of information obtained from the other. This facilitates better judgements, evaluations and decision making. Both may start by reviewing their current situation to identify areas of potential deception before taking more active combative measures.

The candidate's proactive strategies

Candidates' lack of knowledge is a crucial element in their susceptibility to deception. This may stem from inadequate, incomplete or incorrect details about the job, organization and selection process. Alternatively, self deception could be involved, as lack of self awareness about personal abilities can create unrealistic expectations.

The candidate's proactive strategies, shown in Figure 10.1, can be very effective in the short term, though do not guarantee employment. At all stages the applicant has the option of withdrawing from selection.

Operating from a sound knowledge base helps a candidate. Instead of readily accepting information given by an organization, the candidate can evaluate its quality and veracity, so facilitating informed judgements and decision making. Increased possession of as much reliable, factual knowledge as possible can be achieved in several ways.

Increasing self awareness

Greater knowledge of one's personality, skills and career interests reduces self deception. Those unsure of career directions can seek career counselling, or complete interest inventories such as Gradscope or the Rothwell Miller interest blank, whilst identifying transferable skills may help the redundant. Such services are available through public careers services, training and enterprise councils (TECs) or private consultancies. Examination of past experiences in work and job search can identify mistakes and avoid future repetition. Feedback from previous applications, however unpalatable, may be enlightening.

| PURPOSE | STRATEGIES | |
	PROACTIVE	REACTIVE

Strengthen the candidate's position against deception by others	• awareness of sources and types of deception
	• awareness of rights under equal opportunities and relevant legislation
	• keep records of job search
	• clear contracts with agencies
	• thorough checks of job and organization
	  – job description
	  – person specification
	  – terms and conditions
	  – realistic job preview
	  – site visit
		• adopt a more wary approach
		• attempt to clarify discrepancies with selectors
		• check with other candidates
		• complain to
		  – senior management
		  – professional association
		• publicize
		  – letters to media
		  – contact media
		  – pressure groups
		• redress
		  – tribunals
		      equal opportunities
		          race
		  – law

Strengthen the candidate's position against charges of deception	• honesty	

CANDIDATE VARIABLES

★ current employment position
★ amount of job search experience
★ access to training in selection techniques and specialist knowledge

Figure 10.1   Strategies available to the candidate in combating deception

Increasing general awareness of jobs and the selection process

Inexperienced candidates or those contemplating a career change may want more realistic information about their proposed employment. This may be gained indirectly by conversations with people already doing the job or from careers information through brochures, videos, presentations or open days. Previewing the job by direct sampling may be possible through work experience whilst at school, Saturday jobs, work shadowing, work trials whilst unemployed, university sandwich courses, vacation work or specific longer term placements.

In researching the selection system, individuals can ascertain their employment rights and responsibilities through information from the citizens advice bureau, pressure groups or government bodies. EOC and CRE publications outline and explain the Sex and Race Discrimination Acts. Job centres provide informative leaflets, job clubs to improve the jobseeking skills of unemployed individuals and disability employment advisers to assist the disabled.

Candidates seeking work through agencies can 'shop around'. They can check whether agencies belong to the Federation of Recruitment and Employment Services, and can clarify their policies, especially those concerning CV despatch. There is frequently a choice of agencies for people who feel misled or dissatisfied.

Applicants may also wish to check with referees that they are able, willing and happy to provide references. A copy of a current CV may refresh the referee's memory of biographical details they may be expected to recall, so avoiding the referee's inadvertent factual deception.

Gaining information on a specific employment position

Individuals considering particular job applications may seek information on the job, the organization and selection procedures.

The job and the organization

Uninformative advertisements can be supplemented by research through formal and informal sources. The obvious solution is to contact the organization for a job description, personnel specification, details of salary and other relevant matters. Should these be unforthcoming or inadequate, research in the local press, library and on the Internet may yield information on the company, its reputation and possibly staff turnover. If appropriate, a company's annual reports may furnish additional facts. Networking with current employees, existing contacts or other jobseekers through job clubs may provide useful information. If jobseekers proceed with the application, the assembled data become invaluable. It enables candidates to display background knowledge at interview, ask salient questions and check the honesty of any given information.

Practical information may be gained through familiarisation with the actual work site and its accessibility, and reality testing can reduce self deception or wild optimism. A thirty mile journey on an urban motorway may appear feasible from the armchair but the reality of rush hour conditions may prompt second thoughts. These considerations may be especially pertinent if interviews are offsite.

Selection procedures

Applicants may wish to clarify selection details. Written confirmation avoids misunderstandings, especially if reimbursement of considerable expenses is involved. Failing this, it could be useful to note the name and position of any person supplying details. Some undergraduates record details of specific organizational selection procedures, which are filed by the university careers service for students' benefit.

If research achieves limited success, candidates may weigh probabilities and judge whether to proceed or withdraw from selection. Much depends on the availability of job vacancies and personal circumstances. Withdrawing limits candidates' exposure to further deception, terminates investment of time and effort and enables them to concentrate on more promising opportunities. Proceeding may necessitate other strategies.

Strategies during selection

When completing the application form, applicants can choose to ignore questions which are perceived to be unethical, discriminatory or intrusive. This may be counterproductive. Selectors have expectations that candidates will complete the form and withholding information has a negative or biasing effect (Stone and Stone, 1987). Employers may not distinguish between non-completion of questions for ethical reasons and attempts to deliberately conceal unfavourable details. Some selectors report intense irritation at trying to work out an applicant's age when this has been omitted.

Candidates called for interview may arrive early to further their knowledge. Ten minutes spent waiting in a reception area can reveal much about the organization's efficiency, facilities and staff qualities of courtesy, friendliness and professionalism. Gatekeepers, car park attendants, security staff and cleaners may also be sources of information.

Applicants can use interviews to gain further information and can ask for a tour round the site. In meeting others, especially potential colleagues in the targeted department, they may be able to judge the 'atmosphere' and whether people work well together as a team. Conversation with the leaving incumbent can be extremely helpful, as can ascertaining reasons for his departure.

After the interview jobseekers may wish to record details, especially if issues such as promised training were discussed. Such topics may form part of the psychological contract rather than featuring in the formal contract, though candidates can press for their inclusion. Written confirmation of such topics is advantageous and may be sought in confirmatory letters of job acceptance.

The organization's proactive strategies

Increased awareness of deception, its manifestations and the areas in which it is most likely to occur can be advantageous as a starting point. Deception may be unintentional or deliberate, occurring through the practices of selectors and third parties. Organizations are deceived in several areas. First, there is an element of self deception if companies judge their selection system to be good when in fact it is the opposite. It may be unprofessional or employ methods of doubtful validity which could lay the organization open to allegations of unfairness. Complications arise if the selection system is not operating as anticipated by Personnel staff, perhaps because people interpret and apply it idiosyncratically. The second element is external deceit from two sources: candidates who may misrepresent their skills, experience and attributes, and third parties such as agencies or referees who may demonstrate underhandedness.

Organizations have several defences against deception and an overview of available strategies is shown in Figure 10.2. As with candidates, proactive and reactive strategies can be adopted, both within the organization or externally, and choice of emphasis may be governed by organizational ethos.

Proactive strategies focus on reviewing and strengthening the selection procedure, increasing the provision of information so applicants have

PURPOSE	STRATEGIES	
	PROACTIVE	REACTIVE

Strengthen the candidate's position against deception by others	• awareness of sources and types of deception
	• awareness of rights under equal opportunities and relevant legislation
	• keep records of job search
	• clear contracts with agencies
	• thorough checks of job and organization
	  – job description
	  – person specification
	  – terms and conditions
	  – realistic job preview
	  – site visit
		• adopt a more wary approach
		• attempt to clarify discrepancies with selectors
		• check with other candidates
		• complain to
		  – senior management
		  – professional association
		• publicize
		  – letters to media
		  – contact media
		  – pressure groups
		• redress
		  – tribunals
		      equal opportunities
		      race
		  – law

Strengthen the candidate's position against charges of deception	• honesty	

CANDIDATE VARIABLES

★ current employment position
★ amount of job search experience
★ access to training in selection techniques and specialist knowledge

Figure 10.2   Strategies available to the organization in combating deception

less need for deceit and encouraging candidates to be honest. Like candidates, the first line of defence may be to take stock of the existing position.

A review of selection

Scrutiny of selection methods, practices, personnel and other facets such as candidate care may be helpful. It gives the Personnel department an accurate picture of how their espoused policies are actually implemented, so that any discrepancies can be identified and addressed. Enquiries into any company specific examples of deception or particularly poor selection could stimulate discussion on remedial measures. Improving the selection system generally is a good defence against deception practised by some selectors, candidates and third parties.

The overview

A review of the selection system could be multifunctional. It could audit:

• general efficiency

• effectiveness of selection methods

• cost effectiveness

• fairness and consistency in treatment of candidates

• training needs to increase efficiency.

It could be undertaken by the Personnel department or by external consultants. An internally conducted review has the advantage of familiarity with the system and personnel involved. External consultants may be more impersonal and therefore more effective in challenging established practices which are accepted unquestioningly by the organization. Subsequent discussion may stimulate a reappraisal of existing practice. The awareness of widespread deception influenced the authors to develop a selection audit, and typical questions are shown in Figure 10.3.

A review may be accompanied by checking selection procedures against those advocated in best practice guides produced by professional bodies such as the Institute of Personnel and Development (IPD). Guides are also produced by the CRE and EOC. Some guides are specific to particular functions such as the administration of psychometric tests.

How are the applications received?

0   No system, depends on who is in the office when they come in.
1
2   They are collected at a central point and held there until needed.
3
4   They are collected and held at a central point and logged
    in a specific document.
5
6   They are held and logged at a central point and stored securely.

**Would the information sought for the application forms
seem relevant to the candidate?**

0   The application form is for our benefit, not theirs.
1
2   A lot of it would seem irrelevant.
3
4   Some of it would seem irrelevant.
5
6   Doubtful if any of it would seem irrelevant.

Does the test procedure give a good image of the organization?

0   Testing is obnoxious and officious; likely to give a negative image.
1
2   The testing procedure is likely to be neutral.
3
4   An attempt is made to explain the tests and convince
    the candidate that testing is reasonable.
5
6   Invitation letter clearly explains why tests are used, testing session is
    planned, candidates are put at ease and reasons for choosing
    specific tests are explained.

Does the test procedure give a good image of the organization?

0   Not at all. The tests come as a surprise.
1
2   They are notified in advance that tests are used and the
    duration is given.
3
4   They are told the type of test, given some reassurance and sent a
    test-taker's guide.
5
6   They are told most things about the test in advance **and** given practice
    items to complete in their own time. Candidates are given a name and
    contact telephone number in case they wish to clarify anything.

Figure 10.3   Typical questions from a selection audit

Organisations may wish to paint a broader canvas from supplementary information, as detailed below.

Selectors

An analysis of selectors' professionalism and skills may help to identify any training needs, as interviewers' blind faith in their abilities can contribute to the deception of the organization. It may also consider awareness of public relations, since selectors may not appreciate that their behaviour to candidates, the image they project of the company and the information they impart can be critical factors in 'losing' preferred candidates.

The policies

A policy review could evaluate whether candidates' deception arises directly or indirectly from the organization's own selection practices and possible incompetence. Instead of rushing to fill a vacancy immediately, lengthier reflection could determine whether redeployment or reorganization of existing jobs are alternatives. Organizations may consider a review stage in which the replacement of staff has to be justified to others, though this can prolong the process and introduce bureaucracy. Focused discussion could establish whether the organization wants a large pool of poorly qualified, often inappropriate applicants or a smaller pool of suitable candidates. This could affect the location and content of advertisements.

The methods

A specific review of selection methods is obviously a precursor to improvements in this area. It can focus on the choice of methods, their validity, administration and interpretation. This is discussed more fully in Chapter 11.

Feedback from candidates

The candidate's perspective on selection may be gained from formal or informal research. Feedback from unsuccessful candidates may be helpful, since successful entrants to the organization may be reluctant to jeopardize their new position by airing any discontent. Exit interviews with departing staff may reveal shortcomings in the selection system which contributed to the employee's commitment and intention to quit. Empty promises, falsely raised expectations and broken psychological contracts are possible topics of investigation.

Provision of information to candidates

Organizations may decide that an open and honest outlook on selection could help to eliminate deception. This involves supplying comprehensive information in the advertisement and subsequent despatch of job description, personnel specification, details of the organization plus terms and conditions of employment. Some companies advise applicants not to apply if they do not meet at least 70% of the requirements or may emphasize the essential qualifications required. If candidates have sufficient information on the job and selection procedures, they can reach considered judgements on whether to continue or self select out of the process. Encouraging ineligible or wildly optimistic candidates to withdraw ultimately benefits all parties and focuses concentration on serious contenders.

Companies may be similarly open about their wider ethos, training schemes, work climate and career paths. Proactive provision of information fosters realistic expectations which are more likely to be met and empowers candidates in decision making. Hopefully this reduces the need for deceit. Similarly, alerting candidates to selection procedures helps them to perform well, so facilitating better selection decisions. This is especially important for internal candidates, as was seen with Levi's (see Chapter 9).

Encouraging candidates to be honest

The information itself and the way in which it is communicated can convey an organization's culture of trust and openness. Companies which pride themselves on integrity may expect it to be reciprocated and this may act as a self fulfilling prophecy. They may believe that most candidates are honest and are not prepared to offend them by suspicion and extensive checks in order to reveal an unscrupulous minority. This may encourage candidates contemplating deception to discard it as counter-productive. Fear of discovery could be a deterrent, as the organization's aversion to deceit would render the candidate unsuitable and unacceptable.

Dealing with third parties

Organizations may review their role and relationship with agencies and clear demarcation of rights and responsibilities may eliminate misunderstandings. Similar openness may be needed in providing agencies with detailed job information, preferably documented, which can be made available to applicants. This reduces agencies' misrepresentation of jobs and increases their efficiency in selecting suitable and interested jobseekers. Applicants with inflated expectations would not attend interview, only to learn the truth of the situation and withdraw precipitously, refuse job offers or fail to turn up for work.

Other ways of combating deception

Selection rarely affords candidates or organizations the time or opportunity to reach considered, realistic conclusions about each other. Expectations may not be realized and each party may discover inconsistencies, errors or downright untruths in the other party's information. In order to reduce these discrepancies, organizations may suggest other ways in which they and candidates can discover whether they are mutually compatible.

Organizations may opt for probationary periods for new entrants or temporary/short term contracts, both of which provide time to check an individual's skills and ability to fit into the organization. Training ability, potential and personality can be more realistically assessed over longer periods. Equally it is only by experiencing true working conditions, organizational culture, work colleagues and management that the candidate can fully appreciate the job's implications. A more controversial proposal is offering unpaid work, as at Cable Channel Live TV (*Personnel Today*, 16 July 1996). This is defended as an attempt to break the syndrome that you cannot get work without experience but cannot get experience without work.

Some organizations proactively prepare potential candidates for selection. This avoids losing good applicants because they lack certain qualities which could be remedied comparatively easily. *Personnel Today* (16 July 1996) reported that the army is offering new recruits fitness training programmes to help them pass its initial training level. This aims to help raise the proportion of recruits passing phase one selection from 63% to 90%, so giving the army more choice from a larger pool of applicants.

The proactive strategies of third parties

All third parties, particularly agencies, may protect themselves against deception by clarifying contracts, roles and responsibilities. Agencies may persuade or insist that organizations invest sufficient time for comprehensive briefings on job descriptions and personnel requirements, with written confirmation. This can eliminate potential confusion, and its subsequent transmission to clients. Agencies also have legal redress if organizations try to avoid their financial obligations over the agency's successful staff placement.

Some agencies operate on the premise that there will be no fee if the candidate leaves within a specified period such as six months. This is a very strong, financial inducement to ensure candidates are thoroughly briefed and hold realistic expectations. Both agencies and headhunters may refuse to act for apparently dishonest organizations or candidates, so defending themselves against deception and possible collusion.

Referees can guard against unintentionally misleading others by exercising care in the compilation of references. An awareness of the legal implications and suggested improvements in the reference procedure, described in the following chapter, may be beneficial.

REACTIVE STRATEGIES

Not all organizations wish to adopt reactive strategies. Those with cultures of openness and trust may be reluctant to sacrifice such principles by using tactics which imply suspicion and doubt. Some may combine elements from proactive and reactive policies. Others, with a more utilitarian ethos, may have little hesitation in vigorously pursuing reactive policies.

Readiness to behave reactively is not always activated. Action may be determined by the discovery of deception and personal perceptions of its intention, nature and seriousness. Attitudes towards deceit are also relevant. These factors are considered before describing the candidates' and organizations' reactive strategies.

Attitudes towards deception

The discovery of deception

Candidates and selectors will not react to deception if it remains undetected. This may happen if deceit is innocuous or so well planned that discovery is virtually impossible. Sometimes a company feels it has made a bad appointment without necessarily discovering active deceit. Raised suspicions may prompt enquiries with varying degrees of success. A worker's claim of vast experience is belied if he cannot perform basic tasks, but excuses of procedural differences may be used as camouflage.

Reprisals tend to be minimal if deceit is discovered sooner rather than later, as there will have been less investment of time, effort, cost and commitment. A jobseeker receiving a job information pack at variance with a misleading advertisement can easily withdraw. Reaction is stronger from the worker who left satisfactory employment only to discover six months later that promised opportunities fail to materialize. Similarly uncovering lies on application forms during shortlisting produces less organizational annoyance than discovering discrepancies on the P45 of a newly appointed candidate who was appointed after a protracted selection procedure.

Personal and organizational attitudes to deception

Attitudes to general deception and specific manifestations can be crucial and complex. They can also affect the implementation and degree of retribution. Some selectors and candidates, viewing 'economy with the truth' as inevitable, may accept deception with resignation and forbearance. Action may not occur if individuals and organizations dismiss deception as isolated incidents caused by errors or misunderstandings. Others believe that fabrication indicates a generally dishonest and unreliable character and should be eradicated. Occasionally organizations may regard 'inventions' as originality deserving grudging admiration. A salesman who embroiders the truth may be credited with the creativity needed in selling. This re-evaluation of deception is discussed later.

Closely intertwined with attitudes are perceptions of the seriousness of deception and these can influence the scale and scope of reactivity. An individual's manipulation of age to satisfy selection criteria may be regarded more tolerantly than the embezzler trying to access a financial institution through a false CV. Enhancement of qualifications may be seen as commonplace whilst a forged reference may invoke greater comment.

The candidate's reactive approach

What can the candidate do about the organization's deception? Probably the short answer is 'not a lot', but this is not entirely true. Positive action is possible and choice of tactic depends on when the deception is discovered. Individuals may withdraw from selection if they discover deceit before, during or after selection.

During selection

Candidates may appreciate an interviewer's impression management tactics. Faced with apparent deception or misinformation, they may remain silent and draw their own conclusions. If unethical questions are asked, candidates may use combative answers they have prepared earlier. If they perceive questions to be discriminatory, they can subsequently check with other candidates whether they were asked the same questions. Applicants may probe points which are glossed over or actively challenge certain statements or inferences.

Candidates who feel deceived by other selection methods may try to redress the situation. Discussion of ability and personality tests in interviews, especially in assessment centres, allows candidates to voice their concerns about test administration and the accuracy of their results. Consequently, the assessor may adjust the report or produce it in conjunction with the candidate. If references are felt to be deceitful, they can be challenged privately or through law courts.

After the selection decision

Successful and unsuccessful candidates may adopt different strategies. There is a high cost in taking the wrong job and candidates may feel that they do not wish to prolong their relationship with a devious organization. Withdrawal at the job offer stage is an option for candidates who discover stated terms and conditions are unexpected and not as previously agreed. The Case Study of Anita (Chapter 9) illustrates that legal redress can be sought if deception is discovered after an offer of appointment has been accepted. If this is not appropriate, rapid departure from the firm is an alternative.

Unsuccessful applicants may accept the situation passively, 'put it down to experience' and become more suspicious or cynical in further jobseeking. There may be psychological benefits in taking more positive action, though caution suggests a balance of potential gains against possible emotional and financial costs. Although reactive measures may not gain candidates employment, they may reduce the sense of powerlessness, create a certain sense of satisfaction in 'getting it off your chest' and attempt to eliminate the repetition of unethical behaviour. Candidates may feel justified if their actions generate apologies or compensation.

Specific complaints may focus on selection methods or the selectors' behaviour. Allegations of unfairness, improper suggestions or other unethical activities may be made to the organization's senior management or relevant professional associations. Frustrated applicants can communicate their disapproval, outrage or sense of injustice to a wider audience. The media may be contacted or letters to professional journals may highlight concerns and call for change. In some specific instances, such as sexual harassment, legal redress may be sought. If individual pressure is felt to be ineffective, candidates may join pressure groups to achieve remedies.

If candidates feel that questions or psychometric tests are blatantly discriminatory they can seek justice and recompense under the Race, Sex or Disability Discrimination Acts. The associated commissions can help in pursuing cases to tribunals, though sex discrimination cases may be conducted by the individual or with the help of unions, citizens advice bureaux or legal representatives. Access to personal details through the Data Protection Act may be helpful for corroboration of facts which candidates have recorded independently. Awards for damage to feelings is tangible compensation for deception practised by selectors.

The organization's reactive approach

Some organizations may feel cynical about proactive policies. They may believe that manipulative applicants or third parties pursuing ulterior motives will maintain dishonesty regardless of deterrents or fear of discovery. Companies may decide that detecting dishonesty and taking appropriate action is the most realistic deterrent. The adoption of a no-nonsense attitude may be interpreted as professionalism, though an aggressively suspicious approach could alienate honest applicants.

If candidates' deceit is uncovered during the selection process, organizations can disqualify applications. Employers faced with a questionable reference may challenge the referee about its authenticity. The current employer of the seemingly 'too good to be true' applicant may admit that he hoped to offload the poorly performing employee onto someone else. Crosschecking with a previous employer may help, as there is less likelihood of a hidden agenda.

If discovery is made at a later stage, companies may hold enquiries, invoke disciplinary procedures, summarily dismiss employees or take legal action. Prosecution may be especially pertinent if deceivers have gained financial advantage through their misrepresentations, as in the case of Alison Durbar (see Chapter 1). Action against staff detected in deception, even if perpetrated several years previously, can be a salutary deterrent. Internal staff will soon learn of these examples and word may spread more widely through gossip or media coverage. The organization's stance may be applauded. An established reputation for stringency may deter potential deceivers and divert them to more apparently gullible targets.

ALTERNATIVE WAYS OF DEALING WITH DECEPTION

Re-evaluation of deception

Whilst direct deceit through deliberate lies, forged documents and fraudulent misrepresentation may be condemned, more ambiguous views are held about the widespread use of impression management during selection.

Deception and impression management are detrimental and dysfunctional if they obstruct the relationship between selector and candidate. The creation of falsely positive images and information distortion may result in erroneous evaluations and decision making. Consequently selectors may regard impression management negatively and wish to eliminate it. Alternatively, selectors and candidates may expect some deceptive behaviour in selection and are prepared to tolerate it. Impression management frequently straddles deception and such behaviour.

An alternative perspective of deception and impression management views it as a positive attribute. According to Rosenfeld et al. (1995) impression management is advantageous when it facilitates positive interpersonal relationships, accurately portrays positive persons or events or products and facilitates successful decision making.

Impression management as a positive attribute

Fletcher (1995) suggests impression management may be recognized as a skill, not a deficit. This perspective regards individuals as social chameleons who change attitudes and behaviours in order to fit into the immediate social situation. The skill involves a strong concern for behaving in a socially appropriate manner and paying great attention to the behaviour of others as cues for their own impression management. Good impression managers use impression management with finesse and are adept at modifying and controlling their tactics. They successfully exhibit different behaviours in different circumstances.

In certain jobs impression management might be a valuable attribute in its own right, especially with the rapidly growing number of people engaged in service industries. Here social influence and persuasiveness are important as in public relations and sales personnel. Consequently, ability in impression management may become an additional competency required for many jobs. Alternatively, impression management may be a more general organizational skill, valuable in increasing the effectiveness of interpersonal relations or in mastering organizational politics to achieve organizational success.

Ways of assessing impression management

If this positive view of impression management is adopted, then there is a strong argument that the skill should be assessed. This may be done in three ways. First, through the social desirability scales contained in many personality questionnaires, described in Chapter 6. Second, using specific measures designed to assess the nature and amount of the individual's propensity for impression management. Rosenfeld et al. (1995) provide a detailed description of four scales – 'Self-Monitoring Scale, Balanced Inventory of Desirable Responding, Self-Presentation Scale and Measure of Ingratiatory Behaviors in Organisations'. Whilst measures are mainly used *within* organizations, Riordan (1989) believes they could be used 'to predict those positions in which different abilities and motivations can promote job success'. Third, re-evaluate the purpose of the interview.

Using the interview as a means of assessing impression management

The interview can be regarded as a sample of the applicant's impression management skills. As these abilities may be very important for success in some jobs, the selector could judge whether the candidate could successfully utilize impression management when needed in future job settings. This may depend on whether ability in impression management is a dispositional characteristic or a behavioural response to situations.

Fletcher (1989b) recounts Anderson's (1988) argument that 'far from seeking to control or eliminate impression management in the interview, we should be deliberately using the interview as a vehicle for eliciting and assessing impression management skills'. Indeed, this was suggested as the sole purpose of the interview. However, it could be inappropriate if self presentation skills lack relevance to subsequent job performance. Arguably interviewers may have actually been evaluating these skills, but deluded themselves they were judging personality.

Rewrite the rules of the interview and convey them to candidates

A more revolutionary way of addressing potential deception is to clarify the behaviour expected in interviews. Fletcher (1990) suggests established rules could be written and conveyed to candidates, forming a 'role description of candidate behaviour in interview'. This would seem a compromise position between the traditional interview approach and the more radical suggestion of using interviews only for investigating and assessing self presentation skills.

Fletcher propounds several advantages of this approach. By specifying the 'rules of the game' both selectors and interviewees would know what was expected of them. The considerable ambiguity and uncertainty currently surrounding behaviour in interviews would be removed and the effects of impression management would be minimized. Common expectations could offset differences in candidates' impression management skills, especially those arising from differential training for interviews. He maintains that the provision of common rules would provide interviewers with some basis for assessing the extent to which candidates can adopt appropriate role behaviours. Such differences as were observed between candidates could be evaluated against that background.

SUMMARY

Deception may be more widespread than selectors imagine. Whilst the impression management component may be regarded as a positive attribute for some jobs, selectors may prefer to tackle deception through proactive or reactive strategies. Proactive methods centre on reviewing and improving the extent and accuracy of information. Reactive measures may involve internal disciplinary action or dismissals whilst external action includes recourse to tribunals and the law.

Organizations may introduce realistic job previews to deflate exaggerated expectations and provide lengthier opportunities to directly observe candidate skills, ability and attributes. This may also be achieved through improving selection methods to combat deception.

Improving selection methods to combat deception

11

Improving the selection system involves both processes and Personnel. Its predominant aim is to focus on verifiable facts and/or behaviour, and selectors may need training to sharpen their skills in this area. Increasing the professionalism of methods, enhancing the effectiveness of personnel and heightening selectors' awareness of strategies used by deceptive candidates constitutes a three pronged attack on deception.

The chapter starts by outlining the general training of personnel and reviewing the choice of selection methods. It then concentrates on the classic trio, initially suggesting adaptations of application forms and interviews to guard against deception. A more specific emphasis on training interviewers to minimise deception is included. Attention then turns to references. As references are the most common way of verifying information, this section is given particular prominence. The legal context is explored before considering ways of improving traditional references or using alternative measures.

TRAINING PERSONNEL

Within the context of deception, training selectors has two objectives:

- to increase professionalism
- to heighten awareness of candidates' deceptive strategies.

Greater professionalism centres on paying more attention to verifiable details, so reducing the candidates' opportunities to deceive. Whilst this is critical for interviewers, it is advantageous for everyone involved in selection.

Some companies insist on compulsory training in selection. Training advocates good practice, emphasizes objectivity, identifies common biases, highlights errors and usually incorporates a module on equal opportunities policy and practice. Practice sessions and videoing give delegates the chance to learn from observations of their own behaviour. Regular refresher courses ensure selectors keep abreast of current and proposed legislation, so avoiding illegal practice.

Whilst training heightens selectors' awareness of good practice, there is no guarantee that guidelines will be implemented, especially by selectors who remain convinced of their innate ability. A possible means of reducing this self deception is to increase selectors' accountability. This focuses their attention on detail and promotes increased objectivity. It encourages keeping documentary records, which generally have to be behaviourally specific and are also a useful defence against possible challenges. Justifying decision making to others tends to discourage personal bias which could be discriminatory.

Selectors also need to be aware of deceptive practices adopted by some candidates. Those used in particular selection methods were described previously, but a more comprehensive recognition of impression management could be incorporated into training. Personnel's appreciation of tactics, their frequent success and the reciprocity of impression management could be valuable. Rosenfeld, Giacalone and Riordan (1995) maintain that Personnel often do not recognize that their own impression management provides behavioural cues which affect the strategies adopted by others.

CHOICE AND USE OF SELECTION METHODS

Best practice suggests that selection methods are used independently. However, as thorough checking of candidate information regarding facts and attributes is central to detecting deception, subsequent verification and crosschecking of key points seems sensible. This may be done in interviews through probing apparent discrepancies and weaknesses or by careful examination of references, qualifications, identity and other relevant information.

The foundation of efficient selection is sound job analysis, from which accurate, up to date job descriptions and personnel specifications are derived. If these are absent or out of date, selectors, agencies and candidates are misled about the qualities needed to fill the vacancy. Advertisement content deserves scrutiny for possible exaggeration of qualities which are unnecessary for successful job performance. Much deception is a response to meeting requirements which may in themselves be misleading.

Specific examination of selection methods, relevant administrative practices and the scoring and interpretation of results could focus on their validity, suitability, ease of faking, job relevance and standardization. It can highlight any poor practices or those which may appear acceptable or justified but disenchant candidates. Organizations may wish to fire-proof themselves against accusations of discrimination, deceit or breaches of employment contract, whether justified or not. Monitoring of selection procedures and test results for adverse impact on minority groups could establish whether practices are unfairly discriminatory. Proof, rather than supposition, can then determine whether strategies are effective or alternatives need to be adopted.

Increasing the use of robust selection methods decreases the likelihood of candidates' practising and succeeding in deception. More valid methods also lessen the chances of candidates' pressing charges of discriminatory practice against the organization. It may be necessary to consider the trade off between test effectiveness and their acceptability to candidates, though Mabey and Iles (1991) suggest that acceptability could be improved with feedback.

Organizations may wish to introduce selection methods which provide more objective and quantifiable assessments of the candidate. Work samples or assessment centres afford direct observations of a candidate's skill, rather than relying solely on candidates' descriptions of their ability. Psychometric tests of personality and ability may be other options. Increasing the length of the selection process, either by multiple methods or several interviews conducted by different staff, allows more people to see the candidate and perhaps form more accurate judgements. Collating all aspects of selection can facilitate the detection of any discrepancies. However, this in itself can create false confidence, and selectors are advised to recall that fraudsters can be clever and well organized.

Should organizations prefer the classic trio, improvements to these methods are suggested in the following sections, beginning with application forms.

APPLICATION FORMS

In minimizing deception, selectors may use application forms for two purposes. Primarily, application forms are the source of verifiable details. Ensuring that all essential information is requested may require job specific forms or additional, specific subsections used in conjunction with general forms. Careful checking of forms can identify omissions or apparent inconsistencies, which may be investigated later.

Improvement of questions

Opportunities for impression management could be reduced by improving the format of open ended questions as follows:

- Ensure questions are relevant, either to the job or the applicant.

- Provide appropriate guidelines on what sort of information would be relevant, e.g. instead of asking candidates to describe a group project specific subheadings could be suggested such as planning, research and task allocation.

- Focus on describing concrete past behaviour rather than abstract future aspirations. This allows recruiters to make their own assessment of candidates.

- Replace blatantly transparent questions on topics such as ambition with subtler questions, so that it is not obvious what information is sought by the selector.

- Reduce self appraisals which could involve self deception or hypothetical responses if applicants lack sufficient work experience to facilitate sound judgements (Keenan, 1983).

Application forms may also be used to channel and highlight the organization's policy towards deception. Forms may deter potential dishonesty by categorical warnings that canvassing will disqualify and advising candidates that appointments will be subject to satisfactory references and any specific checks deemed relevant by the organization. Declarations themselves and explicit statements on the consequences of dishonesty may have more impact.

Declarations

Declarations direct candidates' attention to honesty and nullify subsequent pleas of ignorance. They usually concentrate on three areas – first, the completeness and accuracy of information, second, the omission, withholding, misstating or wilful suppression of facts and third, the consequences of inaccuracies or false information.

Consequences of deception may be detailed as:

- the application is prejudiced
- the application is disqualified

- offer of employment is withdrawn

- disciplinary action will result

- employment is terminated

- summary dismissal

- summary dismissal without notice

- summary dismissal without compensation.

Although declarations refer to information on application forms, some explicitly state that verbal material in interviews will be recognized as contributing to falsehoods. Declarations vary in style, content, compre-

---

DECLARATION

- I declare that to the best of my knowledge and belief the information given on the form is correct.

- I declare that to the best of my knowledge and belief the information given on the form is correct and that I have not withheld any information.

- I declare that to the best of my knowledge and belief the information given on the form is correct and I understand that any information which is deliberately misleading or incorrect, whenever discovered, could lead to my application being disregarded.

- I declare that the information given on this form is true. I understand that if it is subsequently found that any statements are false or misleading, this could lead to the withdrawal of offer or dismissal without notice and without compensation if I have commenced work.

Signed . . . . Date . . . .

Figure 11.1 Typical declarations on application forms

hensiveness and tone, as shown in Figure 11.1, reflecting shades of organizational culture.

INTERVIEWS

In order to reduce deception, improvements could be made in the technical quality of the interview and the interviewer's awareness of deception.

Improving the technical quality of the interview

Many companies are moving away from sole interviews to panel interviews, so that more than one person's judgement is available. This is also advantageous as the board interview is less susceptible to impression management (Fletcher, 1989). The inclusion of someone the candidate is going to work with may moderate self assessments and self promotion, since the candidate's subsequent performance will have to correspond with the given impression.

Structure in interviews is advantageous. It promotes consistency and concentrates on job relevant areas. Focusing on verifiable information makes responses more productive, so limiting the opportunity and likelihood of self presentation and aggrandizement. Structure has other benefits. It reduces ambiguity and uncertainty, which favour impression management, and prevents candidates from controlling the topics of discussion. It therefore will help select qualified candidates and not impression managers (Rosenfeld et al., 1995).

Training of interviewers to minimize deception

In order to minimize deception, interviewers would be trained to:

- **Establish rapport**
  This facilitates candidate self disclosure and encourages authenticity.

- **Focus on verifiable behaviour**
  This encourages candidates to use more accurate self presentation strategies, and present themselves in a way that is closer to what they really believe. 'Individuals moderate their self-assessments when they know they will be subject to subsequent external checking' (Fletcher, 1989, p.275).

Key verifiable areas centre on achievements, work responsibilities and job competence. If the reality of the information cannot be checked, interviewees have free rein to let their imagination run wild. The more difficult information is to check, the more likely candidates are to aggrandize.

- **Recognize impression management techniques**
  Recognition of different strategies is an additional perspective which illuminates candidate behaviour. It enables interviewers to identify impression management techniques and the situations in which they are likely to occur and to take account of them in decision making. If impression management tactics are regarded as deceptive, they can be eliminated. If they are perceived more positively, they can be assessed as personality attributes and characteristics of self presentation style. Awareness also assists interviewers to distinguish between candidates who are deliberately deceiving from those who are misleading unintentionally through over-confidence and optimism. Familiarity with impression management could therefore increase the fairness of the interview.

- **Be prepared to probe answers**
  Probing could check information, uncover weaknesses and reduce tendencies to exaggerate.

The focus on verifiable material necessitates accurate checking of information. Traditionally this is achieved by using references, which are the subject of the following section.

IMPROVEMENT OF REFERENCES

References are the most widely used method of substantiating candidate claims. Although they are open to abuse, the fundamental principles governing the process appear to be sound. The best predictor of future behaviour is past behaviour, which ideally has been ascertained from an independent assessor's lengthy observations of the candidate in a natural setting. The assessor can therefore verify the applicant's accounts, especially previous job performance, and provide independent assessments of his abilities and other work related behaviours.

Maximizing the potential of references necessitates obtaining the information without the fallibility described previously. Their accuracy and validity may be enhanced by improving the reference request and report, with a special emphasis on the quality, precision and relevance of information. Stronger vigilance in selection of referees could be beneficial, as referees' integrity is crucial. Similarly it may be possible to upgrade the effectiveness of Personnel's checking procedures.

In this section an initial summary of the law on references establishes a broader context. This is followed by devising an organizational policy, improving the format of references, checking their content, authentication and consideration of alternatives to traditional references.

THE LAW ON REFERENCES

Spring v. Guardian Assurance plc (1994)

Spring was a sales manager with Guardian Assurance. He was appointed in conformity with the rules of LAUTRO, the self regulatory body governing the life assurance industry. He was dismissed without warning and had his name removed from the LAUTRO register of Guardian Assurance representatives.

He then applied to work for Scottish Amicable, another LAUTRO member. Under LAUTRO rules, Scottish Amicable had to write to Spring's previous employer asking for a character and experience reference. The reference was damning and described as a 'kiss of death'. It accused Spring of dishonesty, misselling and giving poor advice to clients. The reference was not compiled maliciously, but the individual writing it had not made the proper checks to confirm the information provided to her was accurate. Scottish Amicable decided not to employ Spring, as did two other companies.

The High Court decision

Spring took Guardian Assurance to the High Court. He claimed damages for loss of earnings due to their falsehoods and/or negligent misstatements. Furthermore he claimed that they had breached an implied term in his contract that any reference would be compiled with care. His claim was upheld in the High Court. Judge Lever accepted that:

- there had been a negligent misstatement

- the employer owed a duty of care to employees over the preparation of references

- the employer had not acted out of malice but had not carried out the kind of detailed investigation which would have shown that Spring had not acted dishonestly.

The Court of Appeal

Guardian Assurance appealed and the appeal was upheld. The Court of Appeal ruled that:

- there was no such thing as duty of care to an employee in the preparation of a reference

- the only remedy available to an employee in circumstances such as those facing Spring was to sue for defamation.

Spring could not have won such an action, since under the libel laws the employers would have had the defence of qualified privilege, which arises where there is a need for frank and free communication provided there is no evidence of malice.

Lord Justice Glidewell said employers should be able to express honest opinions fully and frankly about something they believed to be true, even if it is not, provided the motive was not one of malice.

The House of Lords

Spring appealed to the House of Lords. Five senior judges heard the case. Lords Woolf, Lowry, Slynn and Goff, by a majority, gave a judgement in favour of Spring. They concluded that his claim that employers did have a duty of care in preparing a reference was valid. Lord Keith dissented, arguing that the outcome of the ruling would be to inhibit employers from giving frank references and that the proper course of action when an individual was aggrieved was in a claim for defamation. The key points of the judgement are:

- Employers owe a duty of care to employees that the facts are accurate when providing references.

- There may be an implied term in an employment contract that if a reference is supplied it will be supplied with due care and skill.

- Such an implied term might exist even where there was no legal obligation on an employer to provide a reference.

- The obligation arising from the implied term can apply even after the employee has left the employer.

- If employers fail to do this and, as a result, an employee suffers a financial loss, employers can be liable to compensate that employee for the consequences of their negligence.

Lord Keith felt that referees might be deterred from speaking frankly, may prefer not to give references at all or may give bland, unhelpful references. However, Lord Slynn argued that if fewer references are given they will be of higher quality. He said referees could state whether there were any limitations in the parameters of the reference, e.g. limited acquaintance as to time or situation, and that employers could make a disclaimer of liability to the subject and recipient of the reference.

DEVISING AN ORGANIZATIONAL POLICY ON REFERENCES

A review of current strategy could evaluate the importance of references and consider available options. These include formulating an organizational policy, delegating reference checks to outside agencies, replacing references with other checks or abandoning the whole reference procedure.

If it is concluded that the reference procedure adds value, then upgrading and strengthening the process would appear sensible, especially if the current system is half hearted and implemented spasmodically. The more structured and precise the policy about references, the more likely it is to be taken seriously by all concerned. If agencies are involved in the selection procedure, organizational policy should clearly demarcate responsibilities.

Identify the information needed

It is important to adopt specific goals and identify the proof that will be needed. An organization may wish to decide whether it seeks details of qualities, facts or characteristics about a prospective employee. Such decisions will determine the comprehensiveness of information required and whether the company devises general or job specific references. In turn, the detail and length of request may influence the choice of referees and method of contacting them.

The choice of referees

Most organizations require two or three references for each candidate and may draw these from one source such as a previous employer or from several areas such as a previous employer and a personal reference. The timing of reference requests may also affect choice. If reference checks are sought for shortlisted candidates, character references and past employers may be favoured, as they can be contacted at any time. Issues of time and cost may have to be balanced against perceived benefits of additional information available before selection decision making. If references are taken at later stages, current employers may be more appropriate.

A structured approach

It is important that referees can actually pinpoint and describe the qualities the organization wishes to check. Determining the category of referees instead of allowing candidates free choice gives the company greater control, indicates a more structured approach to references and signals to candidates that references are taken seriously. As a general principle it appears that the more detail a candidate is asked to supply, the greater the difficulty in faking.

Guidance on suitability of referees

Choice of referee is largely determined by the perceived function of the reference. If detail is sought on work experience, then the reference has to be sent to someone who has observed the candidate and can supply relevant details. This tends to be the line manager rather than a more senior manager or personnel department.

Some organizations stipulate clearly who can and cannot be a referee. Detailed guidance may clarify suitability and eligibility, whilst specifically identifying unacceptable referees as a relative, contemporary, person under eighteen or a friend. Employers are usually the most acceptable referees for people with work experience and personal or academic referees are acceptable for those entering the job market. The latter may be more clearly defined as a specified tutor, head of department or professor.

Obtaining referee details

Essential details of referees – their full names, titles, positions, phone numbers and full addresses – need to be established at some stage. Both address and phone number may be requested, regardless of whether checks are to be made in writing or orally, since the other medium may be used to authenticate references. Relationship to the candidate and length of time known are also salient.

Seeking information in interviews provides an opportunity to emphasize the importance of references and helps the candidate to identify the most relevant person, but is difficult if candidates do not have the necessary details to hand. The benefit of asking candidates to provide written information on referees is that time allows research and inclusion of detail such as postcodes and phone numbers which may ultimately hasten the whole procedure.

Informing the candidate

Emphasizing the importance of references to candidates at an early stage may minimize subsequent exaggeration and false claims. The application form, interviewer and offer of employment may state clearly that the job offer is made subject to satisfactory references. Candidates may be informed about the company's preference for phone or written references and the point at which referees are approached may be indicated on the application form. The main alternatives are:

• as required

• before offering employment

• when posts or provisional offers have been made

• when employment offers have been made and accepted.

Candidates' permission to approach a referee may be sought as a question such as 'Do you wish to be consulted before an existing employer is contacted?' or a statement such as 'Referees will be contacted at any time unless you indicate otherwise.'

THE REFERENCE REQUEST

Format

Structured references appear to be infinitely preferable to unstructured references. They enjoy increasing popularity, largely because the organization rather than the referee is directing the amount and content of information. Structured references facilitate consistency. Gaps are more readily apparent and it is easier to compare references.

Ways of seeking information

Reference requests may adopt one of two basic approaches, each having its advantages and disadvantages. One method requests the referee to confirm information given by the candidate. This is usually quicker. However, if the referee notices apparent inaccuracies she may be reluctant to spend time on further investigation, especially if the discrepancies appear slight, faulty memory causes self doubt or if she appreciates that disclosure could reflect on the candidate's veracity.

Generally the referee is expected to answer specific questions. This has the advantage of supplying the organization with completely independent data. However, assembling the information may require more time and effort, resulting in the referee's temptation to rely on memory or seek the information directly from the candidate.

The recording of answers

There are also two approaches to recording answers. Answers may be written in the spaces next to the questions or elsewhere. The latter gives the referee greater freedom to provide information which may be very valuable to the organization, while the former allows gaps to be identified more readily and also controls the amount of information provided. Some requests involve rating scales where appropriate alternatives are marked.

Method of contacting referees

The complexity and length of the reference may determine how the manner of its completion. Sending references by fax or post allows the referee time to assimilate accompanying material before completing the reference, but completion may be delayed. Phoning the referee is speedier, but means that the referee usually lacks additional written information. The selector may use the reference form to conduct an interview, record the referee's answers then send the completed form to the referee for signature and confirmation of the information's accuracy.

Content of the reference request

Basic rules

A number of basic rules helps to obtain a good reference:

- Provide as much structure as possible.

- All information requested should be job related, whether concerned with facts or attributes. Job analysis should be used to identify behaviour forming the content of questions and Schmitt (1976) believes that this should improve the reliability and validity of references.

- It is improper to ask the referee something you are not permitted to ask the applicant unless these are job related, e.g. details about marital status.

- Information sought should be as specific as possible, especially if required on personality or behaviour, and sought consistently about all applicants.

- Seek facts and behaviours rather than evaluations.

Type of information sought

References may seek three types of information – facts, behaviours and evaluations. There is a strong argument that they should be limited to facts rather than opinions, as more objective information is less prone to error than subjective evaluations of the candidate's personality. In order to achieve greater objectivity, companies may adapt existing references by changing the phraseology of questions, for example by asking how many days the candidate was absent rather than for an opinion as to whether attendance is good or poor. Figure 11.2 lists the main types of factual and judgemental information obtained in references.

Subjective reference assessments, whilst potentially valuable, are prone to inaccuracy. Their accuracy is likely to be enhanced by increasing specificity and establishing whether the referee has had opportunities to observe relevant behaviours. Rather than asking about personality in general, it might be preferable to ask the referee to supply specific examples of identified traits or behaviours. This specificity can prompt the referee to re-evaluate original judgements and offset errors.

Bias in references may be overcome or reduced through the use of closed questions, so strengthening comparisons between different applicants. Dobson (1989) suggests other methods:

- **Forced choice items** to measure specific attributes, e.g. which of the following is most characteristic of the individual?

  a dynamic   **b** calm   **c** a good problem solver

- **Ranking methods**. The referee selects and ranks the individual's five main strengths and weaknesses from a list of relevant and equally desirable characteristics. These may include energy, self assurance, sociability, equability, leadership, problem solving ability and forcefulness.

- **Behaviourally anchored rating scales**, where each part of the scale is behaviourally defined, as shown in Figure 11.3.

- **Relative comparisons** where the referee is asked to judge a person in relation to their peers or those of similar age and experience.

Conclusion of the reference

The final question of many structured references asks whether there is any reason why an employee should not be hired. Frequently an open ended section is included in which the referee can add anything else judged to be important.

For clarification of records, reference requests may seek further detail from the referee at the point of signing and dating the request. This may include position, name and address of organization, telephone number and extension. Such information should confirm details given by the candidate and can be useful if subsequent checks are made. Additional details may be sought such as the referee's position, length of time known to the applicant and in what capacity.

OBJECTIVE INFORMATION

Job related   Academic

job title/position   degree
duties   class
responsibilities   A level subjects, grades and dates
number of people supervised   GCSE subjects, grades and dates of
                                         any failed examinations
                                         NVQS – subjects and levels

Personnel

length of time employed at that company
starting and finishing dates – in years and months
full time or part time
number of hours per week if part time
basic salary at commencement of employment
current basic salary
number of days absent in a year and/or sickness
number of days late in a year
presence of any past or current disciplinary proceedings and details
reason for leaving

SUBJECTIVE INFORMATION

ability to do job   strengths
competencies   weaknesses
experience   personality
interpersonal skills   certain qualities
e.g. get on with peers   e.g. leadership
     supervisors   initiative
     clients   honesty
     customers

Figure 11.2 Main objective and subjective information obtained from references

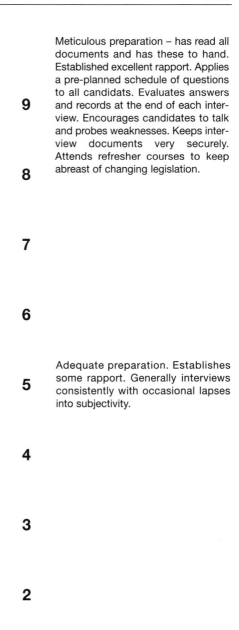

Meticulous preparation – has read all documents and has these to hand. Established excellent rapport. Applies a pre-planned schedule of questions to all candidats. Evaluates answers

9 and records at the end of each interview. Encourages candidates to talk and probes weaknesses. Keeps interview documents very securely. Attends refresher courses to keep

8 abreast of changing legislation.

Sound preparations. Has read most
relevant documents. Establishes good   **7**
rapport. Interviews consistently. Is
security conscious.

6

Adequate preparation. Establishes
some rapport. Generally interviews
5 consistently with occasional lapses
into subjectivity.

4

Makes little attempt to establish rapport. Does not always listen carefully to   **3**
responses. Makes subjective judge-
ments which are not recorded.

2

Conducts unprepared interviews in
unsuitable surroundings. Asks irrele-
1 vant and discriminatory questions.
Does not keep to interview schedule.

Figure 11.3   Example of interviewer behaviourally anchored rating scale

Alternatives to the traditional reference

Not all references need to be complex. Some may consist of just three questions:

• How long have you known the candidate?

• Is there any reason why we should not employ him/her?

• Is there anything that you wish to add in support of his/her application? (Hyde, 1982).

Sometimes more precise questions may be asked if the reference request has been specifically designed on the basis of the job description. Figure 11.4 shows some characteristics needed in managerial positions, and the organization can determine whether the referee responds with a brief answer or is given space to elaborate.

Recently situational references have been used (O'Sullivan, 1996). These are job specific and centred on key competencies: ability to do the job, interpersonal skills, motivation, ability to work in a team, reliability and ability to cope with pressure. A seven point scale was used to anchor the competencies, as illustrated in Figure 11.5.

Does he/she generally meet deadlines?

How many job appraisals does he/she conduct in a year?

Has he/she been involved in recruitment and selection?

How many staff has he/she had line responsibility for?

Figure 11.4 Part of a specific job related reference

ACCOMPANYING MATERIAL TO BE SENT TO THE REFEREE

Accompanying material serves many purposes, including gaining the referee's co-operation. This may be vital in obtaining a valid reference. Information may help the referee to complete the reference as efficiently and easily as possible and can be a good public relations exercise. The reference request is therefore likely to be accompanied by the following three items.

A letter

This needs to state the candidate's name and target job fully, clearly and unambiguously, especially if a change of name has occurred. The letter also expresses recognition and appreciation of the referee's time and effort. Some letters stress the importance of the reference, but this may put unwelcome pressure on the referee, as the applicant's failure to acquire a job may be attributed to the referee.

General guidance

Relevant background information such as a job description and person specification is useful, as is advice on the type of information sought by the organization. Referees may not have met certain behaviour in the applicant and advice on whether to provide hypothetical responses or 'Not Applicable' answers helps referees and furthers consistency for the organization.

A stamped envelope addressed to the appropriate person

This speeds up the return of the reference, eliminates uncertainties and is courteous. If this is omitted, the referee may delay responding or ignore the request.

THE ORGANIZATION'S CHECKING PROCEDURE

An effective checking procedure encompasses the following four strands:

- **Administration**. An efficient documentation system logs all stages, pinpointing unanswered reference requests.

- **Assessing and checking information** against details already provided by the candidate in the CV, application form or interview. Careful verification of factual details, e.g. salary and dates may be crucial and there may be an opportunity to compare applicant and referee handwriting. Staff may need to be trained to assess more detailed information.

- **An established policy to deal with discrepancies**. This needs to make provision for at least two eventualities – the unfavourable reference and the one that fails to materialize. Although negative references may be taken at face value, it may be advisable to probe the facts on which the opinion was founded and ascertain whether there were any unusu-

ABILITY TO DO THE JOB

The job requires a high level of skills either dealing with people or dealing with products/equipment which are damaged. How would the applicant be likely to react to situations where customers or colleagues are confronting him/her or where resources need to be stretched?

He/she will always consistently apply knowledge and experience and be able to overcome most major problems which confront him/her.	6
	5
He/she would usually apply knowledge and experience and be wholly able to overcome some problems which confront him/her.	4
	3
He/she would not be able to deal with a situation of this kind without help and supervision because he/she lacks the technical knowledge or the necessary inter-personal skills in dealing with people.	2
	1
He/she would not be able to cope in any situation of this kind even with support or help.	0

Figure 11.5 A typical item in a situational reference
Source: O'Sullivan (1996)

al or mitigating factors. This may also apply when previous employers are silent about key attributes, e.g. when honesty is not mentioned in a reference for someone handling money. Missing references present other problems. Follow up necessitates persistence, which may be costly and time consuming, but possibly worthwhile.

* **A system of checking the authenticity of references.** This may be done systematically, or by random spot checks. Thanking the referee by follow up phone calls or written acknowledgements is a courtesy which also alerts the designated referees and the selector if references have been intercepted or substituted. The applicant who has used references fraudulently is unlikely to have planned for this contingency. However, the system is not infallible since it is often impossible to outmanoeuvre someone who is determined to deceive.

In conclusion, organizations may improve their reference procedure by reviewing and clearly defining their reference system, and then following it consistently. Reference requests are likely to be more valid if they are structured, job related, behaviourally specific and concentrate on facts. Completion by appropriate people who are able to furnish meaningful comments is essential. The organization's policy will have determined the type of information required and the best people able to provide this. A clearly formulated system for checking references is crucial and needs consistent implementation. Without this, the procedure is nullified.

SUMMARY

The proposed methods of minimizing deception have focused on increasing the professionalism of selectors and their awareness of deception. Application forms can be used to draw candidates' attention to honesty and provide verifiable information. Increased structure in interviews may reduce impression management and also highlight detail which can be corroborated. A more structured and systematic approach to references could enhance their effectiveness.

Although improvements to references have been suggested, there are other ways of authenticating candidates' claims, achievements and attributes. Consequently organizations may choose to use supplementary or alternative checks.

Other checks on candidates

12

Selectors may wish to substantiate the information supplied by the candidate, and investigate whether any potentially damaging facts have been omitted. There are two main types of checks – factual verification and enquiries into candidate characteristics such as honesty. The necessity for supplementary checks and their nature may be determined by the responsibilities of the job and in certain occupations there are legal requirements to confirm information.

This chapter initially deals with factual confirmation of matters of public record. Other measures designed to check a candidate's general ability and/or work behaviour are examined, followed by health issues. The focus then shifts to specific attributes, especially honesty, with a detailed review of integrity testing. The chapter concludes by considering employers' attitudes to checks.

FACTUAL CHECKS

Authentication of qualifications, identity, criminal record and financial standing tend to be made in two ways – by the organization itself or by outside bodies conducting general status checks. The distinction is not always clear cut, e.g. some organizations conduct their own investigations into a candidate's financial position whilst others may limit this to a credit rating check which is entrusted to an independent body.

Qualifications

Authenticating educational achievements or other qualifications can be achieved by requesting applicants to produce relevant certificates. Candidates can be asked to bring examination certificates, degrees and certificates of professional membership to the interview. Photocopied material is unacceptable because it is difficult to detect an original which has been altered before photocopying. The possession of a current driving licence is essential for some occupations and can be proved in the same way. Inspection of other relevant documents, such as a motor insurance certificate, may be required for some company insurance schemes. However, production of documents is of limited value, unless they are validated by someone familiar with them who can detect alterations and inconsistencies, or notice features such as the presence of ten penalty points on a driving licence. It is not unknown for forgeries to be presented or for foreign educational qualifications to be accepted without checking their equivalence to British qualifications.

Identity

Checks on the candidate's identity commonly include inspection of relevant documentation such as a birth certificate or passport. Sometimes a marriage certificate may be needed to verify a change of name, otherwise candidate Pearl Overly could be unchallenged when she produces a degree in the name of Pearl Underly. Sometimes photographic evidence is sought.

In some cases identity may need to be established to comply with legislation on immigration status under the Asylum and Immigration Act 1996. However, in these circumstances a document has to be produced before the employment begins, and has to:

- appear to relate to the employee
- be one of the documents listed in Figure 12.1
- be made in accordance with the regulations and kept by the employer.

Other factual checks

Banks and other financial institutions have a strong interest in the financial integrity of prospective staff and may conduct their own enquiries in these areas. There is also a core of other important personal data that can be assembled at low cost. This includes credit ratings, which are derived from the information about the failure to complete previous credit transactions, and county court judgements.

Other areas for verification may include school and university records, all employers for at least the previous five years, doctors, bankers, credit

1. A document issued by a previous employer, the Inland Revenue, the Benefits Agency, the Contributions Agency or the Employment Service, which contains the person's National Insurance number.

2. A passport describing the person as a British citizen, or as having the right of abode in or re-admission to the United Kingdom.

3. A passport containing a certificate of entitlement to right of abode.

4. A certificate or registration or naturalization as a British citizen.

5. A birth certificate issued in the UK or Republic of Ireland.

6. A passport or national identity card issued by a member state of the European Economic Area which describes the person as a national of that state.

7. A passport or other travel document endorsed to show that the person has current leave to enter or remain in the United Kingdom and is not precluded from taking the employment in question, or a Home Office letter confirming this.

8. A UK residence permit issued to a national of a member state of the European Economic Area.

9. A passport or other travel document endorsed to show that the person has a right of residence in the UK as a family member of a named person who is a national of a member state of the European Economic Area and resident in the UK.

10. A letter issed by the Home Office indicating that the person has a permission to take employment.

11. A letter issued by the Home Office indicating that the person is a British citizen.

12. A work permit or other approval to take employment issued by the DfEE.

Figure 12.1 Suitable documents to check status under the Asylum and Immigration Act 1996

Source: CRE (1996) The Asylum and Immigration Act 1996. Implications for racial equality. Provisional guidance for employers on compliance with the Race Relations Act 1976.

card companies, checking with neighbours, the electoral roll and the telephone directory.

Criminal records and court activities

Application forms may ask applicants whether they have criminal records or ongoing court activities. Many organizations rely heavily on the honesty of applicants. However, specific investigations may be undertaken in certain areas where there is a responsibility to ensure that new employees are fit people to work with particularly vulnerable groups such as the elderly, the ill or children. Some public sector departments such as social services and education have access to centrally held criminal records, though this facility is not generally available.

Rehabilitation of Offenders Act 1974

Criminal records of about seven million people are held on computer at Scotland Yard. Some criminal convictions can become 'spent' or ignored after a 'rehabilitation period'. This is set from the date of conviction, and a general outline is provided in Table 12.1, though sentences with varying rehabilitation periods have not been included. Currently once an offence is spent under the Act, a person's name should be removed from the register of criminal records, though a custodial sentence of 30 months or more is never spent. Generally, after the rehabilitation period, ex-offenders are not obliged to mention the conviction when applying for a job.

Health questionnaires and medical examinations

Employers' concern over candidates' fitness for work is not just a matter of personal interest. It may have implications for health and safety legislation, the well being of other employees, customers and the public, and damage to property and equipment. The applicant's fitness to operate machinery, propensity for accidents and likelihood of experiencing stress are all areas the organization may wish to investigate.

Checks may be in the nature of questions on the application form or a longer and more specific health questionnaire. Number of days absent from work through sickness may be investigated and verification sought in a reference request to a previous employer. Some organizations require their

Sentence	Rehabilitation period	
	People aged 18 18 or over when convicted	People aged under 18 when convicted
Prison sentence of 6 months or less	7 years	3½ years
Prison sentence of more than 6 months but less than 2 ½ years	10 years	5 years
Borstal (abolished in 1983)	7 years	7 years
Detention centre (abolished in 1988)	3 years	3 years
Fines, probation, compensation, community service, combination order and curfew order	5 years	2½ years
Absolute discharge	6 months	6 months

Table 12.1 The 'spending' of offences under the Rehabilitation of Offenders Act 1974

candidates to undergo a medical examination by the company's doctor or the individual's GP. Checks on specific attributes of direct work relevance may be conducted. For example, a company wishing to check colour vision may use the Ishi Hara test. A candidate's smoking behaviour may be judged relevant if the firm bans smoking on site, and staff may be asked to sign agreements that they will not smoke on company premises.

Drugs testing

Drug abuse is an increasing problem within organizations and an IPD survey showed that employees were taking drugs in one in six firms (Howlings, 1996). Organizations are increasingly considering whether they should have a drugs policy and whether drugs testing is appropriate. In the USA drugs testing is now standard practice and according to the American Management Association's latest research, 90% of major US companies test employees or recruits for illegal drug use (Greenberg, 1996). The survey found that 94% of companies that test job applicants will withdraw the job offer if the results are positive. British firms appear reluctant to follow the American route and there is uncertainty about the extent of drugs testing in Britain. However, in September 1996, Grampian Police became the first force to adopt this practice. It introduced random drugs testing for employees and all recruits have to take a compulsory drugs test.

Whilst the above methods focus on a candidate's specific attributes, in other cases it may be considered more helpful to have a broader picture. This may be gained informally by networking with others who have knowledge of the person, or by the use of agencies which can vet the applicant on the employer's behalf.

Comprehensive checks

It is comparatively rare for organizations to conduct comprehensive checks on potential employees, though these are done for applicants to the police force and entrants wishing to work in some government departments. Security clearance involves lengthy, in-depth checks where other people are questioned about the applicant, his affiliations, friendships and both general and specific behaviour. This is invariably costly and time consuming. Private companies may employ investigative agencies to undertake similar tasks, though their role and value may be limited. Ways of improving service from this source appear to consist of checking the company's reputation, and ascertaining clearly what can and cannot be achieved by its efforts.

CHECKS ON ABILITY, HONESTY AND INTEGRITY

Reliance on the classic trio of methods sometimes precludes a practical assessment of whether candidates can actually demonstrate their professed skills. A company may consider including work samples such as typing tests, or a candidate may be requested to produce samples of work, as in a portfolio of art, photography, fashion drawings or architectural plans. Whilst these could be the work of someone else, close questioning about the composition or construction of such samples should not only confirm authenticity, but may provide additional knowledge of the applicant's practical and technical skills. Alternatively, a candidate may be given data and asked to prepare a presentation within the confines of the selection process. This has the further advantage of measuring a candidate's resourcefulness and ability to work within time constraints.

Sometimes it may be thought necessary to attempt to judge a candidate's honesty objectively rather than through normal selection methods. The two main attempts to detect dissimulation have been the lie detector and honesty tests.

The lie detector

To some people, all deception in selection could be stopped dead in its tracks if only employers routinely screened all applicants with a lie detector. Lie detectors have been available for decades and have been used by a number of very prestigious employers such as the FBI and the CIA where matters of national and international security have been at stake. The lie detector is seen by many people as an easy, high-tech solution to the problems of disloyalty, crime and dishonesty. Others are not so sure. They see the lie detector as a capricious, unreliable tool which, while masquerading in a scientific and technical guise is, in fact, a threat to the civil liberties of all freedom loving peoples throughout the world. The lie detector is a device which arouses strong and opposing views.

The basis of the lie detector

The lie detector has its basis in the structure of the human nervous system. Broadly speaking our nervous systems can be divided into two parts: the *central nervous system* and the autonomic nervous system. The central nervous system controls our conscious behaviour such as moving our face so that we can smile, synchronizing fingers so that we can type and orchestrating the muscles of our larynx so that we can speak. Because these and other actions are under conscious control we can easily change them in order to meet our goals. If our goal is to deceive other people we can smile in order to obtain their approval, write an untruthful CV or tell lies at an interview.

The other part of our nervous system, the *autonomic nervous system*, looks after body systems such as breathing, regulation of body heat, digestion and some sexual functions such as orgasms. Normally, these activities are not under conscious control. An important function of the autonomic nervous system is to prepare our body systems to meet emergencies and cope with emotional situations. If we are facing an emergency or emotional situation, one part of the autonomic nervous system, the *sympathetic nervous system* (SNS), goes into action. Digestion is stopped. Glucose is released into the blood stream ready to supply the muscles with energy. Breathing becomes quicker to provide an abundant supply of oxygen. Some of the blood supply to the skin is diverted so it is available to the muscles involved in either fighting or running away. Heart rate is increased so that blood and its supplies of energy circulate faster. We also sweat more in order to keep our temperature down when huge amounts of energy are released. All this happens without our conscious control. If the emergency or the emotional situation is intense we will be aware of many of these changes. Under normal circumstances the processes of the sympathetic autonomic system are not noticed. But they are constantly active in order to maintain our bodies in the proper state of readiness to deal with our environment. If we are relaxed, the sympathetic autonomous system will be quiet. Its activity will increase slightly if we need to mobilize resources for a routine task. The sympathetic nervous system will be quite active when we face a challenge. It will go into overdrive if we encounter an emergency.

The lie detector is founded on the idea that when we tell lies we feel challenged and emotional. Unbeknown to our central nervous system, the level of our autonomic activity will increase. Hence, if we measure the level of activity in the sympathetic autonomic system and it shows an unexpected increase, one explanation might be that we are lying.

Furthermore, we will have no conscious control and will not be able to suppress these tell tale signals.

The lie detector hardware

The lie detector is simply a machine which picks up and graphs the activity of the sympathetic autonomic nervous system. It would be unwise to graph just one facet of the SNS such as breathing because this might be influenced by an artifact such as a stuffy room where the air contains little oxygen. Usually a lie detector records and graphs several aspects of the SNS and hence the more accurate and and more technical name for the lie detector is the 'polygraph'. Typically, the polygraph will measure heart rate, blood volume, blood pressure, breathing rate, and sweating. Cardiovascular activity is well recognized as responding to emotion and our language has many phrases linking the two concepts. Often we talk about the blushing bride, being white with fear, being chicken-hearted, and our hearts falling into our boots. The most easily accessed index of cardiovascular activity is the heart rate or pulse. In the polygraph, the measurement of the heart rate is more sophisticated than a nurse with a watch counting the number of beats per minute. The polygraph will work from an electrocardiogram (ECG) which captures the electrical activity of the beating heart by means of electrodes attached to the chest wall. The blood pressure and blood volume are measured by plethysmograph which takes the form of a rubber cup which fits around a finger. Sweating is usually measured by electrodes attached to the hand and they measure how well the skin conducts electricity. When we perspire our sweat contains minute amounts of salts. These salts allow electricity to pass more easily. These changes are therefore called the galvanic skin response (GNS). Breathing rate is often measured by a pressure device (manometer) that is activated rubber bands placed around the chest.

A crucial point is that these devices are measuring minute changes. The changes in the galvanic skin response, for example, involve only fractions of a volt – much less than a hundredth of the electrical potential contained in a typical battery. Such small changes mean that the instruments must be applied by skilled people: a badly applied electrode can produce wildly misleading information about the level of activity in the sympathetic autonomic nervous system. Typically, polygraph operators undergo eight weeks' training and many recruits are drawn from the ranks of retired police officers (British Psychological Society, 1986).

Another complication arises from the sheer volume of data that are produced. Computers are now used to average data over several seconds in order to remove the erratic and spiky fluctuations seen in earlier devices. Of course, the computer programming is arbitrary to the extent that someone needs to decide the precise details of the averaging process and the appropriate time base that is used. Each of these decisions has an impact on the results from a polygraph test.

A final complication is produced by the fact that there is a time lag in some autonomic functions but not in others. For example, breathing rate usually changes a few seconds after an emotional experience whilst the galvanic skin response follows almost immediately. These lags need to be taken into account by the procedures which are adopted when attempting to use the polygraph to detect deception in selection or other settings.

Polygraph procedures

After setting up the equipment the procedure is demonstrated to the subject. Research suggests that the demonstration is a crucial part of the process because they induce the suspect to have faith in the accuracy of the polygraph. Sometimes, polygraph operators use deceit to achieve credibility. They demonstrate the ability of the polygraph to detect which card the subject has extracted from an ostensibly normal pack of playing cards. In fact, the pack of cards is often rigged or marked (Bull, 1985; Elliot, 1982) After the demonstration, the next stage is to calibrate the readings obtained from the polygraph. People show great differences in the activity of their sympathetic autonomic nervous systems. Some people are very 'jittery' and show high levels. Some people are so relaxed that their SNS shows little reaction to a bomb blast in the neighbourhood. The first stage is to establish the base rate of activity which will be later used as a comparison. The base rate is usually established by asking a series of innocuous questions such as 'is your name . . . ', 'are you employed by . . . ', 'is the day today . . . ' and 'is the weather cloudy'. About half the 'base rate questions' will require a 'yes' response and about half the questions will require a 'no' response.

Once the base rate has been established, the interrogation may proceed in two ways. With the direct question method, the person will be asked questions such as, 'Have you ever been dismissed by a previous employer?', 'Have you ever been involved in fraud?', 'Have you ever been involved in a sexual activity with people below the age of 16?', 'Have you ever stolen valuables or money from an employer?'. This direct questioning technique is probably the only method which could be used in employment settings. The alternative technique is the guilty knowledge technique which is more applicable to criminal settings. In the guilty knowledge technique a list of words is read to the person under interrogation. Some words will be neutral and others will involve information which is known only to the guilty person and the authorities. For example suppose that an emerald necklace was the only item of jewellery included in the haul from a robbery. The suspect attached to the polygraph would be read a list of items such as ruby ring, emerald necklace, diamond bracelet. Unfortunately, the guilty knowledge technique can sometimes implicate innocent witnesses or people who accidently happen to know the details of a crime.

When the interrogation is over the analyst would compare the polygraph results on sensitive questions with the results on neutral questions. If the ECG and GSR readings during and shortly after the subject replied 'no' to a question about sexual episodes with children was similar to the base rate readings she would be judged to be telling the truth. If the autonomic responses were two or three times higher when the emerald necklace was mentioned she would be judged to be guilty of the theft.

Polygraph weaknesses

The polygraph has several weaknesses. First, it assumes that people are emotional when lies are told. This assumption is probably true for a large majority of people. But there are some people such as psychopaths or unscrupulous people who believe that telling lies is the normal way to behave and who feel little or no emotion when engaging in quite exploitative deceptions. With these people, any system of detection which is based on autonomic activity engendered by emotion is bound to fail. In practice, the situation is made worse by the fact that the people whose deception tends to be on the biggest scale and whose deceptions it is most important to detect are likely to be the very people who show least emotions and hence the least autonomic activity.

The second weakness is that even very sensitive and expressive people can bring their autonomic processes under control. It is not totally accurate to say that autonomic activity is automatic. There are whole technologies of biofeedback which are designed to achieve this aim. In biofeedback, a person is linked to one of the devices used in the polygraph such as a cardiograph which measures heart rate and a display showing the heart rate is easily visible. A reasonable target for the heart rate is set and the person relaxes while at the same time tries to bring the heart rate down to the target level. After a little time the person learns the frame of mind, the actions and thoughts which tend to lower the heart rate. Slowly but surely they are able to control their pulse and bring the heart rate down to the target level. The approach need not be so high-tech. Many yoga classes and relaxation classes teach techniques such as concentrating on one's being and use of constructive imagination which help bring the processes of the sympathetic autonomic system under con-scious control. Indeed, anyone faced with an unwelcome lie detector test would be well advised to enrol at the local relaxation classes!

Someone really intent on beating a lie detector can easily take extra action. They can alter the base rate levels that are used to calibrate their replies. If the base rate levels can be elevated then the elevated responses to lies will not stand out and the lies will not be detected. Elevating the base rate is easy. All that needs to be done is to think of something embar-rassing while the neutral questions are being asked. Another effective strategy is to inflict pain on oneself by, for example, biting one's lip or pressing one's foot on a sharp tack in one's shoe, while the base rate data are being obtained.

The cumulative impact of these problems is considerable. Even an experienced polygraph operator would have problems detecting lies told by a moderately psychopathic person who bit their lip during the cali-bration stage, who then used biofeedback techniques when the crucial questions are posed and who liberally sprayed himself with anti-perspirant before attending the lie detector session!

Informed opinion about the use of polygraphs

Critics of the polygraph recite these weaknesses in their case to have the polygraph banned. In particular, critics are concerned about the high rate of false positives given by the polygraph: these are people who are truly innocent but whom the polygraph results indicate are guilty. It has been claimed (British Psychological Society, 1986) that a rate of 50% false posi-tives is not uncommon. One of the best studies suggests that the poly-graph results are not the crucial part of the process (Carroll, 1985; Ginton et al., 1982). Half of a group of subjects were induced to cheat in a mathe-matics exam. All subjects were then subjected to a polygraph test and data were collected in three modes:

- **Mode one** was a normal polygraph situation where the operator administered the polygraph, saw the person's behaviour and also saw the polygraph charts.

- In **mode two** an observer saw the person's behaviour but did not have access to the polygraph charts.

- In **mode three** only the charts were available and a decision was made solely on the basis of the polygraph.

On analysis it was found that the decisions made in mode three were no more accurate than random guesses. However, the results from mode one and from mode two were equally accurate. These results suggest that by itself, the polygraph adds little to the detection of guilty people – it is the observation of their behaviour which matters. Furthermore, the complicated and expensive piece of equipment would seem superfluous since behaviour can be observed in other, more orthodox situations.

Critics of the polygraph claim that the inaccuracies, especially the false positives, are particularly dangerous because the polygraph seems so scientific and credible. Consequently, when mistakes are made it can have a considerable and often irreversible impact on people's lives – even strong and justified protestations of innocence are unlikely to be believed if it is known that someone has failed a 'lie detector test'. Because the ethical issues are so immense, prestigious bodies such as the British Psychological Society and the American Psychological Association have set up committees to investigate its use. There is a very clear consensus of these bodies against the use of polygraph tests. For example the report of the British Psychological Society (1986) states that polygraphs 'are unlikely to be accepted in the British context of employment staff screening'. Similar reports have led a number of American states to make the use of the polygraph illegal. In Canada, Germany and Israel the courts have explicitly ruled against the evidence of the polygraph. In France, it is an administrative offence to use the polygraph.

Employers contemplating the use of polygraphs to screen applicants should consider one further point – the image they project to prospective employees. The culture in many countries does not readily accept the use of devices such as the polygraph and it is used in only a tiny percentage of organizations. Those organizations which do use the polygraph therefore project an organizational climate of suspicion and distrust. The best employees, often those with other career avenues, will seek employment elsewhere. Employers who use the polygraph could well be left with the unappetizing prospect of an applicant pool that is an amalgam of people who are unemployable elsewhere and near psychopaths who relish the thought of 'taking on' the lie detector test.

In full knowledge of all these arguments some organizations continue to use the lie detector test. They know that it does not work but they reason that if applicants believe it to work, they will be more accurate when they write their CV and answer questions at an interview. There may have been some basis for this rationale. In security circles a number of important confessions have been obtained from suspects who were about to be given a 'lie detector test'. This strategy is losing its force as the weaknesses of the polygraph become more widely known. The strategy also poses ethical issues. At the very least an employer who uses the polygraph for these reasons is acquiescing to a misunderstanding and at the worst the employers are, themselves, perpetrating a deception. Perhaps it should be a rule that before applicants take a lie detector test the employer should be given one first!

Integrity testing

Need for integrity tests

Many employments offer considerable temptations to employees to steal from or cheat their employers. Classic examples are in retailing and warehousing where employees could help themselves to supplies. Indeed this kind of stealing has been given a term of its own and is called 'shrinkage'. Shrinkage can easily account for 5% of a company's inventory. Of course this 5% is not financed from thin air. The cost is ultimately passed on to the organization's customers and amounts to a 'shrinkage tax'. Recent advances in computerization, automatic warehousing and the appropriately named 'shrink-wrapping' of goods are making substantial reductions in the 'shrinkage tax' but it remains a significant problem. Handling cash is another area where the integrity of employees is important. Large financial institutions have tight procedures to minimize the loss. However, the problem is acute where money is handled on an informal basis such as charity collections.

Difficulties of this kind have led many employers to seek ways of predicting whether an applicant is honest and this, in turn has led psychologists to develop 'honesty tests' or, as they are more usually called 'integrity tests'.

Description of integrity tests

Integrity tests usually take the form of a paper and pencil test which is easily incorporated into a battery of selection tests. Some of the first tests of this kind were the Reid Report developed in the USA, the Personnel Selection Inventory (PSI) and the Keeler Pre-Employment Opinion Survey. At least eight other tests are available. Generally, the tests have between 60 and 160 questions. Most of the questionnaires attempt to measure propensity to theft and, to a lesser extent alcohol and drug abuse. Some tests also attempt to measure other forms of counterproductive behaviour such as hostility to authority, poor job performance and the likelihood of changing jobs after a short period.

Integrity tests use four main types of questions. The first and most blatant questions are *point-blank enquiries* about anti-social behaviour. The point of the questions and their rationale are obvious. Typical examples would be:

What is the highest value item you have ever
stolen from your employer?

a never
b under £1
c £2–5
d £6–25
e £26–100
f £101–500
g over £500

How many times in the past have the results of a drinking session interfered with your performance at work?

a never
b once or twice
c up to ten times
d more than ten times

How often have you stolen things from an employer?

a never
b once or twice
c up to six times
d up to 20 times
e up to 100 times
f more than 100 times

The second type of question used in integrity tests are *estimates of anti-*

social behaviour. The technique is a little less direct and rests on the rationale that someone who engages in theft or other anti-social behaviours perceives that anti-social behaviour is frequent. Typical examples of questions in this category are:

What percentage of the population would you estimate steals items worth more than £5 per year from their employer?

a less than 20%
b between 20% and 29%
c between 30% and 39%
d between 40% and 49%
e between 50% and 59%
f between 60% and 69%
g 70 percent or more

In a typical retail store, what is the level of goods taken by staff without paying?

a less than 1% of turnover
b 1 to 2% of turnover
c 3 to 5% of turnover
d 6 to 10% of turnover
e 11 to 20% of turnover
f more than 20% of turnover

The third type of questions used in integrity tests asks about *rationalizations for theft* and other disruptive behaviour. Again there is a clear logic for questions of this kind. Presumably, if you can easily find reasons and excuses for theft you are less likely to refrain from stealing. Typical questions of this genre ask people whether they agree or disagree to statements of the following kind:

• Taking small things from an employer who pays low wages is only a way of evening things up.

• Shrinkage of stocks doesn't matter because the loss is usually covered by insurances.

The final type of questions concerns punitive *views on retribution* for theft and other misdemeanours. The logic behind these questions is that if misdemeanours are thought to justify only small penalties, then the misdemeanours may be worth the risk and their occurrence will increase. Questions concerning punitive attitudes might be:

What would be an appropriate punishment for an employee who is caught stealing £20 worth of goods?

a   a reprimand
b   a fine of £100
c   suspension
d   dismissal
e   prosecution
f   prosecution and bad publicity

The penalty for being drunk when in charge of a slicing machine is:

a   a reprimand
b   a fine
c   suspension
d   a fine and suspension
e   dismissal
f   prosecution

Some tests such as the Wilkerson Pre-employment Audit try to soften the impact of the test and disguise its purpose by embedding the questions among other, innocuous questions concerning TV viewing, current affairs and general opinions.

DO INTEGRITY TESTS WORK?

Integrity tests raise an ethical dilemma. On the one hand, is it fair to deny someone the chance of employment on the basis of their answers to a test which suggests they have a higher probability of stealing or engaging in disruptive behaviour? On the other hand, is it fair to force customers and consumers to pay the 'shrinkage tax' caused by employees who steal when employers could use a simple paper and pencil test to reduce the problem? The only way off the horns of the dilemma is to establish the accuracy of integrity tests. If they are inaccurate, then it would be unfair to reject employees on the basis of their scores. If they are accurate, then it would be unfair to consumers and fellow employees not to use them. The importance of this problem has attracted the attention of a large number of researchers.

One of the most influential and realistic studies was conducted by Terris and Jones (1982). They obtained monthly shrinkage figures for a chain of 30 convenience stores in the USA over a period of 23 months. During the 23 months the stores were using polygraphs as a part of their employee selection procedures. During this polygraph phase, shrinkage was $515 per store per month which was 2.35% of turnover. The use of the polygraph was ended and an integrity test (the PSI) was used in its place for 19 months. During the integrity test phase the shrinkage per store per month dropped to $249 which was 0.97% of turnover. Although it was influential, the study had a major weakness. According to textbooks on experimental design there should have been a third stage where neither the polygraph nor the integrity test was used. This would have provided important data for a control situation. However, this information is missing, presumably, because when management saw the savings that were being made, they were reluctant to discontinue the use of integrity tests. Perhaps understandably, they put profits before scientific purity (see Figure 12.2).

Another study by Jones and Terris (1981) produced similarly convincing results. Eighty people who made collections ('kettlers') for the Salvation Army were given the PSI integrity test. They employed all eighty people but kept track of the dollars they turned in at the end of each day. The average return of those who 'passed' the integrity test was $81.00. In comparison, those who failed the test returned an average of $62.77 per day. It should be noted that the Salvation Army study made an attempt to compensate for the fact that some kettlers had better pitches than others. A complete cynic with the benefit of hindsight might observe that the Salvation Army had behaved unethically and had deprived the needy of substantial sums of money by not heeding the results of the integrity test.

A third study by Selection Research Publishing (1983) adopted a different approach which examined individual scores rather than the average scores of groups of people. An integrity test was given to all applicants for jobs in a department store. At the end of a nine month period 91 of those employed had been dismissed for theft. Their scores were compared with a sample of 191 people who had not been dismissed for theft. The analysis revealed a high correlation of 0.48 between the integrity test score and being dismissed for theft. This correlation is notable because it arose in spite of contamination caused by the fact that some of the 191 remaining employees would have committed thefts but had not been caught and dismissed.

These three studies are only a selection from those available on the

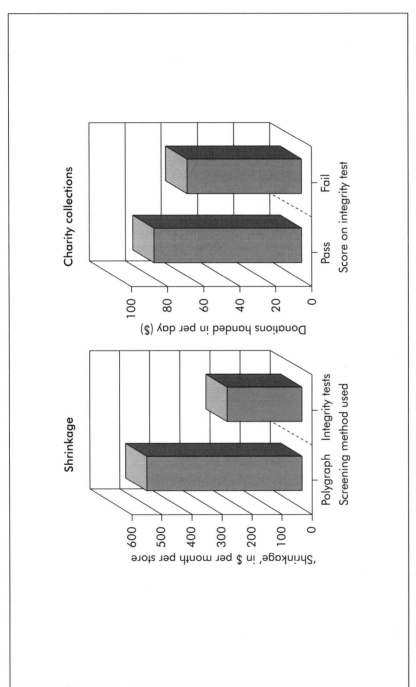

Figure 12.2 Financial impact of using integrity tests

validity of integrity tests. Several authors have attempted to review all studies and arrive at a general conclusion using the techniques of meta-analysis. The main meta-analytic reviews have been conducted by Ones, Viswesvaran and Schmidt (1993); Sackett, Buris and Callahan (1989) and Sackett and Harris (1984). They unanimously come to the conclusion that integrity tests are valid measures for employee selection. The analysis by Ones et al. is particularly impressive. Their meta analysis involved 665 validity coefficients based on data for a huge sample of 576,460 people. They found that the validity of integrity tests was 0.41 and concluded that they predict a broad range of organizationally disruptive behaviours, job performance, theft, disciplinary problems and absenteeism.

WHY DO INTEGRITY TESTS WORK?

At a superficial level, it is astounding that integrity tests are so useful. The questions they ask are so very transparent. Surely, only fools would incriminate themselves? Bernadin and Cook (1993) suggest one possible answer. They suggest that people who obtain low scores on integrity tests and people who are dishonest and counterproductive do not think that there is anything wrong with the way they behave and therefore they have nothing to hide. Low scorers simply believe that they are 'average' people who are operating in a basically dishonest and corrupt world – and they are not ashamed of that!

EMPLOYERS' ATTITUDES TO CHECKS

Generally, the above measures can be introduced with comparative ease, speed and little cost. However, employers frequently do not use them. One cogent argument is that further checks may be deemed irrelevant, costly and unnecessary, especially if selectors are convinced that they are excellent judges of character. The fallibility of checks may be recognized and it is nearly impossible to unmask the determined 'con artist'. Consequently, many people's dishonesty may be undetected, and their possession of apparently unblemished records inaccurately reflects previous activities.

A tendency to trust others may be both a personal inclination and a feature of an open organizational culture. There may be a reluctance to doubt and question prospective employees' honesty, and selectors may believe this an inauspicious start in a new relationship with a new employee. This is particularly true of using lie detectors. Alternatively employers could believe that candidates may take umbrage at checks and decline job offers, so damaging the whole utility of selection. The use of outside agencies could have repercussions, since the candidate's discovery of such clandestine methods could cause discontent and a disinclination to work for such an organization. Employers may also have ethical concerns that such tactics are an invasion of privacy, and be mindful of civil liberties groups.

SUMMARY

A variety of checks is available to selectors but there may be practical and ethical reasons which limit their implementation. Time, effort and verification by a knowledgeable person are needed for factual checks. Lie detectors are problematic and integrity tests raise ethical dilemmas, though appear to be valid measures. Organizations may be loathe to adopt measures which question a candidate's honesty, especially as some are fallible.

Whilst checks can help to detect deceit, they are not infallible and candidates and selectors may prefer the more proactive strategies described in previous chapters. One such tactic was to increase the knowledge base, especially in regard to the manifestations of deceit. This book aimed at increasing the understanding and appreciation of deception. Hopefully, awareness of deception is in itself a defence against it.

Glossary

Ability test   A psychometric measure of a person's ability, such as intelligence, physical ability and specific abilities such as numeracy and verbal reasoning.

Agency   A recruitment agency whose clients are employers wishing to fill vacancies. The agency matches their needs with those of potential candidates, drawn from the agency's database of jobseekers.

Aptitude   A person's potential for achievement.

Assessment centre   Not a place, but a number of selection methods applied to candidates, who are observed and evaluated by several assessors on multiple dimensions or competencies.

Behaviourally anchored rating scale   A rating scale which consists of two parts: clearly defined characteristics to be rated and a scale with descriptions of specific observable behaviours. The behaviours are at different levels, ranging from minimum and maximum of performance.

Bias   A predisposition towards or against an individual or group, which is usually related to prejudice and stereotypes.

Biodata   A specialist method of collecting biographical information and, with the use of a formula, predicting suitability for a job. It involves more than simply asking for biographical information and making subjective judgements.

Correlation   The relationship between two or more factors. An increase in one is accompanied by a systematic increase or decrease in the other. The strength of the relationship is expressed as a correlation coefficient ranging from -1 to +1 and the stronger the relationship the further the distance from zero. Hence a correlation of 0.8 is greater than one of 0.40.

Criteria   The standards taken in making judgements. They usually reflect some aspects of work performance.

Curriculum vitae (CV)   The resumé of the salient details of a person's life and work history which jobseekers frequently present to prospective employers.

Cut-off score   The level of scores on tests or other measures which is used to determine whether a candidate has reached an acceptable standard. These scores are not necessarily fixed but may be set according to the number and calibre of candidates.

Department for Education and Employment (DfEE)   The government department with responsibilites for helping jobseekers find employment.

Discrimination   Fair discrimination is the just differentiation between candidates. this become unfair discrimination if it is based on gender, race, ethnic origin or other unfair attributes and is not related to ability to do the job.

Distributive justice   Justice which is concerned with the fairness of the results or outcomes of selection.

Enhancements   A form of impression management which maximizes achievements and qualities.

Entitlements   A form of impression management which maximizes responsibility for positive events.

Face validity   The acceptability of a selection method to the candidate.

Faking   Giving a false impression of oneself, to create a socially desirable effect. It may occur in many methods of selection.

Feedback   Information given to candidates about their performance in the selection procedures. It frequently focuses on strengths and weaknesses and should usually be constructive.

Graphology   The analysis of handwriting which is claimed to be a means of assessing people's characteristics.

Headhunter   A recruitment specialist who actively seeks candidates on behalf of an employer. The candidates may already be in employment and the headhunter may outline the opportunities and attractions of alternative employment.

Impression management   The tactics adopted by individuals in order to create a favourable impact on the impressions of another about the individual.

Integrity testing   Sometimes called 'honesty testing'. This is a psychometric tool and can be a pencil and paper test or a lie detector. They are used to determine an individual's tendency to engage in dishonest or disruptive activities.

Interview   A social encounter between the selector and candidate in which information is exchanged, primarily through the interviewer questioning the candidate in order to assess her suitability for the job.

Intra-rater reliability   The similarity of results found among a number of different people assessing the same candidate.

In-tray exercise   A role play exercise in which candidates are given a file or basket containing memos, correspondence and other material which would typically be found in a manager's in-tray.

Job analysis   The process of examining a job in order to identify its salient features and activities. From this information, the characteristics of the ideal job holder can be inferred and incorporated into the personnel specification, and criteria can be developed.

Job description   A written document describing the details of the job in terms of component tasks. It also includes the incumbent's activities and the minimum standards of competence. It is usually derived from a job analysis.

Job-knowledge test   A test of the candidate's information about a particular job.

Leaderless group exercise   Commonly experienced in an assessment centre, candidates are given a topic of discussion and no roles are allocated, so that the discussion has free rein. It is usually designed to assess inter-personal and problem-solving skills.

Leniency effects   Favourable ratings which are not fully justified.

Norm table   The table of comparative scores of the comparable norm group. Usually available in the manuals of psychometric tests.

Norms   The scores of a specific group of comparable people against which an individual's scores on psychometric tests are compared.

Outplacement   An organizational shedding of staff. Outplacement consultants assist and advise outplaced staff in their search for work.

Patterned behaviour interview   A structured interview in which the applicant is asked to describe how she behaved in the past in a given situation.

Person specification   The skills and attributes a person needs in order to do a specific job. They are derived from the job analysis and formally documented.

Personality questionnaires   An inventory used to establish an individual's characteristic traits, disposition and preferences.

Personnel function   The part of an organization which tries to maximize the effectiveness of the people in the organization. The Personnel function includes selection and other work affecting Personnel. In this book the term is used interchangeably with the term 'human resources' (HR) function.

Polygraph   An instrument designed to mesaure a candidate's physical responses to questions, in order to ascertain whether the candidate is telling the truth.

Procedural justice   Justice which occurs within the process of an event such as selection.

Psychological contract   An unwritten agreement between a potential employee and an organization, pertaining to generally intangible matters such as career development.

Psychometric tests   Measurements of psychological attributes and samples of behaviour. They may relate to ability, personality and other characteristics.

Realistic job preview   Accurate, practical, common sense information given to a candidate about a job.

Reference   Information provided by a third party, often an employer, about the applicant's suitability for employment. It usually provides details on character or job related behaviour.

Reliability   The consistency of test measurement which indicates its dependability. It is the extent to which repetition of the test produces the same results, if other conditions are similar. The most usual index of reliability is a correlation coefficient, which is a statistical coefficient measured between 0 and 1. The higher the score, the greater the reliability.

Situational interview   A structured interview in which the applicant is asked to describe how she would behave in a given situation. It focuses on future intentions.

Social desirability   The individual's presentation of herself in a favourable light and a way which she feels ought to, rather than an accurate reflection of the truth.

Stereotypes   A view of a person which is based on group characteristics rather than the individual's own attributes. Often has negative connotations.

Trainability test   A test measuring an applicant's ability to learn new skills and successfully undertake and complete training.

Validity   There is a number of types of validity. The most important is predictive validity which is the ability of a selection method to predict success on future work performance. The most usual index of validity is a correlation coefficient, which is a statistical coefficient measured between 0 and 1. The higher the score, the greater the validity.

Work sample test   A test which directly samples employment by mimicking its key characteristics.

Bibliography

Adams, D. (1991) 'Pre-selection in graduate recruitment and the re-taking of tests', *Guidance and Assessment Review* **7** (2): 4–5.

Adams, D. (1995) 'Psychometric testing – through the eyes of some test users', *Selection and Development Review* **11** (3) 4–7.

Anastasi, A. (1988) *Psychological Testing* 6th edn, Macmillan, New York.

Anderson, N. (1991) 'Decision making in the graduate selection interview: an experimental investigation', *Human Relations* **44**: 403–17.

Anderson, N. and Shackleton, V. (1986) 'Recruitment and selection: a review of developments in the 1980s', *Personnel Review* **15** (4): 19–26.

Anderson, N. and Shackleton, V. (1990) 'Decision making in the undergraduate selection interview: a field study', *Journal of Occupational Psychology* **63**: 63–76.

Anderson, N., Payne, T., Ferguson, E. and Smith, T. (1986) 'Assessor decision making information processing and assessor strategies in a British assessment centre', *Personnel Review* **23**: 1–62.

Anonymous (1995) 'Lies, damned lies and CVs', *Management Accounting* **73** (10): 6–8.

Argyle, M. (1972) *The Psychology of Interpersonal Behaviour*, Penguin, Harmondsworth.

Arvey, R.D. and Campion, J.E. (1982) 'The employment interview: a summary and review of recent research', *Personnel Psychology* **35**: 281–322.

Arvey, R.D. and Campion, J.E. (1984)' Person perception in the employment interview', in M.Cook (ed.) *Issues in Person Perception*, Methuen, London.

Arvey, R.D. and Faley, R.H. (1988) *Fairness in Selecting Employees*, Addison Wesley Longman: Harlow.

Arvey, R.D. and Renz, G.L. (1992) 'Fairness in Employee Selection', *Journal of Business Ethics* **11**: 331–40.

Asher, J.J. (1972) 'The biographical item: can it be improved?', *Personnel Psychology* **25**: 251–69.

Asher, J.J. and Sciarrino, J.A. (1974) 'Realistic work sample tests: a review', *Personnel Psychology* **27**: 519–33.

Baker, B.R. and Cooper, J.N. (1995a) 'Fair play or foul? A survey of occupational test practices in the UK', *Personnel Review* **24** (3): 3–18.

Baker, B.R. and Cooper, J.N. (1995b) 'Psychometric assessment: selected findings from a survey of UK organizations', practices' *Development Review* **11** (2): 4–6.

Barber, A.E., Hollenbeck, J.R., Tower, S.L. and Phollips, J. M. (1994) 'The effects of interview focus on recruitment effectiveness: a field experiment', *Journal of Applied Psychology* **79**: 886–96.

Baron, H. (1991) 'Does practice make perfect?', *Guidance and Assessment Review* **7** (2): 1–3.

Barrick, M.R. and Mount, M.K. (1996) 'Effects of impression management and self-deception on the predictive validity of personality constructs', *Journal of Applied Psychology* **81**: 261–72.

Bartram, D. (1991) 'Addressing the abuse of psychological tests', *Personnel Management* **23** (4): 34–9.

Bartram, D. (1995) 'Predicting adverse impact in selection testing', *International Journal of Selection and Assessment* **3** (1): 52–61.

Bartram, D., Ashley, N. and Wright, S.J. (1995) 'Test instructions: the importance of getting them right', *Selection and Development Review* **11** (6): 1–3.

Baxter, J.C., Brock, B., Hill, P.C. and Rozelle, R.M. (1981) 'Letters of recommendation: a question of value', *Journal of Applied Psychology* **66**: 296–301.

Beardwell, I. and Holden, L. (1994) *Human Resource Management - A Contemporary Perspective*, Pitman Publishing, London.

Beason, G. and Belt, J.A. (1976) 'Verifying applicants' backgrounds', *Personnel Journal* **55**: 345–8.

Ben-Shakar, G. (1989)' Non-conventional methods in personnel selection', in P. Herriot (ed.) *Assessment and Selection in Organizations*, Wiley, Chichester.

Ben-Shakar, G., Bar-Hillel, M., Bille, Y., Ben-Abba, E. and Flug, A. (1986) 'Can graphology predict occupational success? Two empirical studies and some methodological ruminations', *Journal of Applied Psychology* **71**: 645–53.

Bernadin, J.H. and Cooke, D.K. (1993) 'Validity of an honesty test in predicting theft among convenience store employees', *Academy of Management Journal* **36**: 107–108.

Bies, R.J. and Shapiro, D.L. (1988) 'Voice and justification: their influence on procedural fairness judgments', *Academy of Management Journal* **31**: 676–85.

Blinkhorn, S. and Johnson, C. (1990) 'The insignificance of personality testing', *Nature* **348**: 671–2.

Blinkhorn, S. and Johnson, C. (1991) 'Personality tests: the great debate', *Personnel Management* **23** (9): 38–42.

Blum, M.L. and Naylor, J.C. (1968) *Industrial Psychology: Its Theoretical and Social Foundation*, Harper and Row, New York.

Bolster, B.I. and Springbett, B.M. (1961) 'The reactions of interviewers to favourable and unfavourable information', *Journal of Applied Psychology* **45**: 97–103.

Bordwin, M. (1994/1995) 'Firing 101: before, during and after', *Small Business Forum* Winter: 44–57.

Borislow, B. (1958) 'The Edward's Personal Preference Schedule and fakability', *Journal of Applied Psychology* **42**: 22–7.

Boyle, S., Fullerton, J. and Wood, R. (1995) 'Do assessment/development centres use optimum evaluation procedures? A survey of practice in UK organisations', *International Journal of Selection and Assessment* **3** (2): 132–40.

Brannick, M.T., Michaels, C.E. and Baker, D.P. (1989) 'Construct validity of in-basket scores', *Journal of Applied Psychology* **74**: 957–63.

Brindle, L. and Ridgeway, C. (1995) 'UK occupational assessment survey – experts' views on current practice and future perspectives', *International Journal of Selection and Assessment* **3** (2): 141–6.

British Psychological Society (1986) 'Report of the working group on the use of the polygraph in criminal investigation and personnel screening', *Bulletin of the*

British Psychological Society **39**: 81–94.

British Psychological Society (1989) *Psychological Testing Guidance for the User*, BPS, Leicester.

British Psychological Society (1993) *Graphology in Personnel Assessment*, BPS, Leicester.

Buckley, M.R. and Eder, R.W. (1988) 'B.M. Springbett and the notion of the "snap decision" in the interview', *Journal of Management* **14**: 59–69.

Bull, R. (1985) *Questioning Strategies used by Polygraphers*, Paper presented to Annual Conference of British Psychological Society, Swansea.

Callen, A. and Geary, B. (1994) 'Best practice – putting practice testing to work', *Selection and Development Review* **10** (3): 4–7.

Campion, M.A. (1978) 'Identification of variables most influential in determining interviewers' evaluations of applicants in a college placement centre', *Psychological Reports* **42**: 947–52.

Carlson, R.E. (1967) 'The relative influence of appearance and factual written information on an interviewer's final rating', *Journal of Applied Psychology* **51**: 461–8.

Carroll, D. (1985) *The Accuracy of Polygraph Lie Detection*, Paper presented to Annual Conference of British Psychological Society, Swansea.

Carroll, S.J. and Nash, A.N. (1972) 'Effectiveness of a forced choice reference check', *Personnel Administration* March-April: 42–6.

Cascio, W.F. (1975) 'Accuracy of verifiable biographical information blank responses', *Journal of Applied Psychology* **60**: 767–9.

Cavanagh, G.F. and Moberg, D.J.(1981) 'The ethics of organizational politics', *Academy of Management Review* **6**: 363–74.

Childs, R. (1991) 'In search of excellence – should we use high ability psychometric tests?', *Guidance and Assessment Review* **7** (4): 5–7.

Christine, B. (1994) 'Liability for negligent hiring: the importance of background checks', *Risk Management* **41** (7): 96.

Clark, T. (1993) 'Selection methods used by executive search consultancies in four European countries: a survey and critique', *International Journal of Selection and Assessment* **1** (1): 41–9.

Closs, J. (1995) 'Ipsative personality tests: unsound and unfair', *Selection and Development Review* **11** (4): 4–7.

Cohen, B.M., Moses, J.L. and Byham, W.C. (1974) *The Validity of Assessment Centres: A Literature Review*, Development Dimensions Press, Pittsburgh.

Cohen, D. (1993) *How to Succeed in Psychometric Tests*, Sheldon Press, London.

Commission for Racial Equality (1996a) *A Fair Test? Selecting Train Drivers for British Rail*, Belmont Press, London.

Cook, M. (1995) *Personnel Selection and Productivity*, Wiley, Chichester.

Cooper, D. and Robertson I.T. (1995) *The Psychology of Personnel Selection*, Routledge, London

Cornwall, H. (1987) *Datatheft: Computer Fraud, Industrial Espionage and Information Crime*, Heinemann, London.

Cottringer, W. (1995) 'Selecting the best of the bunch', *Security Management* **39** (10): 21–2.

Courtis, J. (1995) 'When it's incompetent not to discriminate', *People Management* **1** (11): 23.

Commission for Racial Equality (1996b) 'The Asylum and Immigration Act, 1996. Implications for racial equality. Provisional guidance for employers on compliance with the Race Relations Act 1976', CRE, London.

Cronbach, L.J. (1955) 'Processes affecting scores on understanding others and assumed similarity', *Psychological Bulletin* **52**: 177–93.

Dalessio, A.T. and Silverhart, T.A. (1994) 'Combining biodata test and interview information: predicting decisions and performance criteria', *Personnel Psychology* **47**: 303–15.

Daniels, A.W. and Otis, J.L. (1950) 'A method for analysing employment interviews', *Personnel Psychology* **3**: 425–44.

Dipboye, R.L., Arvey, R.D. and Terpstra, D.E. (1977) 'Sex and physical attractiveness of raters and applicants as determinants of resume evaluation', *Journal of Applied Psychology* **62**: 288–94.

Dobson, P. (1989)'Reference reports', in P. Herriot (ed.) *Assessment and Selection in Organizations*, Wiley, Chichester.

Donnelly, H. (1994) 'Store security: the retail perspective', *Stores* **76** (11): 57–8.

Downs, S. (1989) 'Job sample and trainability tests', in P. Herriot (ed.) *Assessment and Selection in Organizations*, Wiley, Chichester.

Drakely, R.J. (1989)'Biographical Data', in P. Herriot (ed.) *Assessment and Selection in Organizations*, Wiley, Chichester.

Driver, R.W., Buckley, M.R. and Fink, D.D. (1996) 'Should we write off graphology?', *International Journal of Selection and Assessment* **4** (2): 78–86.

Dulewicz, V. (1989) 'Assessment centres as the route to competence', *Personnel Management* **21** (11): 56–9.

Dunnette, M.D., McCartney, J., Carlson, H.C. and Kirchner, W.K. (1962) 'A study of faking behavior on a forced-choice self-description checklist', *Personnel Psychology* **15**: 13–24.

Eastwood, L. (1990) 'The introduction of a structured reference to select civil service administrators', *Guidance and Assessment Review* **7** (1): 2–4.

Elliot, D.W. (1982) 'Lie detector evidence: lessons from the American experience', in Campbell and Waller (eds) *Well and Truly Tried: Essays on Evidence in Honour of Sir Richard Eggleston*, Law Book Company, Melbourne.

Equal Opportunities Commission (1990) *Fair and Efficient Selection*, Equal Opportunities Commission, Manchester.

Feltham, R.T. (1989)'Assessment Centres', in P. Herriot (ed.) (1989) *Assessment and Selection in Organizations*, Wiley, Chichester.

Feltham, R.T. (1991) 'Practice effects in graduate testing – reply to Hunter, Keys, Wynne and Corcoran', *Guidance and Assessment Review* **7** (1): 1–2.

Feltham, R.T. and Smith, P. (1993) 'Psychometric test bias – how to avoid it', *International Journal of Selection and Assessment* **1** (2): 117–22.

Feltham, R.T., Baron, H. and Smith, P. (1994) 'Developing fair tests', *The Psychologist* **7** (1): 23–5.

Ferguson, J. (1989) 'Improving the validity of selection interviews', *Guidance and Assessment Review* **5** (5): 4–5.

Fletcher, C. (1986) 'Should the test score be kept a secret?', *Personnel Management* **18** (4): 44–6.

Fletcher, C. (1989a) 'A test by any other name', *Personnel Management* **21** (3): 46–51.

Fletcher, C. (1989b) 'Impression management in the selection interview', in R. A. Giacalone and P. Rosenfeld (eds) *Impression Management in the Organization*, Lawrence Erlbaum Associates, Inc., New Jersey.

Fletcher, C. (1990) 'The relationships between candidate personality, self-presentation strategies, and interviewer assessments in selection interviews: an empirical study', *Human Relations* **43**: 739–49.

Fletcher, C. (1991) 'Personality tests: the great debate', *Personnel Management* **23** (9): 38–42.

Fletcher, C. (1992a) 'Indicators of quality in the use of psychometric tests', *Selection and Development Review* **8** (2): 1–3.

Fletcher, C. (1992b) 'Ethics and the job interview', *Personnel Management* **24** (3): 36–9.

Fletcher, C. (1992c) 'Ethics in the selection interview', *Journal of Business Ethics* **11**: 361–7.

Fletcher, C. (1993) 'Testing times for the world of psychometrics', *Personnel Management* **25** (12): 46–50.

Fletcher, C. (1994) 'Validity, test use and professional responsibility', *The Psychologist* **7** (1): 30–1.

Fletcher, C. (1995) 'What means to assess integrity?', *Personnel Management* **1** (17): 30–1.

Fletcher, C. and Wood, R. (1993) *The Efficacy of Coaching Test Taking: a Preliminary Investigation'*, Paper presented at the British Psychological Society Annual Conference, Blackpool.

Ford, C.V. (1995) *Lies! Lies! Lies! The psychology of deceit*, American Psychiatric Press Inc., Washington.

Fowler, A. (1995) 'How to make the best use of CVs', *People Management* **1** (7): 44–5.

Fusilier, M.R. and Hoyer, W.D. (1980) 'Variables affecting perceptions of invasion of privacy in a personnel selection situation', *Journal of Applied Psychology* **65**: 623–6.

Gatewood, R., Thornton, G.C. and Hennessey, H.W. (1990) 'Reliability of exercise ratings in the leaderless group discussion', *Journal of Occupational Psychology* **63**: 331–42.

Gaugler, B.B. and Rudolph, A.S. (1992) 'The influence of assessee performance variation on assessor's judgements', *Personnel Psychology* **45**: 77–98.

Giacalone, R.A. and Rosenfeld, P. (eds) (1989) *Impression Management in the Organization*, Lawrence Erlbaum Associates, Inc., New Jersey.

Gill, B.W. (1994) 'Running a background check', *American Printer* **213** (6): 152.

Gilliland, S.W. (1993) 'The perceived fairness of selection systems: an organizational justice perspective', *Academy of Management Review* **18**: 694–734.

Gilliland, S.W. (1994) 'Effects of procedural and distributive justice on reactions to a selection system', *Journal of Applied Psychology* **79**: 691–701.

Gilliland, S.W. (1995) 'Fairness from the applicant's perspective: reactions to employee selection procedures', *International Journal of Selection and Assessment* **3** (1): 11–19.

Gilmore, D.C. and Ferris, G.R. (1989) 'The effects of applicant impression

management tactics on interviewer judgements', *Journal of Applied Management*
15: 557–64.

Glinton, A., Daie, N., Elaad, E. and Ben-Shakar, G. (1982) 'A method for evaluating
the use of the polygraph in a real life situation', *Journal of Applied Psychology* **67**:
131–7.

Goldstein, I.L. (1971) 'The application blank: how honest are applicant responses?', *Journal of Applied Psychology* **55**: 491–2.

Gottfredson, L.S. (1986) 'Reconsidering fairness: a matter of social and ethical pri-
orities', *Journal of Vocational Behaviour* **33**: 293–319.

Graves, L.M. and Powell, G.N. (1995) 'The effect of sex similarity on recruiters'
evaluations of actual applicants: a test of the similarity–attraction paradigm',
Personnel Psychology **48** (1): 85–98.

Gray, J.A. (1994) 'Reforms to improve client protection and compensation against
personal financial planners' unethical business practises', *American Business
Law Journal* **32** (2): 245–76.

Greenberg, E.R. (1996) 'Drug-testing now standard practice', *HR Focus* **73** (9): 24.

Greenberg, J. (1986) 'Determinants of perceived fairness of performance
evaluations', *Journal of Applied Psychology* **71**: 340–2.

Greenberg, J. (1987) 'Reactions to procedural injustice in payment distribution: do
the means justify the ends?', *Journal of Applied Psychology* **72**: 55–61.

Greenberg, J. (1990) 'Organisational justice: yesterday, today and tomorrow',
Journal of Management **16**: 399–432.

Griffiths, P. and Goodge, P. (1994) 'Development centres: the third generation',
Personnel Management **26** (6): 40–3.

Harlan, A., Kerr J. and Kerr, S. (1977) 'Preference for motivator and hygiene factors
in a hypothetical situation: futher findings and some implications for the
employment interview', *Personnel Psychology* **30**: 557–66.

Harn, T.J. and Thornton, G.C. (1985) 'Recruiter counselling behaviours and
applicant impressions', *Journal of Occupational Psychology* **58**: 57–65.

Hartigan, J.A. and Wigdor, A.K. (1989) *Fairness in Employment Testing*, National
Academy Press, Washington, DC.

Hartshorne, H. and May, M.A. (1928) 'Studies in the nature of character', vol. 1
Studies in Deceit, Macmillan, New York.

Heilman, M.E. and Saruwatari, L.R. (1979) 'When beauty is beastly: the effects of
appearance and sex on evaluations of job applicants for managerial and non-
managerial jobs', *Organisational Behaviour and Human Performance* **23**: 360-72.

Herriot, P. (1985) 'Give and take in graduate selection', *Personnel Management* **17**
(5): 33–5.

Herriot, P. (1989a) 'Selection as a social process', in J.M. Smith and I.T. Robertson
(eds) *Advances in Selection and Assessment*, Wiley, Chichester.

Herriot, P. (1989b)'The selection interview', in P. Herriot (ed.) *Assessment and
Selection in Organizations*, Wiley, Chichester.

Herriot, P. and Fletcher, C. (1990) 'Candidate-friendly selection for the 1990s',
Personnel Management **22** (2): 32–5.

Herriot, P. and Rothwell.C. (1981) 'Organizational choice and decision theory:
effects of employers' literature and selection interview', *Journal of Occupational*

Psychology **54**: 17–31.

Herriot, P. and Wingrove, J. (1984) 'Decision processes in graduate pre-selection', *Journal of Occupational Psychology* **57**: 269–75.

Hertzberg, F. (1954) 'Temperament measures in industrial selection', *Journal of Applied Psychology* **38**: 81–4.

Hollandsworth, J.G., Kazelskis, R. Stevens, J. and Dressel, M.E. (1979) 'Relative contributions of verbal communication to employment decisions in the job interview setting', *Personnel Psychology* **32**: 359–67.

Hough, L.M., Eaton, N.K. Dunnett, M.D., Kamp, J.D. and McClay, R.A. (1990) 'Criteria-related validates of personality constructs and the effects of response distortion on those validates', *Journal of Applied Psychology* **75**: 581–93.

Howlings, J. (1996) 'Sober solutions to help tackle substance abuse', *People Management* **2** (24): 43–4.

Hunter, J.E. and Hunter, R.F. (1984) 'Validity and utility of alternative predictors of job performance', *Psychological Bulletin* **96**: 72–98.

Hunter, J.E. and Schmidt, F.L. (1989) 'Meta-analysis: facts and theories', in J.M. Smith and I.T. Robertson (eds) *Advances in Selection and Assessment*, Wiley, Chichester.

Hunter, R. A., Keys, A., Wynne, K. and Corcoran, R. (1990) 'Graduate testing – the problem of practice effects', *Guidance and Assessment Review* **6** (5): 1–4.

Hyde, B. (July 1982) 'First job referees – a different ballgame', *Personnel Management* **14** (7): 5.

Iles, P.A. and Robertson, I.T. (1988) 'Getting in, getting on, and looking good: physical attractiveness, gender and selection decisions', *Guidance and Assessment Review* **4** (3): 6–7.

Iles, P.A. and Robertson, I.T. (1989)'The impact of personnel selection procedures on candidates', in P. Herriot (ed.) *Assessment and Selection in Organizations*, Wiley, Chichester.

Industrial Relations Law Reports (1994) *Spring* (appellant/plaintiff) v. *Guardian Assurance plc and others* (respondents/defendants) **23**: 460–1

The Industrial Society, (1994) *Managing Best Practice 4: Recruitment and Selection*, The Industrial Society, London.

Institute of Personnel and Development (1996) *The IPD Guide on Recruitment*, IPD, London.

Institute of Personnel and Development (1997) *The IPD Guide on Psychological Testing*, IPD, London.

Institute of Personnel Management (1994) *Graphology Information Note*, IPM, London.

Jackson, D. and Rothstein, M. (1993) 'Evaluating personality testing in personnel selection', *The Psychologist* **6** (1): 8–11.

Jacobs, A. and Barron, R. (1968) 'Falsification of the Guiford-Zimerman temperament Survey. Making a poor impression', *Psychological Reports* **23**: 1271–7.

Jagacinski, C.M. (1991) 'Personnel decision making: the impact of missing information', *Journal of Applied Psychology* **76**: 19–30.

James, J. (1989) 'Practice tests in occupational selection', *Guidance and Assessment Review* **5** (2): 3–6.

Janz, T. (1989) 'The patterned behaviour description interview: the best prophet of the future is the past', in R.W. Eder and G.R. Ferris (eds) *The Employment Interview*, Sage, Beverly Hills, California.

Jenner, L. (1994) 'Employment-at-will liability: how protected are you?', *HR Focus* **71** (3): 11.

Johnson, C.E., Wood, R. and Blinkhorn, S.F. (1988) 'Spuriouser and spuriouser: the use of ipsative personality tests', *Journal of Occupational Psychology* **61** (2): 153–62.

Jones, J.W. and Terris W. (1981) *Predictive Validation of a Dishonesty Test that measures Theft Proneness*, Paper to 18th Congress of Psychology, Santo Domingo, Dominican Republic.

Judge, T.A. and Ferris, G.R. (1996) 'The interview: expecting a quick decision?', in G.R. Ferris and M.R. Buckley *Human Resources Management – Perspectives, Context, Functions and Outcomes*, Prentice-Hall, Eaglewood Cliffs, New Jersey.

Keenan, A. (1976) 'Interviewers', evaluations of applicant characteristics: differences between personnel and non-personnel managers', *Journal of Occupational Psychology* **49**: 223–30.

Keenan, A. (1980) 'Recruitment on campus: a closer look at the tools of the trade', *Personnel Management* **12** (3): 43-6.

Keenan, A. (1982) 'Candidate personality and performance in selection interviews', *Personnel Review* **11** (1): 20-2.

Keenan, A. (1983) 'Where application forms mislead', *Personnel Management* **15** (2): 40-43.

Keenan, A. (1995) 'Graduate recruitment in Britain: a survey of selection methods used by organizations', *Journal of Organizational Behaviour* **16**: 303–17.

Keenan, A. and Wedderburn, A.A.I. (1980) 'Putting the boot on the other foot: candidates' descriptions of interviewers', *Journal of Occupational Psychology* **53**: 81–9.

Kellett, D. (1991) 'Practice tests in occupational selection – further steps', *Guidance and Assessment Review* **7** (5): 1–3.

Kellett, D. and Toplis, J. (1989) 'Quality standards for the development and use of psychological tests', *Selection and Development Review* **5** (4): 4–7.

Kellett, D., Fletcher, S., Callen, A. and Geary, B. (1994) 'Fair testing: the case of British Rail', *The Psychologist* **7** (1): 26–9.

Kent, S. (1997) 'Mettle fatigue', *Personnel Management* **2**: 24–7.

Kinder, A. and Robertson, I.T. (1995) 'Getting the best out of personality questionnaires', *Selection and Development Review* **11** (1): 1–4.

Klein, S.P. and Owens, W.A. (1965) 'Faking of a scored life history blank as a function of criterion objectivity', *Journal of Applied Psychology* **49**: 452–4.

Kluger, A.N., Reilly, R.R. and Russell, C.J. (1991) 'Faking biodata tests: are option-keyed instruments more resistant?', *Journal of Applied Psychology* **76**: 889–96.

Knouse, S.B. (1989) 'Impression management and the letter of recommendation', in R. A. Giacalone and P. Rosenfeld (eds) *Impression Management in the Organization*, Lawrence Erlbaum Associates, Inc., New Jersey.

Kolenko, T.A. (1996) 'Human resources planning and staffing college recruitment: realities and guidelines for the 1990s', in G.R. Ferris and M.R. Buckley *Human*

Resources Management – Perspectives, Context, Functions and Outcomes', Prentice-Hall, Englewood Cliffs, New Jersey.

Kravitz, D.A., Stinson, V. and Chavez, T.L. (1996) 'Evaluations of tests used for making selection and promotion decisions', *International Journal of Selection and Assessment* **4** (1) 44–8.

Kwiatkowski, R. (1994) 'Testing in the workplace', *The Psychologist* **7** (1): 10.

Landy, F.J. (1976) 'The validity of the interview in police officer selection', *Journal of Applied Psychology* **61**: 193–8.

Langtry, R. (1994) 'Selection', in I. Beardwell and L. Holden (eds) *Human Resource Management – A Contemporary Perspective*, Pitman Publishing, London.

Latham G.P. and Saari, L.M. (1980) 'The situational interview', *Journal of Applied Psychology* **65** (4): 422–7.

Latham G.P. and Saari, L.M. (1984) 'Do people do what they say they do? Further studies on the situational interview', *Journal of Applied Psychology* **69**: 569–73.

Leventhal, G.S. (1980) 'What should be done about equity theory? New approaches to the study of fairness in social relationships', in K.J. Gergen, M.S. Greenberg and R.H.Willis (eds) *Social Exchange: Advances in Theory and Research*, Plenum, New York.

Lewis, C. (1985) *Employee Selection*, Hutchinson, London.

Liden, R.C. and Parsons, C.K. (1986) 'A field study of job applicant interview perceptions, alternative opportunities, and demographic characteristics', *Personnel Psychology* **39**: 109–22.

Littlefield, D. (1996) 'Hackney's former HR chief alleges racism', *People Management* **2** (11): 7.

Loewenthal, K. (1975) 'Handwriting and self-presentation', *Journal of Social Psychology* **96**: 26–70.

Loewenthal, K. (1982) 'Handwriting as a guide to character', in M.D. Davey and M. Harris *Judging People*, McGraw-Hill, London.

Longstaff, H.P. (1948) 'Fakability of the strong interest blank and the Kuder Preference Record', *Journal of Applied Psychology* **32**: 360–9.

Lowry, P.E. (1994) 'The structured interview: an alternative to the assessment centre?', *Public Personnel Management* **23** (2): 201–15.

Lowry, P.E. (1995) 'The assessment center process: assessing leadership in the public sector', *Public Personnel Management* **24** (4): 443–50.

Lynch, B. (1985) 'Graphology – towards a hand-picked workforce', *Personnel Management* **17** (3): 14–18.

Mabey, B. (1989) 'The majority of large companies use occupational tests', *Guidance and Assessment Review* **5** (3): 1–4.

Mabey, C. and Isles, P. (1991) 'HRM from the other side of the fence', *People Management* **23** (2): 50–3.

Mabey. C. and Iles, P. (1993) 'The strategic integration of assessment and development practices: succession planning and new manager development', *Human Resource Management Journal* **3** (4): 16–34.

Macan, T.H. and Dipboye, R.L. (1988) 'The effects of interviewers' initial impressions on information gathering', *Organisational Behaviour and Human Decision Processes* **42**: 280–96.

Macan, T.H., Avedon, M.J., Paese, M. and Smith, D.E. (1994) 'The effects of applicant reactions to cognitive ability tests and an assessment centres', *Personnel Psychology* **47**: 715–38.

McDaniel, M.A., Whetzel, D.L., Schmidt, F.L. and Maurer, S.D. (1994) 'The validity of employment interviews: a comprehensive review and meta-analysis', *Journal of Applied Psychology* **79**: 599–616.

McFarlin, D.B. and Sweeney, P.D. (1992) 'Distributive and procedural justice as predictors of satisfaction with personal and organizational outcomes', *Academy of Management Journal* **35** (3): 626–37.

McHenry, R. (1997) 'Tried and tested', *People Management* **17** (3): 32–7.

Mackinnon, D.W. (1977) 'From selecting spies to selecting managers', in J.L. Moses and W.C. Byham (eds) *Applying the Assessment Centre Method*, Pergamon Press, New York.

Malde, B. (1992) 'The brave new world of assessing: the anomalies of a marketplace professionalism', *Selection and Development Review* **8** (4): 6–7.

Marchington, M. and Wilkinson, A. (1996) *Core Personnel and Development*, Institute of Personnel and Development, London.

Mars, G. (1994) *Cheats at Work: An Anthropology of Workplace Crime*, Dartmouth, Aldershot.

Martocchio, J.J. and Whitener, E.M. (1992) 'Fairness in personnel selection: a meta-analysis and policy implications', *Human Relations* **45**: 489–506.

Merrick, N. (1995) 'Men fight for right to do women's traditional jobs', *People Management* **1** (18): 7–8.

Mischel, W. (1968) *Personality Assessment*, New York, Wiley.

Mitchell, T.W. and Klimoski, P.M. (1982) 'Is it rational to be empirical? A test of scoring biographical data', *Journal of Applied Psychology* **71**: 311–17.

Monahan, C.J. and Nuchinsky. P.M. (1983) 'Three decades of personnel selection research: A state-of-the-art analysis and evaluation', *Journal of Occupational Psychology* **56**: 215–25.

Moore, H. (1942) *Psychology for Business and Industry*, McGraw-Hill, New York.

Mosel, J.N. and Goheen H.W. (1958) 'The validity of the employment Recommendation Questionnaire in personnel selection: the skilled trades', *Personnel Psychology* **11**: 481–90.

Mosel, J.N. and Goheen H.W. (1959) 'The Employment Recommendation Questionnaire III. Validity of different types of references', *Personnel Psychology* **12**: 469–77.

Mosel, J.N. and Goheen H.W. (1982) 'Agreement amongst replies to an employment recommendation questionnaire', *The American Psychologist* **7**: 365–6.

Muchinsky, P.M. (1976) 'The use of reference reports in personnel selection: a review and evaluation', *Journal of Occupational Psychology* **59**: 287–97.

Mullins, T.W. (1982) 'Interviewer decisions as a function of applicant race, applicant quality and interviewer prejudice', *Personnel Psychology* **35**: 163–74.

Munro, A. (1995) 'Put your hands together one more time for the "ipsative debate": a response to Closs', **11** (5): 1–2.

Myers, J.H. and Errett, W. (1959) 'The problem of preselection in weighted application blank studies', *Journal of Applied Psychology*, **43:** 94–5.

Nash, A.N. and Carroll, S.J. (1970) 'A hard look at the reference check', *Business Horizons* **13**: 43–9.

Neter, E. and Ben-Shakar G. (1989) 'The predictive validity of graphological inferences: a meta-analytic approach', *Personality and Individual Differences* **10**: 737–45.

Nevid, J.S. (1983) 'Comments: hopelessness, social desirability and construct validity', *IT Journal of Consulting and Clinical Psychology* **51**: 139–40.

Newell, S. and Shackleton, V. (1992) 'Are psychometric tests being used ethically in British industry and commerce?', *Selection and Development Review* **8** (6): 5–7.

Newell, S. and Shackleton, V. (1993) 'The use (and abuse) of psychometric tests in British industry and commerce', *Human Resource Management Journal* **3** (4): 14–23.

Nisbett, R.E. and Ross, L. (1980) *Human Inference: Strategies and Shortcomings of Social Judgements*, Prentice-Hall, Englewood Cliffs, NJ.

Noon, M. (1993) 'Racial discrimination in speculative applications: evidence from the UK's top 100 firms', *Human Resource Management Journal* **3** (4): 35–47.

O'Donnell, S. and Muncar, A. (1993) 'Graduate recruitment: what influences the acceptance of offers and subsequent retention?', *Selection and Development Review* **9** (1): 3–6.

Odom, R.C. (1995) 'Candid candidates', *Security Management* **39** (5): 66–70.

Ones, D.S., Viwesvaran, C. and Reiss, A.D. (1996) 'Role of social desirability in personality testing for personnel selection: the red herring', *Journal of Applied Psychology* **81** (6): 660–79.

Ones, D.S., Viwesvaran, C. and Schmidt, F.L. (1993) 'Comprehensive meta-analysis of integrity test validities: findings and implications for personnel selection and theories of job performance', *Journal of Applied Psychology* **78**: 679–703.

O'Sullivan, M. (1966) 'The situational reference', unpublished MSc dissertation, School of Management, UMIST.

Overell, S. (1996) 'Equality enters the mainstream', *People Management* **2** (4) 26–8.

Paddison, L. (1990) 'The targeted approach to recruitment', *Personnel Management* **22** (11): 54–8.

Parkinson, M. (1993) 'The management of feedback', *Selection and Development Review* **9**(4): 3–5.

Patterson, J. (1976) *Interpreting Handwriting*, McKay, New York.

Paulhaus, D.L. (1989) 'Socially desirable responding: some new solutions to old problems', in D.M. Buss and N.Cantor (eds) *Personality Psychology: Recent Trends and Emerging Directions*, Springer, New York.

Payne, T. (1995) 'Evaluating test fairness', *International Journal of Selection and Assessment* **3** (1): 47–51.

Peres, S.H. and Garcia, J.R. (1962) 'Validity and dimensions of descriptive adjectives used in reference letters for engineering applicants', *Personnel Psychology* **15**: 279–86.

Perry, P.M. (1995) 'The risks of employment references', *Savings and Community Banker* **4** (2): 31–5.

Pickard, J. (1995) 'Prepare to make a moral judgement', *People Management* **1** (9):

22–5.

Pickard, J. (1996) 'The wrong turns to avoid with tests', *People Management* **2** (16): 20–5.

Pocock, P. (1989) 'Is business ethics a contradiction in terms?', *Personnel Management* **21** (11): 60–3.

Pollan, S.M. and Levine, M. (1995) 'Asking your boss for a reference', *Working Woman* **20** (2): 53.

Prewett-Livingston, A.J., Veres, J.G. III, Feild, H.S. and Lewis, P.M. (1996) 'Effects of race on interview ratings in a situational panel interview', *Journal of Applied Psychology* **81** (2): 178–86.

Pynes J., Bernadin, H.J. Benton, A.L. and McEvoy, G.M. (1988) 'Should assessment centre ratings be mechanically derived?', *Journal of Business and Psychology* **2**: 217–27.

Radcliffe, J.A. (1966) 'A note on questionnaire faking with the 16PF and MPI', *Australian Journal of Applied Psychology* **18**: 154–7.

Ralston, S.M. and Brady, R. (1994) 'The relative influence of interview communication satisfaction on applicants' recruitment interview decisions', *Journal of Business Communication* **31** (1): 61–77.

Rasmussen, K.G. (1984) 'Nonverbal behaviour, verbal behaviour, resume credentials, and selection interview outcomes', *Journal of Applied Psychology* **69** (4): 551–6.

Raza, S.M. and Carpenter, B.N. (1987) 'Model of hiring decisions in real employment interviews', *Journal of Applied Psychology* **72**: 596–603.

Rees, C. (1996) 'Psychometrics: topical misunderstandings amongst test users', *International Journal of Selection and Assessment* **4** (1): 44–8.

Reilly, R.R. and Chao, G.T. (1982) 'Validity and fairness of some alternative employee selection procedures', *Personnel Psychology* **35**: 1–61.

Rimland, B. (1962) 'Personality test faking: expressed willingness to fake as affected by anonymity and instructional set', *Educational and Psychological Measurement* **22**: 747–51.

Riordan,C.A. (1989) 'Images of corporate success', in R. A. Giacalone, and P. Rosenfeld (eds) *Impression Management in the Organization*, Lawrence Erlbaum Associates, Inc., New Jersey.

Robertson, I.T. (1994) 'Personnel selection research: where are we now?', *The Psychologist* **7**: 17–20.

Robertson, I.T. and Kandola, R.S. (1982) 'Work sample tests: validity, adverse impact and applicant reaction', *Journal of Occupational Psychology* **55**: 171–84.

Robertson, I.T. and Makin, P.J. (1986) 'Management selection in Britain: a survey and critique', *Journal of Occupational Psychology* **59**: 45–57.

Robertson, I.T. and Smith, J.M. (1989) 'Personnel selection', in J.M. Smith and I.T. Robertson (eds) *Advances in Selection and Assessment*, Wiley, Chichester.

Robertson, I.T., Iles, P.A., Gratton, L. and Sharpley, D. (1991) 'The psychological impact of personnel selection and assessment methods on candidates', *Human Relations* **44**: 963–82.

Rochester, A. (1989) 'Pitfalls in the use of assessment centres', *Guidance and Assessment Review* **5** (4): 1–3.

Rosenfeld, P., Giacalone, R.A. and Riordan, C.A. (1995) *Impression Management in Organizations*, Routledge, London.

Rosse, J. G., Miller, J.L. and Stecher, M.D. (1994) 'A field study of job applicants' reactions to personality and cognitive ability testing', *Journal of Applied Psychology* **79** (6): 987–92.

Rowe, C. (1994) 'Picking the winners: the thorny issue of assessing leadership potential', *Leadership & Organization Development Journal* **15** (6): i-iv.

Rowe, P.M. (1963) 'Individual difference in selection decisions', *Journal of Applied Psychology* **47** (5): 304–7.

Russell, C.J. (1985) 'Individual decision processes in an assessment centre', *Journal of Applied Psychology* **70**: 737–46.

Rynes, S.L., Heneman, H.G. III and Schwab, D.P. (1980) 'Individual reactions to organizational recruiting: a review', *Personnel Psychology* **33**: 529–42.

Sackett, P.R. and Hakel, M.D. (1979) 'Temporal stability and individual differences in using assessment information to form overall ratings', *Organisational Behaviour and Human Response* **23**: 120–37.

Sackett, P.R. and Harris, M.M. (1984) 'Honesty testing for personnel selection: a review and critique', *Personnel Psychology* **37**: 221–45.

Sackett, P.R. and Wilson, M.A. (1982) 'Factors affecting the consensus judgement process in managerial assessment centres', *Journal of Applied Psychology* **67**: 10–17.

Sackett, P.R., Burris, L.R. and Callahan, C. (1989) 'Integrity testing for personnel selection: an update', *Personnel Psychology* **42**: 491–529.

Sackett, P.R., Burris, L.R. and Ryan, A.M. (1989) 'Coaching and practice effects in personnel selection', in C.L. Cooper and I. Robertson, *International Review of Industrial and Occupational Psychology*.

Schmitt, N. (1976) 'Social and situational determinants of interview decisions: implications for the employment interview', *Personnel Psychology* **29**: 79–101.

Schmitt, N. (1989) 'Fairness in employment selection', in M. Smith and I.T. Robertson (eds) *Advances in Selection and Assessment*, Wiley, Chichester.

Schmitt, N. and Coyle, B.W. (1976) 'Applicant decisions in the employment interview', *Journal of Applied Psychology* **61** (2): 184–92.

Schmitt, N., Schneider, J.R. and Cohen, S.A. (1990) 'Factors affecting validity of a regionally administered assessment centre', *Personnel Psychology* **43**: 1–12.

Schrader, A.D. and Osburn, H.G. (1977) 'Biodata faking: effects of induced subtlety and position specificity', *Personnel Psychology* **30**: 395–404.

Seay, S. (1995) 'Hiring good employees', *Savings and Community Banker* **4** (1): 38–41.

Seisdedos, N. (1993) 'Personal selection, questionnaires and motivational distortion: an intelligent attitude of adaptation', in H. Schuler, J.L. Farr and M. Smith (eds) *Personnel Selection and Assessment: Individual and Organisational Perspectives*, Erlbaum, Hillsdale, NJ.

Selection Research Publishing (1983) *Development and Validation of the Personal Outlook Inventory*, Selection Research Publishing, Chicago, IL.

Shackleton V. and Newell S. (1991) 'Management selection: a comparative survey of methods used in top British and French companies', *Journal of Occupational Psychology* **64**: 23–36.

Sheets, T.L. and Bushardt, S.C. (1994) 'Effects of the applicant's gender-appropriateness and qualifications and rater self-monitoring propensities on hiring decisions', *Public Personnel Management* **23** (3): 373–82.

Silvester, J. and Brown, A. (1993) 'Graduate recruitment: testing the impact', *Selection and Development Review* **9** (1): 1–3.

Silvester, J. and Chapman, A.J. (1996) 'Unfair discrimination in the selection interview: an attributional account', *Selection and Development Review* **4** (2): 63–9.

Sleight, R.B. and Bell, G.D. (1954) 'Desirable content of letters of recommendation', *Personnel Journal* **32**: 421–2.

Sleight, R.B. and Duvoisin (1982) 'Desirable content of letters of recommendation', *The American Psychologist* **7**: 365.

Smith. J.M. and Abrahamsen, M. (1992) 'Patterns of selection in six countries', *The Psychologist* **5**: 205–7.

Smith, J.M. and Robertson, I.T. (1989) *Advances in Selection and Assessment*, Wiley, Chichester.

Smith M. and Robertson I.T. (1993) *The Theory and Practice of Systematic Personnel Selection*, Macmillan, Basingstoke.

Smithers, J.W., Reilly, R.R., Millsap, R.E., Pearlman, K. and Stoffey, R.W. (1993) 'Applicant reactions to selection procedures', *Personnel Psychology* **46**: 49–76.

Springbett, B.M. (1958) 'Factors affecting the final decision in the employment interview', *Canadian Journal of Psychology* **31**: 13–22.

Stevens, C.K. and Kristof, A.L. (1995) 'Making the right impression: a field study of applicant impression management during job interviews', *Journal of Applied Psychology* **80** (5): 587–606.

Stone, D.L. and Stone, E.F. (1987) 'Effects of missing application-blank information on personnel selection decisions: do privacy protection strategies bias the outcome?', *Journal of Applied Psychology* **72** (3): 452–6.

Storey, J. and Sisson, K. (1993) *Managing Human Resources and Industrial Relations*, Open University Press, Buckingham.

Strickler, L.N. (1969) '"Test wiseness" on personality scales', *Journal of Applied Psychology Monograph* **53** (3): part 2.

Taylor, M.S. and Sniezek, J.A. (1984) 'The college recruitment interview: topical content and applicant reactions', *Journal of Occupational Psychology* **57**: 157–68.

Tenopyr, W. and Jones, J.W. (1982) 'Personnel selection and classification', *Annual Review of Psychology* **33**: 582–618.

Terris, W. and Jones, J. W. (1982) 'Psychological correlates of employee theft in department stores', *Technical Report No. 20*, London House Press, Park Ridge, IL.

Torrington, D. and Hall, L. (1987) *Personnel Management: A New Approach*, Prentice-Hall, London.

Tracey, W.R. (1995) 'How to accommodate and interview job candidates with disabilities', *Human Resources Professional* **8** (2): 23–7.

Tullar,W.L. (1989) 'Relational control in the interview', *Journal of Applied Psychology* **74**: 971–7.

Tversky, A. and Kahneman, D. (1988) 'Rational choice and the framing of decisions', in D. Bell, H. Raffia and A. Tversky (eds) *Information Review of Industrial and Organisational Psychology*, Cambridge University Press, New York.

Wade, K.J. and Kinicki, A.J. (1995) 'Examining objective and subjective applicant qualifications within a process model of interview selection decisions', *Academy of Management Journal*, Best Papers Proceedings: 151–5.

Wanous, J.P. (1989)'Impression management at organizational entry', in R.A. Giacalone, and P. Rosenfeld, (eds) *Impression Management in the Organization*, Lawrence Erlbaum Associates, Inc., New Jersey.

Wareham, J.(1995) 'Reference checking gets creative', *Across the Board* **32** (6): 49–50.

Webster, G. D. (1992) 'Background and reference checks: know what to ask – and relax', *Agency Sales Magazine* **22** (8): 26–8.

Weiss, D.J. and Dawis, R.V. (1960) 'An objective validation of factual interview data', *Journal of Applied Psychology* **44**: 381–5.

Wexley, K.N. and Nemeroff, W.F. (1974) 'The effects of racial prejudice, race of applicant and biographical similarity on interviewer evaluations of job applicants', *Journal of Social and Behavioral Sciences* **20**: 66–78.

Williams, R.S. (1994) 'Occupational testing: contemporary British practice', *The Psychologist* **7** (1): 11–13.

Wingrove, J., Glendinning, R. and Herriot, P. (1984) 'Graduate pre-selection: a research note', *Journal of Occupational Psychology*, **57**: 169–71.

Wiseman, R. (1996) 'Towards a psychology of deception', *The Psychologist* **7** (2): 61–4.

Wood, R. (1994) 'Work samples should be used more often (and will be)', *International Journal of Selection and Assessment* **2** (3): 166–71.

Wood, R. and Baron, H. (1992) 'Psychological testing free from prejudice', *Personnel Management* **24** (12): 32–6.

Wynn-Evans, C. (1994) 'References and negligent misstatement', *Industrial Law Journal* **23**: 346–9.

Index